The Travels of IBN BATTUTA *to* Central Asia

The Travels of IBN BATTUTA *to Central Asia*

Ibrahimov Nematulla Ibrahimovich

ITHACA
PRESS

THE TRAVELS OF IBN BATTUTA TO CENTRAL ASIA

Ithaca Press is an imprint of Garnet Publishing Limited

Published by
Garnet Publishing Limited
8 Southern Court
South Street
Reading
RG1 4QS
UK

First Edition

ISBN 0 86372 256 3

British Library Cataloguing-in-Publication Data.
A catalogue record for this book is available from the British Library.

Jacket design by David Rose
Typeset by Samantha Abley

Printed in Lebanon

The Publishers would like to acknowledge the kind permission granted to them by the Hakluyt Society, London, for the use of a section of their translation of *The Travels of Ibn Baṭṭūṭa* AD *1325–1354* in Chapter 4.

Contents

Introduction

The masterpieces of Arabic geographic literature are of great significance when it comes to history and historical geography, the history of culture, arts and other spheres of the social and political life of the peoples inhabiting the territory of the contemporary independent Central Asian states. They represent a wide range of writings in the Arabic language, and are closely connected with each other through the centuries and countries by certain traditions and lines of succession (though written by representatives of different nations). Consider, for example, the works of such scientists as al-Baladhuri, Ibn Khurdadhbih and al-Ya'qubi, which were created in the ninth century; the works of al-Istakhri, Abu Dulaf, al-Muqaddasi, al-Mas'udi, al-Khorezmi, al-Dinawari, al-Tabari, Ibn Miskawayh, Ibn Rusta, Ibn al-Faqih and Ibn Hawqal from the tenth century. The eleventh century is represented by al-Biruni. The writings of al-Idrisi, al-Marwazi and al-Sam'ani preserved from the twelfth century; and those by Ibn al-Athir and Yaqut al-Hamawi from the twelfth to thirteenth centuries. Al-'Umari and Ibn 'Arabshah created their works in the fourteenth century. These and other historians and geographers left us the heritage for the contemporary scientists to stand upon to recreate the picture of historical and cultural development of the peoples of Central Asia, Caucasus and Volga river region. *The Travels of Ibn Battuta* (fourteenth century), to which this work is devoted, occupies a special place in the row of works written by Arabic travellers. "After cosmographies and encyclopaedies of the thirteenth and fourteenth centuries," wrote I.Y. Krachkovskiy "the Muslim literature as a whole comes to a climax . . . the genre of travellings is still very rich in number. However, the important fact is that the last great traveller who had been to all the Muslim countries is also related to the fourteenth century. This traveller is the famous Ibn Battuta, the travellings of whom are still widely used in Arabic schools . . . the very Ibn Battuta without references to whom there is no writing about the Golden Horde or Central Asia . . ." [107, 416–417].

Other orientalists also focused long ago on the data provided by Ibn Battuta over the less studied historical period of Central Asia. Ibn Battuta fills many of the gaps in the local chronicles of that time with his interesting observations and personal impressions. (The full name of his book is *Tuhfat al-nuzzar fi ghara'ib al-amsar wa-'aja'ib al-asfar*.) His narration gives us a bright and realistic picture of cultural, political and social life in Central Asia in the first half of the fourteenth century. Many of Ibn Battuta's stories about the cities and urban life of Central Asia in this century do not have any parallels in other sources.

I.Y. Krachkovskiy called Ibn Battuta "the last universal geographer-practioner, not the bookish compiler but the traveller with a great number of visited countries. According to calculations he had covered more than 75,000 miles" [107, 417]. Over his twenty-eight years of wanderings Ibn Battuta had been to hundreds of cities and settlements in Northern and Western Africa, the Arabic Peninsula, India and Spain, Turkey and Iran, Central Asia, Eastern Europe and finally China. "The Travels" of Ibn Battuta contains so many interesting stories about these far and distant countries that his contemporaries supposed them to be untrue and fantastic. Even such an outstanding scientist as Ibn Khaldun, who met Ibn Battuta, did not take these stories and writings seriously, saying that "the people blamed him for telling lies" [48, 143–144]. European science was also sceptical about the data provided by Ibn Battuta. "The Travels" was a genuine work, but the preconceptions hindered it being given an appropriate evaluation.

"The Travels" of Ibn Battuta as a source of the variety of events – geographical, historical and cultural – is just one facet of the work. But there is another facet. "Tuhfat al-nuzzar" is also a very valuable literary and psychological monument which, compared to different descriptions of ways of life and customs, shows with enough level of authenticity the specific features of the way of thinking of the men of that time: their range of interests, attitudes to circumstances and facts, their evaluation. What were the determining features of the genre and literary trends to which "The Travels" are referred? The notes of Ibn Battuta from this perspective had not yet been studied, but were examined in respect of the route, and authenticity of the data utilised by historians, archaeologists and numismatists. However, Ibn Battuta's book is worthy of careful attention not only by value of the facts given in the book but just for itself. Almost all of the many explorers are unanimous in thinking that his style is completely different from that of other writings of the "Rihla" genre. It is different to books like *The Books of Travels and States* (such as the writings of Ibn Khurdadhbih, Ibn al-Faqih, al-Istakhri and others), and to the most comprehensive. With the development of oriental studies and geographical surveys, scientists from different countries of the world started to believe more and more that the stories of Ibn Battuta are not the result of fantastic conception of the medieval mystifier, but rather the result of evidence based on personal observations of the lands and peoples described.

In the geographical collection of the Middle Ages entitled *Mu'jam al-buldan*, which belonged to the distinguished encyclopaedia scientist Yaqut, the description of the travels of Abu Hamid al-Gharnati is more similiar to *The Books of Travels and States*. Meanwhile, in "Tuhfat al-nuzzar . . ." we feel the influence of the popular hagiographic or "eventual" literature. The latter was expressed in a great number of stories implanted in the plot describing the wonders created by the local saints and *sufi shaykhs*. It is not only the fact that Ibn Battuta travelled as "a Muslim scientist" (which undoubtedly enabled him to gain an additional influence and authority, especially before the newly adopted Muslim rulers), but also the matter of the general psychological atmosphere of the epoch that had been reflected openly in the literary process: "life stories" of the saints, *sufi* poetry in Persian and Arabic languages, widespread recognition of the "Sira" genre directly connected with folk traditions.

Ibn Battuta, like Marco Polo, focused on the events that seemed to be not so important. For example, he described in detail the receptions he received and the gifts presented to him. However, it is not correct to regard this as "exaggerated personification"; it was as important to him as for the court people to know where the *amir* or sultan would like the traveller to sit down. The numerous stories about the wonders, and the graves of the saints were also covered by Ibn Battuta.

While in Central Asia, Ibn Battuta covered one of the most difficult and complicated periods in the history of the local people – the Mongol invasion. The Arabic traveller visited this area a century after the Mongol occupation, but while some cities were flourishing, others had still not recovered, preserving the traces of demolition. This is shown very vividly in "The Travels". Some time later in the fourteenth century, the peoples of Central Asia recovered to some extent from the

Mongol occupation and their former trades and cultural centres started to emerge again. The notes of Ibn Battuta portrayed the impressions of the witnesses of life in this part of the world. Not much of this kind of evidence has been preserved from other sources.

Central Asia was conquered by Mongol tribes headed by Chinggis Khan in the first half of the thirteenth century. Earlier, Chinggis Khan conquered North China. The Mongol troops, headed by his elder son Jochi, subjugated the peoples inhabiting the area along both sides of the River Yenisey, and the troop leader Qubilay occupied the nothern part of the Semirechye valley. From 1218 to 1219, the Mongol tribes under the leadership of Jebe invaded the lands of Qarakhitays in Semirechye and Eastern Turkestan, and made close approaches to the borders of the state of Khorezmshahs (comprising Khorezm, Mawarannahr and a part of contemporary Iran and Afghanistan).

In 1220, the city of Otrar was defeated by the Mongols; Bukhara and Samarqand fell later. Many thousands of people and defenders of the cities perished and others were forced to become slaves. The flourishing rich cities, demolished in the battle, were deserted: in Bukhara, for example, all the defenders of the citadel were killed, the fortifications turned into ruins and the city set on fire; in Samarqand, barely a quarter of the population survived.

After the occupation of Samarqand, Khorezmshah 'Ala' al-Din Muhammad escaped from Central Asia and found asylum on one of the islands of the Southern Caspian Sea; he didn't attempt to defend his dominon against the invaders.

Over the following years, the Mongol troops conquered the remaining territories of the state of Khorezmshahs, destroying everything and capturing the people to turn them into slaves. "They did not feel sorry for anybody," the Arabic historian Ibn al-Athir writes. "They killed the women, men, children . . . the Tatars did not spare any city, leaving them completely destroyed."

It was noted by the academic B. Gafurov that "the Mongol invasion was the cause of an endless row of miseries for the peoples of Central Asia. As a result of robberies and fires the cities of Mawarannahr were turned into heaps of ruins, the population totally perished. The agriculture was abandoned" [89, 452].

In the first third of the thirteenth century, with Chinggis Khan still alive, the Mongols conquered the vast territories, including a large part of Central Asia. In 1227, Chinggis Khan divided the occupied territories between his sons. The territory of Central Asia to the east of Amudarya was given to the second son, Chaghatay, and the western parts of Eastern Iran and Northern India were passed over to his fourth son, Toluy; to the north from the Aral and Caspian Sea stretched the belongings of Batu, the grandson of Chinggis Khan (his father Jochi had died by that time); the title of the Great Khan and the vast lands in Central Asia and Eastern Asia were given to Ogodey.

After the death of Chinggis Khan in 1227, his predecessors continued the combat campaigns, and increased their belongings. Hulagu, the son of Toluy, in the mid-thirteenth century conquered Iran, Mesopotamia and Syria. In 1258, the city of Baghdad was invaded and Caliph al-Musta'sim from the dynasty of 'Abbasids was imprisoned and killed.

In the first half of the fourteenth century, when Ibn Battuta visited Central Asia, its territory was divided into three Mongol states. The north-western part, including Khorezm, was part of the Golden Horde (Ulus Jochi) with the capital in New Saray (Saray Berke). The state was ruled by Uzbek Khan (1312–1341). The south-west belonged to the state of Ilkhanids, and the eastern regions were part of Ulus Chaghatay. However, in reality, in many regions the semi-independent feudals were in power. Some of them originated from the dynasties of Jochi, Chaghatay and Hulagu and the others from the local nobility. Ibn Battuta mentions several Mongol rulers. In Mawarannahr, Semirechye and Eastern Turkestan the representatives of Chaghatayid dynasty dominated: these were Kebeg, from 1318 until 1326; Elchigidey and Duva Temur in 1326; and 'Ala' al-Din Tarmashirin from 1326 to 1334. During the reign of the latter, Ibn Battuta came to Central Asia. The head of the Ilkhanid state was "ilkhan" ("obeyed to the Great Khan") Abu Sa'id (1317–1335) [85, 197–205].

The first Mongol ruler who transfered his headquarters to the territory of Central Asia (in Mawarannahr) was Kebeg, who built his palace near the city of Nasaf (today's Qarshi). The decision taken by Kebeg was of great importance because it showed the beginnings of the tendency for Mongol rulers to change their nomadic way of life into a settled one. However, it did not mean a total denial of nomadic life as demonstrated by the considerable amount of time (mostly in the summer) that Kebeg spent away from the palace. His predecessor,

Tarmashirin, despite the cold weather in winter, received Ibn Battuta in his tent.

The rule of Kebeg was marked by important monetary and administrative reforms, contributing to the process of economic development in the Chaghatayid state. The monetary system conformed with those already existing in the state of Ilkhanids and the Golden Horde; new coins – dinars and dirhams – were minted mainly in Bukhara and Samarqand (six dirhams were equal to one silver dinar weighing 8 grams).

During the reign of Tarmashirin the silver coins were intensively minted in Otrar. One of the characteristic features of the internal political life of the Chaghatayid state of that time was the internecine wars. The local *amirs* denied central power and conducted combat activities between each other as well as with the rulers of the state. For example, during the reign of Kebeg the rebellious Prince Yasawur actually controlled the southern regions of the country, making plundering raids on the big cities. Kebeg's successor, Tarmashirin, was killed in the course of the uprising of local feudals. During the reign of Tarmashirin an important event in the political and ideological life of the state occurred: Islam was declared an official religion. Tarmashirin's predecessor did not adopt Islam but was very keen to talk with Muslim clergymen. As for Tarmashirin himself, his contemporaries said that he was a very devoted Muslim.

The administrative reform of the territory meant division into units – *tumens* – headed by the vicegerents, representatives of the local Turco-Mongolian nobility, and this was also of great importance. The heads of the biggest families occupied the posts not only in the state structures of their own dominions but also in the newly founded *tumens* as well. An example of this was the family of Barlas, which was settled in the valley of Qashqadarya and Jalayir – the area near to Khujand. But the continuing feudal wars made it difficult to conduct reforms and by the end of the first half of the fourteenth century the Chaghatayid state collapsed into a number of independent principalities.

The feudal land ownership in Central Asia during the reign of the Mongol rulers was characterized by four types: state land (the lands of *diwan*); feudal, in the form of "milk" and "inju", *waqf* and peasant farms (milk). The system of feudal land grants was practised widely. For example, the military leader of "a thousand" (a military unit consisting of 1,000 warriors) could be granted a strip of land to be divided among the leaders of "the dozens".

The employed population of Central Asia depended in different ways on the feudal nobility and state. A small number of peasants were the landowners (milkdar), while the majority were simply leaseholders.

The Mongols intensively conducted the policy of serfdom towards peasants and craftsmen. The category of craftsmen with the status of slaves was also much in evidence. Meanwhile, there was a group of relatively independent craftsmen and traders who paid taxes in favour of the state treasury. The slave trade was widely used.

As a whole, the wellbeing of much of the population of Central Asia as well as of the other territories conquered by Mongols greatly deteriorated as a result of devastation, decreases in economy, mass extermination, forcing the local population into the slave trade, high level of requisitions and the general arbitrariness of the Mongol rulers.

From midway through the thirteenth century and especially in the fourteenth century, urban life gradually became developed again. The local architects and craftsmen started to erect new buildings to replace the demolished ones.

Continuing with pre-Mongol artistic traditions, the architectural monuments preserved from that time were mainly mausoleums, one of the earliest being that of al-Bakharzi, which was visited by Ibn Battuta. A few of the mausoleums preserved from the fourteenth century are in Samarqand (Shah-i Zinda), Bukhara, Kunya Urgench and other cities. At that time a number of palaces (the palace of Kebeg in Qarshi), madrasas, mosques and other constructions were built. Many no longer remain, although a few have been partially preserved.

In the thirteenth and fourteenth centuries, the territory occupied by Mongols was also home to eminent poets, scientists and thinkers who made an invaluable contribution to world culture. Among them were such brilliant people as Jalal al-Din Rumi (1207–1273); *sufi* poet, Muslih al-Din Sa'di Shirazi (circa 1210–1292); the poet, thinker and traveller, Fazlallah Rashid al-Din (circa 1247–1318); the outstanding historian of the Middle Ages, Nasir al-Din Tusi (1201–1277); the encyclopaedia scientist, Qutb al-Din Shirazi (1236–1311); astronomers, geographers and many others.

One of the socio-political consequences of the policy of the Mongol conquerors was the reason for the introduction of the Sarbadar movement. The movement was supported by peasants, craftsmen, traders and other middle class people who came out against the domination of the Mongol rulers and the local feudals.

Among the Sarbadars, and it was stressed by V.V. Bartol'd, the Shi'a followers were mostly active – although the movement itself was not initiated by religious motives [79, II, 2,364]. The Shi'as in Ilkhanid state during the reign of Abu Sa'id were "in disgrace" and represented potential opposition to the authourities: Ilkhan brought the country again into the lap of Sunni Islam, whereas with his predecessor Oljeytu Khan (1304–1317), the Shi'a Islam was given the status of state religion [156, I, 110].

The Sarbadars founded an independent state in Khurasan, which existed from 1337 until 1381; it was visited and described in detail by Ibn Battuta. The Sarbadar movement was also very popular in Mawarannahr. In 1365, the Sarbadars headed the uprising in Samarqand. In the country of Sarbadars, their own coins were minted, an army was founded and some taxes raised by the Mongols were lifted.

The success of the Sarbadar movement was, to a great extent, dictated by the considerable instability of the state of Ilkhanids, which had become apparent after the death of Abu Sa'id who did not have a direct descendant. "After . . . the death of the ruler, it was impossible to avoid the collaps of the country", writes V.V. Bartol'd [79, VII, 481].

Ibn Battuta's story about the country of Sarbadars is a unique account (as are the other parts of "The Travels"), because the information about this movement provided by the witnesses is extremely scarce in any other form.

1

The life and travels of Ibn Battuta

The full name of Ibn Battuta was Shams al-Din Abu 'Abdallah Muhammad ibn 'Abdallah ibn Muhammad ibn Ibrahim ibn Muhammad ibn Ibrahim ibn Yusuf al-Lawati al-Tanji. He came from the Berber tribe of Lawata (*ilawaten*) and was born in the city of Tanjier in 703/1304. His date of birth can be determined exactly: "I left the city of Tanja, my motherland, the second Thursday of the Allah month of Rajab 'the lonely' in 725 (June 14, 1325) . . . and I was twenty-two years old" [25, 1, 12–13]. This date is confirmed by Ibn Juzayy al-Kalbi, the editor of Ibn Battuta's "Travels" (1356) who referred to his talk with Ibn Battuta in Granada after which he wrote: "Abu 'Abdallah has told me in Granada that he was born in Tanja on Monday the month of Rajab 17 703/24 February 1304" [25, 1, 13].

Ibn Battuta's family belonged to the middle classes of the city. His father was a small *faqih* who probably did not have enough means to provide an appropriate education for his son. Ibn Battuta did not expect support from his father and decided to head for Mecca on his own to listen to the lectures of eminent Muslim scholars. Thus a brave but very poor young traveller started his way on foot and reached Tilimsan alone. Continuing on, Ibn Battuta made for Milyana, joined a group of Tunisian merchants and together with them left for the Algerian city of Bijaya, where he was confronted by the brutality of the local officialdom and the viceroy of the ruler. Here he became sick, though this did not cause him to abandon his journey.

From this moment on, the wanderings of Ibn Battuta began. The route and chronology of his travels have been investigated in detail by I. Hrbek as well as by other authors (including F. Badawi and G. V. Miloslavskiy [161, 409–486; 140, 115]). Therefore we will not focus in great detail on them. However, as Ibn Battuta is rightfully considered to be one of the greatest travellers of the pre-Magellanes epoch, we will describe in short these wanderings to give us an impression of their scale.

Despite his illness, Ibn Battuta continued his trip. Having reached the city of Constantine with great difficulty, he so moved Abu-l-Hasan, the ruler of the city, to pity by his emaciated appearance and worn out dress that the latter presented him with two dinars and some clothes.

Ibn Battuta stayed for some time in Tunis and as a result we receive a very detailed description of the architectural monuments. Then he continued on his way; leaving Sus he went to Safaqus and joined a pilgrims' caravan.

At the beginning of the month Jumada 726/5 April 1326 the caravan entered Alexandria in Egypt. He spent several months there, describing in detail his meetings with scholars and shaykhs, the events relating to the clashes between Muslims and Christians, the citadel walls, the towers and various other places of interest.

From Alexandria, Ibn Battuta went to Damietta and then up to Cairo by the River Nile. He stayed in Cairo for several months admiring the magnificence and gorgeousness of the capital of Egypt, which by diameter, as he put it, was as long "as a one month's trip" and it "seethed with the crowds of different kinds of people like a storming sea: the scholars and fools, the poor and the rich, the wise and ignorant, the modest and swindle, noble and base, bad and kind". He described Cairo in detail – its mosques and madrasas, pyramids, the River Nile – and narrated the biography of the Mamluk ruler of Egypt, Nasir al-Din and his retinue along with the prominent *qadis* and war leaders. Although there is a lot of historical literature available from the time of the domination of the Mamluks dynasty in Egypt (1250–1517), the stories of our traveller are of great merit from the point of view of their objectivity and simplicity as well as by their number of peculiar details (for example, he gives the data for the taxation system in Egypt, which struck him by its dimensions).

From the very first stage of his voyage the dominating interests of Ibn Battuta were defined. Later on during his continued voyages they became more vivid: he was interested in the people first, and then in the local sights. This peculiarity, which distinguished him from the many other travellers, attracted the attention of scientists on many occasions. Thus the Polish orientalist A. Zajaczkowski believes that the following Arabic saying could serve as a motto for Ibn Battuta's travels:

"One must choose a neighbour first and then a house, one must find a companion to travel with before the road to go along" [14, XIV].

Ibn Battuta left Cairo with the caravan of pilgrims and continued his way to Mecca moving along the Nile. He visited a number of cities in Upper Egypt and finally came to the port of 'Ayzab on the Red Sea. Here the pilgrims intended to find a vessel heading for Jidda, but they failed and the caravan returned back to Cairo.

In March 1326, the traveller started for Syria [25, I, 111]. On the way to Damascus, Ibn Battuta visited many cities in Syria and Lebanon. He witnessed Aleppo, Hims, Hama, Ma'arra, Bayrut, Jerusalem, Antioch, Ladhiqiyya and, Tripoli before finally coming to Damascus. There, he attended the lectures of a number of famous lawyers and acquired the right to teach one of the most important collections of the *hadith* – *al-Sahih* by al-Bukhari.

In August 1326, Ibn Battuta went to Mecca again with a caravan of pilgrims and arrived there one year after he left home. Having accomplished all the necessary rituals of the pilgrimage and also having received the honourable title of *hajj*, Ibn Battuta decided to stay for a while. Life in Mecca stipulated the further route of his travellings. He met with pilgrims from various countries and listened to their stories about unknown places. He was especially impressed by stories about "fairytale India". Ibn Battuta dreamed of far-away journeys. Later, he said that he wished to see the world, let his heart enjoy it, see the different miracles, listen to stories about the wonders, acquire broad knowledge, meet interesting people and seek his place in life.

Thus, a new plan was prepared on the way back to Mecca, and from there he made his way to Iraq (in a special palanquin as a private guest of the amir of the caravan). The Baghdad caravan travelled along the road via Najd and further to Iraq by the main transit tract. In Najaf, the caravan split into two parts. Ibn Battuta did not join the group but went via Wasit to Basra. He visited several cities of Iraq on the way.

Ibn Battuta's stay in Iraq was very fruitful and we inherit from him a beautiful description of Najaf, Wasit and Basra, and the customs, traditions, spiritual and cultural life of the people inhabiting these cities.

The time spent by Ibn Battuta in Iraq is also remarkable for the meetings with many people who brought him to take the final decision to visit India. In Basra, the traveller hired a boat that was used to get to

Ubulla. From there he travelled up to the city of 'Abadan. He intended to go to Port Hurmuz in the Persian Gulf, then on to India by sea. However, as is clear from his stories, he complains of being very tired and lacking the means and necessary facilities to go on with the travel, so he had to change the route.

As a result of this experience he devised for himself one rule – as far as it was possible, not to travel one and the same route twice [25, 11, 21].

In 'Abadan, Ibn Battuta boarded a vessel heading for Majul (Mahshahr), and in four days had successfully landed in the port. There he spent one day, hired a camel and after three days' travel in the desert found himself in Ramiz (Ramhurmuz). From there Ibn Battuta made his way through the Lor steppe to Tustar. From Tustar he went on to the city of Idhaj, which was the capital of Lor Atabegs at that time. Having left Idhaj, Ibn Battuta continued on his way, passing the small city Maqbarat al-Salatin. After ten days he arrived in Isfahan, where he spent several days. He gives us a very interesting description of the city with tales of the regular confrontations between Shi'its and Sunnits and also about the important role played by the craftsmen in the social life of the city.

From Isfahan the traveller left for Shiraz. Thanks to the protection of the well-known theologist and educated shaykh Majd al-Din, Ibn Battuta had open access to all the distinguished scholars, political and religious figures of Shiraz. Here, he received a certificate that recognized him as the judge of two trends – Maliki and Shafi'i. This was of very great use to him during his later ventures.

While in Shiraz, Ibn Battuta collected valuable information on the social and cultural life of this part of Iran and the biographies of many political leaders. He also informs us of the spread of Shi'ism and the attempts to declare it as the official religion in this area.

Once again, despite his great desire to visit India, Ibn Battuta could not manage it.

He therefore left Shiraz and returned back to Kufa in Iraq via Kazarun, al-Zaydayn and Huwayza'. He subsequently made the pilgrimage to the sacred Shi'i cities of Hilla, Karbala', Kazimayn and then went to Baghdad.

Having already been substantially acquainted with Baghdad, which "compared to its glorious past presented the picture of a deal of ruins", he described the preserved mosques and madrasas, tombs of caliphs and prominent scholars. He also received access to the court and therefore recounted information about Sultan Abu Sa'id [25, 11, 114–123].

After some time, Ibn Battuta, together with the encampment of the sultan, left Baghdad for Tabriz. Here he was given the sultan's letter, which prescribed to render assistance to the traveller. With this safeguarding letter, Ibn Battuta returned to Baghdad having visited on the way Mosul, Diyar Bakr, Sinjar, Samarra', Dara, Mardin and many other cities and places, describing, in particular, the oil fields. He received a camel, "travelling reserves, water, food for four" and again headed for Mecca together with the annual caravan of pilgrims, where he stayed throughout the year of 1329 and the pilgrimage season of 1330. In Mecca, he witnessed the riots – which happened in autumn 1330.

At the beginning of November, Ibn Battuta left the "Mother of the cities" and moved towards Yemen. He arrived at the port of Jidda on the Red Sea, where he got on a ship bound for 'Ayzab. But on the third day of the journey the wind changed and brought the ship to Ra's Dawa'ir Bay. Ibn Battuta travelled on by land together with some Bedouins. Two days later, the travellers arrived in Sawakin, boarded another ship and sailed over the Red Sea, but this time in the opposite direction. After six days the ship reached the big Yemen port of Hilli.

Having spent several days as a guest of the ruler of Hilli, the traveller again boarded a ship and safely landed in Zabid, which is forty *farsakhs* away from San'a'. On the way to San'a' he visited the then capital of Yemen – Ta'izz – which was "one of the biggest and most beautiful cities of Yemen". The ruler of Yemen, Sultan Nur al-Din 'Ali al-Mujahid, received the traveller and presented him with a horse. With this new opportunity, Ibn Battuta visited San'a', from where he moved to 'Adan and further across the Red Sea again to the African port of Zayla'. He spent four days in Zayla', then the travellers sailed to the south over the Indian Ocean along the African continent to Kilwa.

Ibn Battuta described this voyage very briefly. Nevertheless, he gave a lot interesting data about the lands he visited. For example, passed the Somali coast the ship was anchored in Muqadishu. "The inhabitants have many camels, they slaughter hundreds of them every day. They have also many sheep and they are very rich merchants. In

Muqadishu they make beautiful clothes to be brought to Egypt and the other countries" [25, 11, 183].

Ibn Battuta calls Muqadishu an important city throughout the coast and gives much interesting detail about its ruler: "Barbar by origin and speaks the Maqdishi language" [25, 11, 183]. The contemporary explorers found that, indeed, in the Middle Ages their own language was quite popular with the citizens of Muqadishu, which was used in parallel with Arabic. Another detail here is also very interesting. The Arab geographer Yaqut, who lived at the end of the twelfth/beginning of the thirteenth century, wrote that the citizens of Muqadishu "do not have a ruler and their affairs are supervised by the senior citizens" [56, IV, 602]. As for the Arabs inhabiting the city he wrote: "They do not have the sultan and every group of citizens obey their own senior" [56, 1, 502]. As for Ibn Battuta he states that the city is ruled by the sultan. "We arrived on the big island of Manbas," Ibn Battuta also details his time in Mombasa, "which is two days of sail from the country of Sawahil . . . The island does not have its own territory on the continent. The bananas and lemons grow there. The people also pick up the fruits of a plant very similar to olive . . . They are not engaged in land cultivating . . . and a great deal of their food consists of bananas and fish . . . The grain is brought from the country of Sawahil" [25, II, 191–193].

A part of contemporary Kenya is meant as the country of Sawahil. It is known that in the middle ages there were big city states, inhabited by the mixed Arab-Negro (*bantu*) population, which later served as the core of the Swahili nation. "There (in Mombasa) we spent a night. Then we went out out to the sea and sailed towards the big city of Kilwa, located on a coast where mainly the Zinjis with an extremely black skin used to live . . . Kilwa is one of the most beautiful and comfortable cities. It is built totally of wood" [25, II, 191–193].

According to Ibn Battuta, the citizens of Kilwa (Kulwa) confessed Islam and even pursued a sacred war against their neighbours – "infidels".

"In Kilwa we got on a ship bound for Zafar . . . It is located at the outskirts of Yemen at the Indian Ocean. From there the horses are brought to India. With the fair wind this journey takes one month. I myself sailed twice from the Indian city of Calcutta and it took me 28 days" [25, II, 191].

From Zafar, Ibn Battuta headed further by sea to the north. Having visited on the way the port Hasik, the volcanic islands of Lum'an and Bird Island (Jazirat al-Tayr), he landed in the city port of Sur. From Sur, by land (and with great difficulties) he travelled on foot to the city of Qalhat. From there he travelled for six days through the deserts of Oman and across the Persian Gulf before coming to Hurmuz where he was received by its ruler.

"The Travels" is one of the most complete sources on the history of fourteenth-century Hurmuz. During Ibn Battuta's life, Hurmuz was the biggest port in the Persian Gulf. The city was well known since the Hellenic epoch, though it acquired the importance of a sea port after it had been conquered by the Arabs. On the islands of the Persian Gulf, Ibn Battuta watched the pearl divers. He also visited Bahrayn and Qutayf, al-Hasa and Yamama.

In Yamama he joined the caravan of Amir Tufayl and together, for the third time, they began a pilgrimage to Mecca. During October and the beginning of November in 1332, Ibn Battuta spent time in Mecca. After the end of the pilgrimage season he went to Jidda so that he could go to India via Yemen over the Indian Ocean. "But," said the traveller with a pity "I could not find a companion and as for means to spend for the travel I did not have it" [25, II, 250–251].

Finally, the traveller decided to cross the Red Sea on a small boat to reach Port 'Ayzab on the African coast. But the wind had brought him again to Ra's Dawa'ir, from where (with great difficulties) he got to 'Ayzab. And then, for the third time moving along the Nile coast, he ascended to Cairo.

His arrival at Cairo puts an end to the first stage of Ibn Battuta's travels related to the Middle East countries, Eastern and Northern Africa. This stage could quite definitely be characterized as a Muslim pilgrimage; his visits to well-known places in the Arab world of that time were supposed to be the traditional places to be visited.

Ibn Battuta's next travels are related to a completely new stage where we see him not as a pilgrim but as a keen and observant traveller, inspired by a great desire to see more and more countries. The circle of his interests was getting wider, and his main attention is attached first of all to the people he encountered [115, 38–39]. His previous travels had been limited by small geographical districts, but now he had begun to cover long distances over land and sea. Very often he is accompanied by the caravan loaded with heaps of provisions, with wives, concubines, bondmen and bondwomen. He arrived in every new city like a rich merchant, making deals and sometimes remaining to serve the local ruler.

The goal of his new venture was the Golden Horde – to travel via Syria and Asia Minor with, finally, the Black Sea to cross.

After a few days in Cairo he headed for Syria via Bilbays. Having visited al-Khalil, Jerusalem, Ramla, Tripoli and Jabal, he found himself in Ladhiqiyya. "In Ladhiqiyya we got on a big ship," Ibn Battuta recalled, "which belonged to the people from Genoa. The name of the owner was Martulumin (Bartolomis). We made our way to the country of Turks, known for us as the land of Romans (Bilad al-Rum)."

Thus, Ibn Battuta reached Anatolia and visited all the big cities, had been received by the rulers and *amirs*, *qadi* and scholars. He was always treated with a great deal of respect and interest. Ibn Battuta recounts the hospitality of the members of the guild or of Akhi brotherhood where he used to stay. He left a detailed description of the structure and organization of the Order.

In Asia Minor, Ibn Battuta was in 'Alaya, Antalya, Akridur, Sparta, Qaysariyya, Siwas, Amasya and Erzurum, and went on along the western border of Turkish territories. He finally arrived, in 1331, in Sinop – a port on the Black Sea. From there, at the beginning of 1332, the traveller reached (by ship) the outskirts of Kerch. "The place where we arrived is called Dasht-i Qipchaq. Dasht is translated from Turkish as a steppe. This steppe is covered by green grass from one end to the other and is very favourable but there are no trees. On the whole landscape of the steppe one can find neither mountains, hills, buildings nor firewood. They travel in the steppe on the carriages and it is as long as a six-month trip: three months over the domain of Sultan Muhammad Uzbek and three more over the territory of the others."

From Kerch the traveller went to Port Kafa (Caffa, Feodosiya) and then further to Soldaya (Sudak) and city al-Qirim (Solkhat). Along the western coast of the Azov Sea he moved as far as the city of Azov (Azaq) and further to Majar. Having learned that Sultan Uzbek Khan was in his summer encampment in a place called Bishtagh (Five Mountains), he went there and later, together with the headquarters of the Sultan, moved to the city of Hajji-Tarkhan (Astrakhan). He spent some time there at the residence of Sultan Uzbek during autumn.

One of the wives of the Sultan – Bayalun, the Princess of Bysantyne – was leaving for Constantinople and Ibn Battuta joined her retinue. He eventually arrived in Constantinople on 18 September 1332.

The city impressed him very much. He spent thirty-six days there and left on 24 October 1332 with great honour and generous gifts presented by the Emperor. Without stopping, he went to Astrakhan through Southern Russia but, having failed to find Uzbek Khan, he made for Saray Berke – the capital of the Golden Horde.

From Saray, Ibn Battuta undertook a short trip to Bulghar. "I wished to make the trip there," he writes "to make sure on my own what I heard before, to see a short night at one time of the year and a short day – in the other" [25, II, 398].

There he scheduled the voyage to Pechora ("the Country of Darkness"), but abandoned the idea due to the great danger, and returned to Saray. The traveller stayed in the capital of the Golden Horde for several weeks. Then, in the middle of January 1333 he set off for Khorezm, the northern province of Central Asia.

According to his words he spent forty days on the way and finally came to Urgench, the capital of Khorezm, which struck him by its richness of nature and a very busy trade. We may come across depictions of medieval Khorezm in many Arabic geographical works. Examples are included in the ninth-century author Khurdadhbih's book entitled *Kitab al-masalik wa-l-mamalik* (*The Book of Roads and States*), in which he makes reference to Marw, which is along the left bank, and Khorezm [51, 33]. The author also gives details of the taxes (*kharaj*) raised from Khorezm, including the county of Kurdak [51, 38], and mentions the title of the ruler of Khorezm [51, 40]. Additionally, he speaks about the river Jayhun [51, 173], enumerates the counties of Khurasan, including Khorezm [51, 243], and very briefly mentions Khorezm when making reference to frontiers [51, 259].

Ibn Khurdadhbih speaks about the things that were useful only from a practical point of view. A little more descriptive detail of Khorezm is given by the tenth-century author Ibn al-Faqih in his writings *Kitab al-buldan* (*The Book of Countries*). The data of this author is more varied:

he quotes a poem about fur being processed in Khorezm [46, 237], mentions the sacred fire of the "magicians" (fire worshippers used to live in Khorezm in ancient times) [46, 246], and refers to the woods and bushes stretching from the Caspian Sea (the city of Barda'a) up to Khorezm [46, 297].

Ibn al-Faqih also relates the story of the "wise man" who once came to one of the caliphs. He had the ability to characterize the people living in different countries. He said about the Khorezmians that "these are the most indocile people inclined more than the others to undo themselves " [46, 320]. Ibn al-Faqih also included Khorezm in his three most cold countries [46, 229].

Al-Muqaddasi (tenth century) or al-Maqdisi gives very detailed information about Khorezm, saying that this is "the area stretching on both sides of the River Jayhun" [67, 234]. He goes on: "This is a vast area with many cities, all cultivated . . . there is an endless row of houses and gardens, many vineries, fields and trees, fruits and different facilities for the trading people. The inhabitants are clever, distinguished by their knowledge and education" [67, 284]. Additionally, al-Muqaddasi says: "Allah granted them the privilege of cheap life and fertility of the land, distinguished them by their ability of good reading of the Qur'an and a common sense. They are hospitable and fond of eating, they are brave and strong in the battle" [67, 285]. About the capital of Khorezm – Jurjaniyya – al-Muqaddasi says, that it is located on the right bank of the river [67, 288]. The geographer also tells us about the palace, built by al-Ma'mun in Jurjaniyya, and the wonderful gate of this palace [67, 288].

The author of the well-known geographic glossary *Mu'jam al-buldan*, Yaqut al-Hamawi (twelfth to thirteenth centuries) gives an example of legendary stories about Khorezm quoted from Ibn al-Kalbi. Referring to Ptolemey, he determines the location of Khorezm asserting that it is situated in the "sixth climate" and names the corresponding constellations. However, his later reference to "Zij" of Abu'Awn asserts that Khorezm is on the edge of the "fifth climate" and gives slightly different co-ordinates [55, II, 480–481]. Having mentioned that Khorezm is not really the name of the city but of the area, Yaqut names the capital of the area as Jurjaniyya and details its history: "The people say that Khorezm is called this way because one of the ancient kings got angry with 400 subjects of his kingdom and especially with those at the court, and ordered them to be exiled to the place far away from any settlements, 100 *farsakhs* away from the nearest one. Only one place was found to fit the order of the king – a place near the city of Kath, which used to belong to Khorezm. They were brought there and left for good. Once the king recalled these people he ordered them to go and see what happened to them. They came and saw that the exiles built the houses, caught fish to feed themselves and there was plenty of firewood. The people sent by the king asked: 'How are you doing?' They answered: 'We have meat – they showed the fish – we have firewood to fry the fish and eat it.' They returned back and told the king. This place was called 'Khawarizm' (Khorezm), because 'khawar' in the Khorezmi language meant 'meat', and firewood – 'rism'. To make it easier for pronunciation they began to call it 'Khawarizm' (not Khawarrism), because to pronounce it with double 'r' was difficult" [55, II, 48].

Yaqut continues describing Khorezm and its capital, the city, the customs of the inhabitants, and their appearance. Paying special attention to the origination of the Khorezmians, he quotes many scholars including 'Abdallah al-Faqir, al-Muqaddasi and al-Biruni.

Yaqut writes about the capital of Khorezm – Urgench: "Khorezm is not the name of the city but of the whole region. As for the main city, it is called now Jurjaniyya as I have mentioned in the right place before. But the local people call it Kurkanj" [55, II, 480]. Kurkanj is a reflection of the name Gurgench in Arabic transcription. Having outlined the history of the city he continued his description: "In this region they built the houses and palaces, their number had been increased and they spread throughout the territory. They built settlements and cities, the people of the neighbouring cities of Khorezm seized ignoring them, they came and settled there. The citizens of Khorezm grew in number and glorified themselves. Khorezm became beautiful and prosperous. I had been there in 616 (1219–1220) and never happened to see the region being more populous and flourishing. It is all tilled, the villages are situated one after another, and there are many separate houses and castles in the steppe. It is very seldom that you can see in *rustaqs* (rural areas) the soil not cultivated and not built on. At the same time there are plenty of trees, mostly mulberry trees, because they (the inhabitants) need it to construct their houses and to feed the silkworm. And there is no difference between those who walk along their *rustaqs* and those who walk in the markets . . . Most of the settlements of

Khorezm are the cities with markets full of goods and shops and it is very seldom that you can happen to see a village without the market" [55, II, 482].

This is how Yaqut depicts the situation in Khorezm before the Mongol conquer, pointing out that the area was flourishing and saying, in his own words, that "there was hardly any land not tilled".

He devoted a separate article to the capital of Khorezm – Urgench and wrote: "This is the name of the capital of the region. Khorezm is a big city on the bank of River Jayhun. The people of Khorezm call it Kurkanj (Gurgench) in their native language. But this name was Arabiated and we pronounce it as Jurjaniyya . . . I saw this city in 616 (1219–1220) before it was conquered and ruined by tatars. I believe I never saw the bigger and more comfortable city. But all this came to an end after the tatars had destroyed it; as I learned there remained only big buildings, and the Mongols killed all the citizens" [55, II, 54].

Yaqut's information is being verified by archeological explorations which are showing a highly developed production and culture of Khorezm at the time he visited (in the early part of the thirteenth century). For further examples, refer to 93, 160.

Ibn 'Arabshah (1389–1450) also writes about Khorezm 'Aja'ib al-maqdur fi-nawa'ib Taymur, where he states: "There capital (that of Khorezmiyans) – the City of Jurjan . . . is a place for eloquent speakers to convene; the scholars unsaddle their horses here [that is, make a stop], the wit minded people and poets find shelter, the educated and the great come visit this place. This is a mountainous spring of mu'tazilits . . . It abounds in benefits and kindness has no limits here . . . [42, 15–16].

Al-'Umari (1301–1349), Ibn Battuta's contemporary, wrote about Khorezm in his book called *Kitab masalik al-absar wa-mamalik al-amsar*. He enumerates in detail all kinds of cereals and goods produced in this region, recounts the peculiarities of the monetary circulation and outlines prices in Mawarannahr, Khorezm and its capital Urgench. He depicts thoroughly the character of the people: "Among cereals you can find in this region wheat, barley, rice, and others . . . different fruits, the best of them being from Bukhara and Samarqand although Khorezmian fruits are even better and delicious . . ." [75, 47]. Further, al-'Umari blesses the hospitality of Khorezmians [75, 42–43], speaks about the abundance of homesteads – *madrasas* – where they were received and fed: "If a stranger happens to come, they argue with each other to invite him home as a guest and spend money competing with each other in hospitality whereas others compete in earning as much money as they can" [75, 47].

His story about the markets of Urgench is peculiar for being simple and businesslike, which is in contrast to the lively and natural narration of Ibn Battuta: "The prices in the region [Khorezm] are extremely low, with the exception of Urgench, the capital of Khorezm, which is sometimes called Khorezm. The prices for the grain are either high or average but never cheap. As for meat, it is rather cheap . . . [75, 68].

After three weeks in Khorezm Ibn Battuta headed for the south towards Bukhara and arrived there eighteen days later. The medieval city of Bukhara was one of the well-known cities of the Islamic world. Arab geographers attached much importance to its description. Ibn Khurdadhbih tells a legendary story of how Bukhara (and Samarqand) was built by Alexander the Great after he returned from China, where he erected a wall to confront the mythological tribes of Ya'juj and Ma'juj: "Having reached the country of Soghd he built Samarqand and the city known as al-Dabusiyya as well as al-Iskandariyya the Far and then he went to the land of Bukhara" [51, 265].

The same facts were repeated by Ibn al-Faqih, who also attached much of his attention to the prominent people originating from Bukhara (for example Barmakids) [46, 324].

Al-Muqaddasi gives much space in his writing to Bukhara – its outskirts [67, 266–268], its *qasaba* comparing it with Fustat in Egypt in terms of richness, abundance of markets, and Damascus for is perfection and density of the buildings [67, 280]. Al-Muqaddasi writes: "The city is extremely comfortable. It has seven iron plated gates (including those at Bab Nur, Bab Fufra, Bab al-Khalid, Bab al-Quhandiz [a castle], which belonged to the sultan. They have a treasury and a custody . . . The mosque is inside the city. It has several yards and all are clean . . . The markets of the city are full with expensive things and in Rabad there are ten big roads . . . and there is not such a comfortable and populous city in this part of this world. One can find there nice food, beautiful baths, broad roads, clean water and beautiful buildings . . . [67, 280–281].

Even the short fragments from al-Muqaddasi's description enables us to gain an impression of this lively and populous city, which the author compares with such urban centres as Fustat and Damascus.

If we look at Yaqut's description, made before the Mongol conquer, we see that in the part devoted to Bukhara, as well as in the other segments of his works, he tries to give as complete a picture as possible of the city, utilizing different sources. He writes: "Undoubtedly this is a very ancient city with plenty of gardens and nice fruits. During my stay in Bukhara the fruits were supplied to Marw, which is eighteen passages away and to Khorezm, which was fifteen days to march . . . The author of the book *Kitab al-suwar* said: 'As far as the beauty of Mawarannahr is concerned, I never saw and never heard of a city among the Islamic countries which has such a beautiful appearance as Bukhara, because on top of the castle one can see the green landscape going up as high as the blue sky and there is not a country throughout Mawarannahr and Khurasan where the people could till the land as well as the citizens of Bukhara . . ." The author of the book [*Kitab al-suwar*], which is quoted by Yaqut says: "As for Bukhara this is on a plain and the buildings have a wooden carcass. All the buildings, including castles, gardens, the shops, paved roads and an endless row of settlements, are surrounded by a wall as long as twelve *farsakhs* composing a unique ensemble to embrace the castles, buildings, settlements and the centre of the city. Nor is there any open space, nor ruins. Besides this wall there is one more surrounding the palaces, dwelling houses, shops and gardens which belong to the city and where people stay throughout the winter and summer. And there is not a city in Mawarannahr more populous than Bukhara . . ." [55, 517–518].

The descriptions of Bukhara are full and have plenty of references from the written sources of al-'Umari [75, 50–51, 54]. Al-'Umari was especially struck by the fact, as he wrote, that only in Paykand there were 1,000 *ribats* [75, 54].

Ibn Battuta did not like Bukhara. He wrote with indignation: "This city used to be the capital of the cities located over the River Jayhun, and the damned tatar Tingiz (Chinggis) . . . destroyed it because many of its mosques, *madrasas* and bazaars lie in ruins. The citizens are humiliated, their testimonies are not recognized in Khorezm and the other countries because they are known for their fanaticism, and false pretensions and rejections of truth. At the present time there are no people with knowledge in science and nobody who can pay tribute to it" [25, III, 22].

These words of the traveller from Morocco are in contrast with the story of al-'Umari praising the people of Bukhara for their "knowledge in *fiqh*, confidence and credibility, good behaviour and friendliness, extending of kindness and favourable deeds" [75, 54]. Al-'Umari describes the picture in such a way as if there had not been a devastating invasion, no periodical destructions of Bukhara and no disruption. He makes use of the sources known to him where Bukhara is described as a "flourishing city", whereas Ibn Battuta mainly relies upon his own eyes. His indignant tone is probably the result of not having received a very friendly reception.

So, who should we believe? Marco Polo, who was absolutely independent of the Arab geographical tradition, writes that Bukhara is big and magnificent . . . Throughout Persia, Bukhara is the best city" [70, 45]. But the Bukhara documents of the fourteenth century [78], the most reliable source, depict the disruption prevailing in Bukhara at that time and prove the words of Ibn Battuta: "The lands of one of the villages of Bukhara (Farkan, Farkand) were occupied by the newly planted gardens and there was much soil to be used and difficulties to be counted because of their abundance and lack of boundaries. All of this soil is suitable for tilling and sowing; as for the estates there is a lonely hill, desolate, with a deserted landscape in place of the former buildings and houses . . . The first boundary of the village (that of Farkan, Farkand), the eastern one, stretches along the salt-marsh bank and serves as a mark to divide the wasteland of Ushmiyun and Farkan, Farkand, and goes further until the wasteland . . . Further on, the eastern boundary continues along the small canal as long as two *pora* of land to reach this wasteland of Farkan, Farkand . . ." [78, 119–120].

The wasteland, newly erected canals (after demolition) and the reconstruction of the gardens are mentioned everywhere in the Bukhara documents of the fourteenth century, presenting an opposite view of the stories about the vast gardens and fields, stretching from Bukhara until Samarqand where one could hardly come across a space not built on and not tilled. Further, the documents say: "The whole village of Ushmiyun in Bukhara was watered by the Nawkhas canal . . . [it turned into *waqf*]. The farmsteads are located on a high hill, which is deserted now. In the old times there were different buildings, including the mosques, buildings, storehouses and the houses of *qadi* brewers and all this had been turned into wasteland" [78, 137].

Having become acquainted with Bukhara, Ibn Battuta headed for the city of Nakhshab, where Sultan Tarmashirin had his residence. He also visited Samarqand, which still had the marks of its previous magnificence, preserved from the epoch before the devastation by the Mongols.

The descriptions of pre-Mongolian Samarqand reached us in many writings of medieval geographical and historical literature. Thus, in one of the earliest Arabic descriptions of the city, given in *Kitab al-buldan* by Ibn al-Faqih, it is said: "Samarqand was built by Iskandar (Alexander the Great), the diameter of its walls is twelve *farsakhs*. There are twelve gates in the city and the distance between the gates is one *farsakh*. On top of the walls there are loopholes and war towers. All the gates are wooden and folding. At the far end there are two more gates with a lodging for the guard in between. When you pass the fields you stop in *Rabad* with buildings. *Rabad* and irrigated lands stretch to as much as 6,000 *jaribs* and the wall surrounds the *rustaqs*, gardens and melonfields together with twelve gates built in this wall. Then you find yourself in the town, which is as vast as 5,000 *jaribs*. There are four gates . . . and then you enter the inner city, which occupies the space of 2,500 *jaribs*. There is a main mosque, *quhandiz*, and the residence of the ruler inside the city. There is running water in the city. And there are rivers and canals flowing behind the wall. Quhandiz has an iron gate at the beginning and at the end . . ." [46, 326].

Ibn al-Faqih goes on with this semi-legendary data, repeated by the other authors, that Samarqand was built (obviously, after Alexander) by King Tubba' (one of the Yemen pre-Islamic kings) [46, 326–327]. Referring to the famous philologist al-Asma'i, Ibn al-Faqih writes: "On the gates of Samarqand there is an inscription in the Himyarite language: 'It is 1,000 *farsakhs* between this city and San'a' and 1,000 *farsakhs* from here to Baghdad and Africa'" [46, 326]. The early name of the city is said to come from the name of one of tubba's, Shammar ibn Ifriqiyas, who is supposed to have destroyed the city [46, 25].

Speaking about the *marhalas*, Ibn al-Faqih mentions Samarqand many times, determines the distance between Samarqand and the other cities and regions [for example, 46, 337, 330, 104] and says that the area surrounding Samarqand could be compared only with the famous

Damascus Ghuta, known for its gardens: "Yahiya ibn Aqsam said: 'There is not a place on earth more pleasant to live than the Samarqand fortress, Damascus Ghuta and River Ubulla in Iraq'." [46, 236].

The author of *Kitab al-buldan* informs us that there was a mysterious inscription on top of the gates of Samarqand (here he does not determine what language it was in) similar to that on the gates of Ghumdan in Yemen, and on the column on the bank of the River Nile and so on, and so forth [46, 251]. With Ibn al-Faqih we see that the real, truthful and legendary notes have been mixed and it is interesting to know that he mentions Samarqand paper as being a world-known item of export [46, 25]. Indeed, Samarqand supplied the paper to all the scribes and writers throughout the Caliphate.

Al-Istakhri gives a very careful account of Samarqand, mentioning the four gates of the city: "The Chinese gate to the east side, the Nawbahar gate to the west, the Bukhara gate to the north, the Kesh gate to the south" [52, 316].

Further, he says that "water in Samarqand flows inside the leaden pipes and there is a deep moat around the city, the ground from which was used for the building of the city wall" [52, 316]. This running water pipe crosses the market at a point called Ra's al-Taq ("top of the arch"), which is the most populous place in the city [52, 317]. Describing Samarqand, al-Istakhri underlines the abundance of the gardens and greenery, and a great number of markets with the centre in Ra's al-Taq [52, 317]. Indeed, he writes: "The centre of the markets in Samarqand is in Ra's al-Taq, where all the streets, markets and shops (two times larger than the palaces and gardens) are located. There is not a street or house without a garden. And if you climb to the top of the castle you will not be able to see the town [that is, the buildings] because of the huge number of gardens and trees. The majority of the markets are in *Rabad* and this is the main shopping centre except for the few people trading in the inner city. This city looks like a harbour of Mawarannahr, where the merchants meet. The majority of the goods from Mawarannahr go to Samarqand and from there to the other regions. The residence of Amir of Mawarannahr at the time of Isma'il ibn Ahmad was in Samarqand, and he transfered it to Bukhara" [52, 317–318].

Al-Istakhri also repeats the note about the mysterious inscription in the Himyarite language written down on the Kesh gate [52, 318].

He gives merit to the fertility of the Samarqand soil and praises the citizens for their beauty and boldness [52, 318]. He also mentions that Samarqand was a large slave centre of Mawarannahr, and the training of slaves and the slave trade earned the local merchants significant income [52, 318].

No less enthusiastic are the impressions of Samarqand of the other geographers. Ibn Khurdadhbih, for example, quotes the Persian poems praising Samarqand [51, 26, 176, 262] and gives a brief description of the city. He also recounts the distance from Samarqand to the other cities of Mawarannahr [51, 26], speaks about its history and the title of its ruler [51, 20] and repeats the story about the settling of Samarqand by Alexander the Great [51, 365].

The notes about Samarqand as well as about the other cities of Central Asia are included in the book *Kitab surat al-ard* by Ibn Hawqal. Similar notes are reported by Ibn Rusta, who classifies the cities of Mawarannahr as "the four climate cities" in accordance with the existing tradition of medieval geographers [44].

A very detailed and interesting description of Samarqand can be found in *Kitab al-buldan* by al-Ya'qubi [54]. He writes: "From Kesh till the great city of Soghd there are four passages. It is the most populous and comfortable among them. The strongest warriors and most steadfast soldiers live there" [54, 293]. Further al-Ya'qubi refers to some data on the history of Samarqand: "It was conquered by Qutayba ibn Muslim al-Bahili [at the beginning of the eighth century] during the time of al-Walid ibn 'Abd al-Malik (705–715); he concluded the peace treaty with the peasants and king. The city was surrounded by a big wall, but it was destroyed and al-Rashid (786–809) built it again. There is a big river, which flows from the country of Turks like Ephratis it is called 'Nasif' ('Yasif') [the editor did not identify the name of the river, which is why the diacritic marks are not clarified]. This river flows over the land of Samarqand and further to the countries of Soghd and then to Usrushana . . ." [54, 293]. Al-Ya'qubi says that in the valley of the river the people find gold [Zarafshan] [54, 294].

Further information about Bukhara and Samarqand can be found in "Hudud al-'Al-am's book, where it states that it is "a big flourishing and very pleasant city, where merchants from all over the world meet. It consists of the city itself [that is, the central part of the town, *shahristan*] a castle and suburbs" [77, 113]. Further, there is information about a Manichaean monastery and reference to Samarqand being the centre of paper manufacturing, for which it is known all over the world [77, 113, 352].

Al-'Umari mainly utilizes the data taken from *Ashkal al-ard*, depicting Samarqand as a flourishing city: "It is a lofty city with a citadel. Looking at the city, one can see the greenery of the trees, the glitter of the palaces, the flowing rivers and bright buildings. Wherever you look you can enjoy the sight and whatever the garden, it is a matter for one's delight. The cypruses are cut in a way that resemble the various animals – elephants, camels, cows and other beasts – attacking each other . . ." [75, 55]. Alternatively, Qutayba ibn Muslim said: "When I was approaching Samarqand we began to look for something to compare it with and could not find anything to match. And I said: 'It resembles the sky by its colour, and the palaces look like the stars, sparkling in the heaven and the springs are similar to the Milky Way!' Everybody liked the comparison" [75, 55].

Al-'Umari continued his detail regarding the four gates, the number of bath-houses, the homesteads and the dwelling houses. "In some places amidst the market the mounds of stone are made where the water from 'al-Saffarin' is running." Al-'Umari repeats the story about the "leaden canal" and the moat around Samarqand [75, 56], the Yemen king and the Himyarite inscription on top of the gate [75, 56–57].

It is very interesting that he also says: "In spite of the misfortunes and misery that made the young people get older during the time of Chinggis Khan and his ancestors . . ." Samarqand still remained the matter of delight [75, 60].

In some high-flown prose, which al-'Umari used frequently in accordance with the demand of the literary style of the time, one could feel that he sincerely sympathized with Samarqand being demolished, inasmuch as he preferred Samarqand to Damascus Ghuta, saying that the latter is but a small "piece of the Soghdian Samarqand" [75, 60]

From Samarqand, Ibn Battuta made his way to Tirmith and then crossed the River Jayhun to get to Khurasan. He described the city of Balkh, lying in ruins and uninhabited at that time: "Everybody who visited Balkh thought against his will that this city used to be a flourishing city with magnificent buildings left partially untouched. Once it was a big city occupying a vast territory. The traces of its mosques and *madrasas* preserved, as well as the inscriptions on the buildings which were decorated by lapis-lazuli" [25, II, 398].

Next Ibn Battuta visited Herat. He called it a big and populous city of Khurasan, and devoted several pages to the Sultan of Herat, Mu'izz al-Din al-Kart: "This is a great Sultan Husayn, the son of Sultan Ghiyath al-Din al-Ghuri; he is unbelievably courageous. He relies upon the support from above and feels happy. Two times the Allah granted him with support and help that was very surprising. The first time it happened in a battle against Sultan Khalil, who revolted against him. The latter was eventually captured as a prisoner. The second time it happened in a battle against Mas'ud, the Sultan of 'Rafidits', which ended in the defeat of Mas'ud, his escape and loss of kingdom. Sultan Husayn ascended the throne upon the death of his brother Hafiz, who succeeded his father Ghiyath al-Din" [25, III, 64].

In a chapter about Herat, Ibn Battuta tells us of the origin of the power of the Sarbadar dynasty, who succeeded in establishing an independent state in Khurasan (Sabzawar and Nishapur), which existed for almost half a century. He depicts a picture of real life in the country of Sarbadar from the point of view of a goodwill man rather than a faithful one. The notes of Ibn Battuta about the movement of the Sarbadar are of great interest for historians as far as they are not repeated anywhere else.

During the whole period of summer 1333, Ibn Battuta travelled in North-Eastern Iran and Afghanistan, visiting the ancient cities of Nishapur, Mashhad, Jam, Bistam and Kabul, then passing by the mountain range of Hindu Kush, and via Gazni and desert land where "the deadly wind *samum* blows". He made his way to India together with the caravan of merchants. On September 12, 1333 the traveller crossed the River Indus and finally arrived in India – the country he had for so long dreamed of reaching.

In India Ibn Battuta spent about eight years at the court of Sultan Muhammad Tughluq (1325–1351), who was the protector of scientists, poets and writers from other Muslim countries.

Ibn Battuta soon became one of the favourites of the Sultan and his mother Makhduma Jahan. He was presented with several villages (to own) and was appointed as a judge of the *maliki* trend in the capital. He also became the trustee of the funds coming from the vast lands, which were sacrificed by the Sultan and his nobility in favour of the mausoleum of Shaykh Qutb al-Din. Ibn Battuta fulfilled his duties vigilantly, engaging in the consideration of disputes between amirs and rulers. He often had meetings with the Sultan who accompanied him on his trips all over the country. He built a house in Delhi and a mosque opposite it. He travelled often with slaves and concubines, musicians, singers, dancing women and men following him.

In 1342 Ibn Battuta found himself in a disgrace. The traveller visited the Shaykh-hermit Shihab al-Din ibn Jam who lived in a cave dug by himself and was popular with the people, and thus made the Sultan angry. The Shaykh was suspected of treason and was executed by Muhammad Tughluq. Ibn Battuta was dismissed from the post of judge. Fearing for his life he gave up all his property, slaves and concubines, and became a hermit. Five months later, the Sultan again sought Ibn Battuta's friendship and suggested he occupy the post of a judge of the *maliki* in Delhi, but Ibn Battuta refused. Then, Muhammad Tughluq suggested that he travel to China as a personal ambassador-at-large, and to convey to the Emperor a message relating to the building of a Buddhist temple in India.

Previously there had been a number of missions from China with this request. Ibn Battuta agreed and went on the trip. But the trip was unsuccessful. They were attacked by a gang of armed Hindus, who robbed the caravan and Ibn Battuta was captured as a prisoner. He managed to escape with great difficulty, reaching the city of Kul from where he advised the Sultan about the misfortune.

Having received letters and gifts from the Sultan, Ibn Battuta once again started his journey. Making for the south-west, he reached a small town at the seashore, where the mission boarded a ship and sailed along the Arabian Sea down to the south. Having visited Sindapur (Goa), Ibn Battuta and his companions got to the biggest port in south-west India – Calcutta. With replenished reserves and having thoroughly accomplished all the pre-travel preparations, the caravan was placed on several ships to sail to China. But the travellers again found themselves in trouble. The boat with the gifts and other members of the mission were lost in a storm – although the captain escaped.

Ibn Battuta wandered all over the south-western ports of India looking for his ship. While in western India (in 1343) travelling from one port to another searching for his property and servants, he learned that Sultan Jamal al-Din, with fifty ships, had undertaken an assault against the island of Sindapur (Goa). He decided to join the Sultan. However, he did not stay long on the island because the local population recovered quickly from the sudden attack, and had undertaken an offensive and surrounded the island.

Ibn Battuta left the Sultan and returned to Calcutta by an independent boat. Eventually he realized that his people and property had gone forever, so the bankrupt traveller decided to travel to the Maldive islands.

The majority of the population of the Maldive islands were Muslims (Jaza'ir dhaybat al-mahl). Thanks to his closeness to Sultan Muhammad Tughluq he was extended a very warm welcome and was soon appointed as a judge. Ibn Battuta had decided to establish family relations with the influential nobility and married Khadija, the step-mother of the ruler of the islands, step-daughter of *wazir* 'Abdallah, the daughter of another *wazir* and the widow of the dead Sultan Shihab al-Din [25, IV, 149].

With the diplomatic mission, Ibn Battuta set off for Ma'bar. However, on the way he decided to visit the island of Ceylon. He arrived there in 1344. After Ceylon, Ibn Battuta went to the principality of Ma'bar, located at the southern edge of Hindustan. Ghiyath al-Din, the ruler of Ma'bar, accepted the traveller with great honour and promised him military support in order to conquer the Maldive islands.

However, soon after an epidemic of cholera broke out and the Sultan died, so Ibn Battuta returned to Maldives. Meanwhile, during this time his close friend, Jamal al-Din, died. Ibn Battuta left the Maldives and sailed to Bengal where he arrived forty-three days later. Having seen the different regions in Bengal and its places of interest in the second half of 1345, he could now resume his voyage to China. On the way, he visited Sumatra, Java, and journeyed via the country of "Tawalisi" (not yet precisely identified). Eventually, after another sea voyage, he reached China.

The stay of Ibn Battuta in Indo-China and China is still a matter of dispute between those who study his travellings. The dispute on this matter was summarized by I.Y. Krachkovskiy [107, 425–426], who proved the truthfulness of the reports of the Moroccan traveller in East and South-East Asia. The conclusion made by I.Y. Krachkovskiy was absolutely right: the analysis of the story told by Ibn Battuta shows that the statement of H. Yule, G. Ferrand and other scientists "that Ibn Battuta had not been to Indo-China" is groundless [172, 157].

It is possible that while in Indo-China, Ibn Battuta did not correctly interpret many things that he had a chance to see, and this is often reflected in the stories of his reporters and translators. First of all, language was often a hindrance to the correct understanding of what he had seen. For example, when he arrived at the port of Tsyu-Tung (Tsuyang), which was known in Muslim countries as Zaytun, it sounded similar to the Arabic word meaning "olive". Ibn Battuta decided that probably the city was so called because of the abundance of olive trees there. But later, having been convinced that this was not so, he found it necessary to stress the following: "The first city that we arrived in after we had stepped off the ship was Zaytun. In reality there are no olives because neither in India nor in al-Sin (China) do olive trees grow. Zaytun – "olive" – is just the name given to the city" [25, IV, 269].

In a similar way he explains the origin of the names of many other cities and places. For example, about the city of Khansa (Khan-Tsufuy) he writes: "The name of the city is pronounced the same way as that of the famous Arabic poetess and I don't know whether it came from the Arabic language or whether it existed as it was in Chinese" [25, IV, 287–288].

The data acquired by the traveller, gathered without the help of interpreters or his agents, is distinguished by the vitality and truthfulness of its narration. The traveller had an acute ability to observe and to outline the most important things. Ibn Battuta frequently describes the features that distinguish his motherland (that is, Morocco) from various other countries. He writes about the immense skill of the Chinese painters, speaks about the usage of paper money, the extraction of coal, the legislation protecting the interests of foreign merchants, and he devotes several stories to animals and plants in China.

The evidence of Ibn Battuta relating to craftsmen is very interesting: "On this square in the premises with cupolas the craftsmen sew luxury clothes and make guns. Amir Qurtay told me that there were 1,600 masters, each having three or four apprentices and all of them were the slaves of the Khan (Emperor). Their legs were shackled and they lived out of the territory of the palaces. They were allowed to go to the markets of the city but were not allowed beyond the city walls. Every day they appeared before the eyes of the amir in groups of 1,000 men and if somebody was absent, the senior in charge of the group was made to give a reason. They had a rule: everybody who served for ten years was set free and given a choice. If he wished, he might stay in service without being shackled, otherwise he could go wherever he liked to any of the countries of the Khan, but never to leave the borders of the state. Whenever they reached the age of fifty they were set free of their job and lived at the expense of the treasury . . ." [25, IV, 287–288].

Continuing on, the traveller tells us about "the great amir of Qurtay": "Qurtay is the chief *amir* of al-Sin . . . We stayed with him for three days and then he sent his son with us to see the canal . . . He was accompanied by musicians and singers who sang Chinese, Arabic and Persian songs. The singers performed one Persian song and by the order of Amir repeated it several times so that I learned the words by heart. The song had a wonderful rhythm" [25, IV, 289–290].

It is clear from the extract that a man who had never been to China could hardly invent these details and then tell us about them so carefully. It is especially interesting that he focused his attention on the Persian song. Ibn Battuta did not know the author of the song, nor did the European explorers. However, the prominent Iranian scientist Muhammad Qazwini (who died in 1949) discovered that the verses were the part of Sa'di Shirazi's (who died in 1291) *ghazal* from his collection "Tayyibat". The correct text of the latter follows:

> Since the time I fell in love with You
> I sail in the ocean of dreams
> I seem to see You in mihrab
> Whenever I pray and do my namaz.

Ibn Battuta arrived in Khan Baliq (Beijing) at a very turbulent time. Although the Muslim officials and shaykhs living in Beijing extended him a very warm welcome he did not succeed in fulfilling the duty for which he had come. What prevented him was the internecine war which had broken out and as a result of which the Mongol Khan, Toghan Timur, left the capital. When the riots in Beijing spread, Shaykh Burhan al-Din Sagharji, with whom Ibn Battuta had made an acquaintance when in India, and who had succeeded in getting the post of "sadr-i jahan" (the leader of Muslims), advised Ibn Battuta to return home.

In the autumn of 1346, the traveller left Beijing along the Great Canal, sailed down to the port of Zaytun and went back to India along the same route that he had used on his way to China. Forty days later, at the beginning of 1347, he arrived at the Indian port of Kulam on the eastern shore of the Arabian Sea; at the end of January, he moved to Calcutta from where he intended to go to the capital, to visit the court of Muhammad Tughluq. However, he soon changed his mind.

From Zafar, the traveller went to Hurmuz. He crossed Persia again visiting Mayman, Shiraz, Yazd, Isfahan, Tustar and Huwayza'. From Huwayza' he went to Basra and Najaf, and from there to Baghdad and finally "right after twenty years found himself in Damascus again".

Ibn Battuta stayed there until April 1348; he then left the city and, passing via Hama and Hims, he arrived in Aleppo in June 1348. There, he found out that in Ghaza, the area to which he was heading, cholera had broken out and "every day thousands of people died". He therefore returned to Hims. But the cholera followed him, so without stopping, the traveller went to Damascus where "cholera was taking 2,400 lives a day". To escape from these further epidemics, Ibn Battuta moved to Egypt via Jerusalem and from there made his fourth pilgrimage to Mecca, where he arrived in November of 1348.

After *hajj* he returned to Palestine with the Damascus caravan and then, at the beginning of 1349, he returned to Cairo. There, he decided to return home and in April 1349 sailed for Tunis. But while at sea they were attacked by Corsars who took their ship. The traveller consequently reached Safaqus in a small vessel, then continued his journey to Tunis by land, where he was eventually received by the sultan of the country, Abu-l-Hasan ibn Abi Sa'id 'Abd al-Haqq.

Ibn Battuta visited the island of Sardiniyya and then in November of 1349 he arrived in Fez where he was received with great honour by the ruling sultan Abu 'Inan (1348–1359) of the Marinids dynasty (1196–1465).

But the wanderings of Ibn Battuta had not ended: having visited the tomb of his mother in Tanjier, he crossed the Hybraltar to go to southern Spain, which was still dominated by the Arabs. This trip was on the order of the sultan, but the exact itinerary was not mentioned in the "Travels". We only know that he went to Rondo, Malaga, Granada and returned back across the Hybraltar. On 18 February 1352, by the order of Abu 'Inan, he began a much longer journey in Africa. Via Sijilmasa, he went to Tinbuktu in the newly Islamized state of Malli. On the way back, and having explored the copper mines of Tagadda, on 12 September 1353 he started a very hard journey across the Agades oasis and, suffering great hardships in a cold winter, crossed the Atlas mountains and returned back to Fez.

The stories of the traveller made a great impression on Sultan Abu 'Inan and his dignitaries, and he ordered Ibn Juzayy al-Kalbi, the historian and writer at the court who was the master of "high-flown writing", to record all the stories and impressions of Ibn Battuta. We do not know when Ibn Battuta and Ibn Juzayy began this work. The only thing that is known exactly to us is that the recording of the stories of the traveller and the editing were finished in February 1356 [25, IV, 451].

We have scarce information about the last years of Ibn Battuta. Thus far, we do not know even the date of his death. As it becomes clear at the end of the book by Ibn Juzayy, after he had returned from his travel to Western Africa Ibn Battuta was included in the staff of local scientists at court. In Fez, perhaps, he intended to live at court. But soon after his book had been completed Ibn Battuta lost his protector (Abu 'Inan died in 1359) and, according to the report of the author of *al-Durar al-kamina*, he spent his last years as a judge in provincial cities throughout Morocco [47, III, 424].

As a rule, and mainly in the studies made by European scientists, it is suggested that Ibn Battuta died in 1377 [107, 420]. But we have not been able to find out the source of that information. As we know, there is only one source with details of the last years of the traveller, and that is the biographical dictionary of Ibn Hajar al-'Asqalani. Ibn Hajar refers to Ibn Marzuq and mentions that Ibn Battuta was still alive in 770/1368–1369.

According to some sources, Ibn Battuta was buried near Tanjier, most probably near the tomb of Saint Ahmad al-Tanji.

The travels of Ibn Battuta may be regarded as heroic acts, but at the same time it was a very hard and exhausting job, demanding not only physical and moral endurance but the flexibility and skill to match the many different circumstances he encountered. The entire life of this man was inseparably connected with wanderings and it is almost impossible to write his biography without mentioning his travels. But what was the aim of these wanderings that became the focus of his life? Ibn Battuta did not expand on his motivation. It is something that one has to piece together from the narrative of his tales.

At first glance, one could suppose that he simply had practical aim facing him – to make a pilgrimage to the sacred cities and thus gain the sympathy of his contemporaries, or to listen the lectures on the law and to obtain the right to teach one of the books of *Hadith*, as happened in Damascus in 1305 [25, I, 248], or to seek gifts from the rulers and influential people of several countries, who, indeed, praised him many times.

Of course, the stories about the fairytale wealth of India had attracted attention and encouraged Afanasiy Nikitin, some Europeans in the Middle Ages and also Ibn Battuta, who first heard about the wonderful generosity of Indian rulers whilst at Mecca.

But it was not the most important reason. Ibn Battuta, as well as many other travellers in the East and Europe, belonged to the elite of pioneer travellers-explorers. These people were moved to travel by their enormous desire to study, rather than by economic and political factors. Knowledge of the world was expanding, and the travellers were not the last to be praised for that.

"The inhabited part of the land" known to the Arabs was getting broader and broader and consequently the interest of others to see these new cities and .countries was increased. As Ibn Battuta put it, aspirations "to see the world, let one's heart enjoy it, see the different miracles, acquire the knowledge, meet interesting people, put one's life at a stake" [25, II, 409] were also encouraged. This very desire – to see and to learn as much as possible – explains Ibn Battuta's rule, which he tried to keep to: "Not to pass one and the same road twice" [25, II, 21]. Neither numerous difficulties nor lack of means or various hardships, of which he very often complained, could make him change his mind.

Although it took him several attempts, reaching India was Ibn Battuta's long-held dream. He wanted to sail towards India, yet in 1332, after the pilgrimage and later, he mentioned sorrowfully: "I could not find a companion; as for the money to use for the trip, I did not have it either [25, II, 250–251].

At the time of his travels Ibn Battuta enjoyed the hospitality of Akhi Order members, and stayed in "zawiyas" (*sufi* apartments) where strangers were provided with free food and lodging. The city rulers used to give him gifts and food, regarding their gesture as "the faithful deed". Indeed, the traveller from Morocco did not hide his closeness with prominent religious officials of that time, and had several "certificates" including one that recognized him as being a judge of two trends – *Maliki* and *Shafi'i*. (Later this helped him to occupy the post of a judge of the *Maliki* trend at the court of Muhammad Tughluq in Delhi.)

However, it is hardly possible to agree with R. Hennig who suggests that the traveller was a "fanatic adherent of Islamic religion" and who "missed the Christian countries on purpose" [132, II, 206]. Probably this statement was motivated by the traditional attitude to Islam in Europe. It was difficult for Ibn Battuta, who had no any other way to earn money except through his profession as an Islamic lawyer and *muhaddith*, to find employment and support himself in any Christian country. He was neither a professional merchant, nor a physician and or the official representative of any state. Perhaps he did not have enough money to stop at the merchants' encampments. The religion was like a pass for him but within the borders of the Muslim world only [114, 15].

It is also difficult to accept that "in some cases the objectivity of the information given by Ibn Battuta is seriously influenced by religious fanaticism and undoubtedly his adherence to all that is connected with Islam" [132, II, 207]. Objectivity as we understand it now was different in the Middle Ages. Undoubtedly the traveller was a faithful Muslim. However, we do not read of any implications against Christians and representatives of other religions (the more so, Christianity was one of the protected religions). He simply did not notice them. As for the word "damned", it was attributed to Chinggis Khan as it was used to show the cruelty of this ruler, and the size of the damage that had been caused in some countries. The other Mongol rulers, even non-Muslims, are treated by Ibn Battuta in a very friendly way.

To our mind, the statement of R. Hennig that "he [Ibn Battuta] was inclined, more than Marco Polo, to report about different false rumours and magical adventures, being of no significance at all" are also unhistoric [132, II, 207]. First of all, the book of Marco Polo is also abound with "false rumours" – maybe much more so than we can find with Ibn Battuta. The second, what was "of no significance at all" for us was of primary importance for Marco Polo and Ibn Battuta. "The magic" of the "saint" was more important for both of them than, for example, the coins minted at that time in various countries.

The history of the book is reflected in the preface written by the editor of "The Travels", Ibn Juzayy al-Kalbi, who had written the book exactly as it was told by Ibn Battuta himself. I.Y. Krachkovskiy, in his book *Arabic Geographical Literature* gave the brief contents and analysis of the preface.

In the epilogue of the book there are two notes, which by their essence could be considered together with what Ibn Juzayy said in the preface. In the first note he writes: "Here end 'The Travels' called 'Tuhfat al-nuzzar fi ghara'ib al-amsar wa-'aja'ib al-asfar' (the gift to those who want to see the wonders of the cities and the magics of the travellings). The last record was made the third day of *Dhu-l-Hijja* in the year of 756/9 December 1355" [7, 681].

The second note is at the end of the book following the quotation where Abu 'Inan is highly praised and the traveller is merited in high-flown style: "This book was finished in Safar of 757/February 1356" [7, 682].

As is clear from the text of the preface and notes of Ibn Juzayy, *The Book of Travels* of Ibn Battuta, in accordance with the style of the time, was given a gorgeous and intricate title, using the rhythm "Tuhfat al-nuzzar fi ghara'ib al-amsar wa-'aja'ib al-asfar".

Neither in the preface, the text nor in the conclusion of the book is there a notice about this title. Ibn Battuta, who was not aware of the "scholastic" style of his time, would hardly have used such a title for his book. Most probably, the quoted note with the title of the book was made by Ibn Juzayy after the completion of the editing of the book. However, this title had not been broadly recognized and the book entered literature under the title of *The Travels of Ibn Battuta*.

The education of Ibn Battuta probably was not of an academic nature at all. All he had learnt was the result of his interaction with the scientists-traditionalists, whom he met in different cities. To a large extent he was interested in studying law. Wherever he had a chance, Ibn Battuta received diplomas and certificates that gave him the right him to teach law or to obtain the post of judge. But he was aware of neither traditional scholastic nor exact sciences. Anyway, the absence of any quotations in his stories from either his own poetic works or references to the other writers and scientists is dear evidence that he was experienced enough in written literature. The lack of experience in stylistic and literary language made him seek the help of an editor, Ibn Juzayy. Naturally, this made a special impact on the book because Ibn Juzayy was a skillful master of literary style. He was the writer and adib at court, aware of all the peculiarities of bureaucratic eloquence.

Ibn Juzayy was born and grew up in Granada. He received a traditional education and entered the service of the ruler from the dynasty of Nasrids Abu-l-Hajj Yusuf (1333–1354). Alongside this work, Ibn Juzayy was engaged in history and literary work: we may know of two of his works devoted to "the deeds" and genealogy of the Prophet Muhammad [107, 422]. After a quarrel with the ruler in Granada, Ibn Juzayy moved to court of Abu 'Inan, where he continued his work as secretary and scribe. Abu 'Inan, who listened to Ibn Battuta many times, came to understand that the traveller was a great master of oral narration but did not use a high-flown style. That is why the literary decoration of the book was charged to the experienced Ibn Juzayy. Ibn Juzayy died in 1356, a short time after the completion of the book.

The stories were recorded in December 1355 and the editing by Ibn Juzayy was completed in February 1356. It is obvious that over only two or three months, however strong his desire to do so, it was impossible for the editor to look closely into the "The Travels". We can guess that he limited himself by writing the preface and a small epilogue, included several poems and added small extracts from the writings of Ibn Jubayr (1145–1217) [43, IV, 304–308] to the description of Syria and Arabia. He collected together distinctly separate stories, which very often were not actually connected with each other, by using a logically consistent narration – in other words he conducted the editing work. Hence, "The Travels" is a literary record of the stories and recollections of Ibn Battuta about his wanderings over the countries of Asia and Africa.

The traveller, having no inclination to obtain knowledge from the many books accumulated during his travels, trained his memory and mastered his skill as a professional narrator. Consequently, when he spoke about his travels he could remember almost all the people whom he had met, and the important features and peculiarities of the foreign countries that he had visited. Naturally, his stories abounded in numerous extravagant details which raised suspicion as to whether they were true or not.

As we have mentioned before, Ibn Khaldun, the contemporary of Ibn Battuta who visited him in Fez in 1350, doubted that all stories were true [48, 143–144]. This suspicion, caused by "the amazing stories" told at the court of the Marinids in Fez eventually played a positive role. Scared of causing blame for the authorship of "the amazing stories" to be laid on the "honourable citizens", Ibn Battuta decided to be as precise and careful as possible. Speaking of his own observations he would say deliberately things like: "I saw it myself" while for other cases he specified: "I heard it from somebody else". For example, speaking about Sultan Muhammad Tughluq he writes the following: "All that I mentioned on the affairs of the sultans of India I was told by others and I heard it largely from Shaykh Kamal al-Din ibn al-Burhan al-Ghaznawi – the chief judge. What concerns the King was what I witnessed myself while I stayed in his country" [7, 427].

While retelling the events Ibn Battuta used the most accurate methods of recording them in the stories and reports, and he bore responsibility for their truthfulness. Meanwhile, in other cases he just referred to the sources and never assumed responsibility for them. This specific feature of his notes makes the book of great value.

As was pointed out by V.V. Bartol'd many times, "To use Arabic geographical literature is slightly difficult because of its bookish character and hence the chronological uncertainty. For example, if we have two authors, one who lived in the tenth century and the other in the eleventh century, it is not correct to suppose that the stories of the latter can be dated to the later period than that of the first; almost all the authors were based on the books but never define the source and the time. It happens very frequently when the document of the eleventh-century writing is older than that of the tenth-century" [79, II, I, 561].

2

The study of "The Travels" of Ibn Battuta: translations and publications

At the end of the seventeenth century, Muhammad ibn Fathallah ibn Muhammad al-Bayluni, an admirer of Ibn Battuta made "The Travels" eligible to the broad masses by reducing it significantly and publishing it under the title of *al-Muntaqa min rihlat Ibn Battuta al-Tanji al-Andalusi* (The extracts from "The Travels" of Ibn Battuta the Andalusian from Tanjier). He wrote his own preface in poems. After the "Extracts" of al-Bayluni came into common use, they stopped scribing the full text of "The Travels". So, most of the copies of "The Travels" that reached us contain the text of "The Extracts" of al-Bayluni rather than the original book by Ibn Battuta.

The European orientalists also came to know about Ibn Battuta through the abridged version of al-Bayluni. U. Seetzen, the German traveller, was the first to notice and to purchase the book for the Gottish Library in 1808. Based on the manuscript of "The Extracts" J.G. Kosegarten published a separate study in 1818, together with the text and Latin translation of the three extracts from "The Travels" related to China, India and Sudan. Major attention was attached to the reports of the traveller concerning Sudan. To make sure that the information of Ibn Battuta was factual J.G. Kosegarten used some other geographical sources. The comparison showed him the great historic and geographic value of "The Travels".

In 1819 H. Apetz, a student of J.G. Kosegarten, published another part of "The Travels" covering the Malabar coast of India and the Maldives. This book, which consisted of the translation, commentary and a small preface, could be viewed as the continuation of the study of J.G. Kosegarten.

In the same year, a book called *The Travel to Nubia* (by the famous traveller J.L. Burckhardt) was published. In the annex to this book was an article about "The Travels" based on "The Extracts" by al-Bayluni.

J.L. Burckhardt bought all three copies of the "The Extracts" in Maghrib. Although he could not make out all the parts of the text, he very appropriately evaluated the significance of his predecessor's book.

J.L. Burkchardt died in Cairo two years before the book was published and after his death two copies of the short version of "The Travels" were transferred to the Cambridge University library.

The English orientalist S. Lee went on exploring this monumental work and translated into English the full text of "The Extracts" by al-Bayluni. However, the translation of S. Lee was not very precise and in some cases looked simply like a retelling of the text.

The first European translation of the complete version of "The Travels" appeared in 1840 in Lisbon. The Portuguese priest J.S.A. Moura, while in Fez in 1797, bought the manuscript of *Rihla* and decided to translate some parts into Portuguese. The first volume of his translation covered the travels of Ibn Battuta to Egypt, Syria, Yemen, Mecca, Asia Minor and the Golden Horde. It appeared in 1840, published by the Lisbon Academy. But the death of J.S.A. Moura prevented the full implementation of his plans.

Several extracts from the genuine text of "The Travels" were translated into French by M.G. de Slane, who published some parts of the material devoted to Sudan in the *Journal Asiatique* in 1848. M.J. de Slane added to his translation the remarks of J.T. Reinoaud, which he received enclosed in a private letter.

The other French Arabist, E. Dulaurier, published in 1848 in the same issue of the *Journal Asiatique* the text and translation (with corresponding commentary) of some chapters from the complete version devoted to the travels to the islands of the Malay archipelago and Tawalisi.

This publication attracted the attention of the French orientalist C. Defrémery and, on the basis of the complete version of the manuscript, he translated into French the chapters describing the wanderings of Ibn Battuta in Iran and Central Asia; the translation was also printed in 1848.

Two years later the following publications appeared: *The Story about the Travel to Crimea and Qipchaq*, *The Travel to Asia Minor* and *The Story about Abu Sa'id, the Mongol sultan of two Iraqs and Khurasan.*

As a result of these publications, orientalists came to understand fully the need to prepare and publish the complete critical text of "The

Travels" in order to undertake the comprehensive study. C. Defrémery was more ready for this work than the other scientists. Together with B.R. Sanguinetti, he settled down to this uneasy task.

By the 1950s, with all the accumulated experience of work on "The Travels", a number of lists were discovered bearing the full text of the genuine writing. The prevailing part of these manuscripts, discovered after the occupation of Algeria by the French, was concentrated in the Paris National (then the Imperial) Library. It made the work on the composition of the text considerably easier.

There were five manuscripts available to the editors but only two of them had the full text. Two more, taken together, made up one more copy. As for the fifth one, there were several important gaps in it. The first manuscript – kept in National Library in Paris under the number 967 – is, according to M.G. de Slane and C. Defrémery, the autograph of Ibn Juzayy. It was copied in 1356. The following is a brief description of this manuscript written by M.G. de Slane, and placed by C. Defrémery and B.R. Sanguinetti without any alterations in the preface of the edition: "The paper, torn in some places, is thick and went yellow of the time. The pail handwriting of the manuscript in some places is very hard to read. Some of the pages were added at the later time to replace the missing ones. These are the lists 1, 2 and probably beginning from 19 through 39. But in general, there is only one handwriting which is a good example of Maghribian and Spanish writing; one can make a notice of the lightness, elegance and boldness of the handwriting which are the evidence for the great skill of the calligrapher and is very rare to come across in purely African handwriting. On the last page, the scribe noted that he finished the work in Safar 757 [February 1356]. The manuscript is not complete and comprises only the second part of the work."

It looks as if M.G. de Slane and, later on, C. Defrémery and B.R. Sanguinetti, didn't have enough evidence to prove their statement that the manuscript was the autograph of Ibn Juzayy. The only evidence that they had in favour of the statement was the inscription in the colophone which read: "Wa kan al-firagh min ta'lifiha fi shahr safar 'am sab'a wa khamsin wa sab'i mi'a."

This remark could in no way serve as a testimony for the manuscript being copied by Ibn Juzayy himself. First of all, it should be mentioned that Ibn Juzayy died at the end of 1356 – that is, several months after the work on the book had been finished. Thus, it was impossible in such a short period of time to create a new copy of "nice, delicate and skillful handwriting", however passionate the desire. Second, the word "ta'lif" never was used in the sense of "making a copy". The said inscription was made by Ibn Juzayy to mark the date of the end of the work on "The Travels" and hence it must be taken as the following: "The composition of the book was finished in Safar 757 (February 1356)."

The second manuscript, N.908, which was used by C. Defrémery and B.R. Sanguinetti to clarify the text, is also not complete and embraces only the first part of "The Travels". The copy was made in Safar 1134 (the end of January 1721). Besides, there are many large gaps in the text. It was pointed out by the editors that the full text could be found in only two of the lists (N.909, 911). One list has no date (N.969) and there is a very interesting inscription in the colophone which reads: "wa kutiba min nuskha fi ghayat at-tashif" – "[this list] was copied from a very distorted manuscript". The other manuscript (N.911) also was undated but according to the editors "looked very ancient". The last of these lists (N.910) is also not complete and has only a section of the whole writing. It was copied in 1766. In the colophone of the manuscript there is an interesting remark saying that the scribe "was very sick during the most part of the work".

"From all the manuscripts at our disposal," the editors wrote, "N.911 was undoubtedly the most complete and correct one although there were plenty of mistakes made by the scribe and omissions which were not so important. That was the very copy which we largely made use of and laid down into the foundation of our edition. This was done mainly for the first part of the text; at the same time we avail ourselves of the right to substitute some of the readings of the second part by the corresponding ones of the manuscript N.967, the autograph of Ibn Juzayy."

Comparing all these manuscripts, the editors prepared and published the first complete text in the Arabic language together with a translation in French (1853–1857). Each volume has a corresponding preface and the notes.

Undoubtedly C. Defrémery and B.R. Sanguinetti carried out enormous work to restore, decipher and describe the text of "The Travels" of Ibn Battuta. This edition was laid down into the foundation of all the numerous translations into European and Oriental languages as well as all the Arabic editions of the text.

However, it has to be stated that the problem of restoring the genuine text of the writing is still on the agenda. As previously mentioned, there were only two manuscripts with the complete text at the disposal of the editors and neither of them was free of omissions, additions, corrections and other varied distortions. With no lists explaining the full text, the editors had to solve the discrepancies and different readings wherever it was possible. Besides, due to technical reasons in this edition, one of the main principles of the composition of the scientific and critical texts was violated – the editors refused to reproduce the rejected versions and secondary readings. On this matter they wrote: "We compared the manuscript N.911 with the other three, but we brought it into the text of the reading only when they seemed to be correct and full. We could have supplied the text with the large number of the versions, as we used to do at the beginning of the work on the edition. But the size of the edition and printing norms designed for such kind of works according to the instructions of Asian Society Bureau did not allow us to have such notes (at least, placed at the points where they could really be of use – that is, under the line); that was why we omitted almost all the versions that could add to author's idea . . . The other versions were marked by figures and numbers of pages at the end of each volume."

The conclusion resulting from this said that the editors, due to objective reasons, could not provide the readers with an original, complete critical text based on the genuine text of the author. This was noticed by the other explorers as well.

To restore the original text of "The Travels", firstly we need to discover all of the oldest manuscripts with the full text of the writing. According to the published catalogues of various book depositories in different countries around the world and other separate information, to date there were five discovered copies with the full text of Ibn Battuta. Two of them, used by C. Defrémery and B.R. Sanguinetti, were described earlier. These copies are kept at the National Library in Paris (N.2,289, 2,291).

The next complete manuscript, as Mahmud al-Sharqawi informs us, is in the Madrid Library (CXIII). We could not determine the place of origin of the latter. In the event that this manuscript is not the one that was used by the Portuguese translator J.S.A. Moura, there should be one more manuscript kept in the libraries of Portugal. Besides, there are two more complete copies – one of them is in the library "Jami' Qarawiyyin" in Fez (N. code 1285), and the other one, copied on 27 October 1747, was in the private collection of Muhammad ibn 'Abd al-Karim al-Lafkun. There are also several copies of the shortened version by al-Bayluni. However, as it was mentioned above, they could not be used as a source to restore the genuine text of "The Travels".

The text of "The Travels" by C. Defrémery and B.R. Sanguinetti had a number of editions. It was used as a source for numerous complete, abridged, common and scientific books published in Arabic countries at different times. Among the most full oriental publications reproducing the Paris edition, the following should be distinguished: the Cairo editions of 1287/1870, 1322/1904 and 1964; the Baghdad edition of 1962; the Bayrut edition of 1962 and 1968. Additionally, there are adapted publications, the ones printed in Cairo in 1934 being the most popular among them.

The Paris edition is still the most authoritative and scientific. Due to its authority it was laid down as the foundation of a number of translations into European and Oriental languages.

There also exist the translations into Swedish, Italian, German, English, Polish and Hungarian. The most precise and scientifically approved are the translations into German by H. Mzik and into English by H.A.R. Gibb.

In the twentieth century, H.A.R. Gibb, the famous English Arabist, carried out a study and made the translation into English. Yet in 1929, he published an abridged translation of "The Travels" with laconic and extremely profound commentaries. He continued this work and eventually, in 1956, finished the translation and commentary. The first volume comprised the preface and translation (with the notes) and covered the travels of Ibn Battuta to Egypt, Syria and the Arabian Peninsula; it was published in 1958. The second volume embraced the travels to Asia Minor, the Crimea and the Crimean steppe, and Central Asia. It was published in 1962. The third volume was published in 1971.

The translation of H.A.R. Gibb opened the way to many new translations into European languages.

The Turkish translation by Muhammad Sharif is considered to be one of the earliest in Oriental languages. In 1897–1901, he published the complete Turkish translation of "The Travels" in three volumes. The second edition of the translation came out in 1916.

The Persian translation by Muhammad 'Ali Muwahhid, published in 1970 in Tehran, is one of the latest. This translation was made from the French edition by C. Defrémery and B.R. Sanguinetti.

Every year in Arabic countries there are various editions of the book for contemporary Arabic readers. To a large extent, they look to be just the re-telling of the story of Ibn Battuta. By character and aim these books are supposed to be the translation of "The Travels" into the Arabic language of today, to be understood by the broad mass of readers. The books of Mahmud al-Sharqawi and Husban Shakir are among the most perfect editions.

In Russia, *The Travels of Ibn Battuta* and the value of his information were noticed long ago. The translation of short extracts from "The Travels" under the headline "The Foreigners about Russia" were published in *Russian Vestnik* as far back as in 1841. The translation, with a small preface, was made on the basis of the English translation by S. Lee, who had used for his translation the abridged edition of "The Travels" by al-Bayluni. "The book of Ibn Battuta continues to be unknown for us" wrote the translator. "We know it thanks to the abridged versions scribed by his compatriots, Ibn Juzayy al-Kalbi and Ibn Fathallah al-Bayluni. G.L. Burckhardt was the first to bring it to Europe. J. Kosegarten and H. Apetz published the abridged versions and, in 1829 in London, a complete translation by S. Lee was published. We refer the readers to an interesting extract from this translation – the travel of Ibn Battuta to the Golden Horde, the description of that menacing Court of Khan . . ." We continue with the extracts of "The Travels" devoted to Crimea, Dasht-i Qipchaq and the court of Uzbek Khan.

Russian readers became acquainted with the stories of a Moroccan traveller in 1864–1865. In a collection named *The Medieval Travellers*, the anonymous author wrote a rather long article on "The Travels" of Ibn Battuta and, along with narration, provided the corresponding extracts. That article, as well as the first translation published in *Vestnik* to which the author referred from time to time, seemed to be based entirely on the English translation, although by that time the perfect edition and translation of C. Defrémery and B.R. Sanguinetti had been made public.

The above-mentioned translation and article do not have any significance today from a scientific point of view. But at the time they were important enough to attract the attention of Russian historians to "The Travels" of Ibn Battuta.

The first relatively precise translation of a considerable number of extracts from "The Travels" was published twenty years later by V. Tizengauzen in the *Collection of materials relating to the history of the Golden Horde*. V. Tizengauzen had a difficult task coping with providing the Russian historians with extracts from the works of *Arabian*, *Persian*, *Tatar writers* in order to create a "fundamental, as full as possible, critically evaluated history of the Golden Horde so as to appropriately define the level of impact on Russia" [74, I, I]. This very task stipulated the choice of extracts for translation into Russian. Together with the text and extracts from the writings of Ibn al-Athir, Ibn 'Abd al-Zahir, Ibn Wasil, Rukn al-Din Baybars, al-Nuwayri, al-'Umari and others, there was a Russian translation of extracts from *The Description of Travellings of Ibn Abi 'Abdallah Muhammad ibn Battuta, written by Muhammad ibn Juzayy, relating to the history of Golden Horde*. The story about Khorezm which was then a part of the Golden Horde was included too.

There is no Arabic text of "The Travels" in *The Collection*, only the translation made on the basis of the edition by C. Defrémery and B.R. Sanguinetti. The work of V. Tizengauzen was an outstanding event in the history of oriental studies of the nineteenth century, although, as it was mentioned by I.Y. Krachkovskiy: "the translation of these materials and the summary made by V. Tizengauzen need to be checked and clarified considering the new sources and editions that became known to our science some sixty or more years since the date of publication of his historical work" [107, 410–411].

We must also mention the extract about Dasht-i Qipchaq translated into Tatar language. The translation, undertaken by an expert of Arabic language Rida al-Din ibn Fakhr al-Din, was published as a separate book in Orenburg in 1917. Despite a large amount of work carried out by the translator, who had compared the various Arabic and European editions of "The Travels" in order to determine the exact spelling of the proper names of the places, the translation is not really a scientific work but rather a free narration of the stories about the Qipchaq steppes told by Ibn Battuta.

A short passage from the Russian translation of "The Travels" was published in a collection *The Past of Kazakhstan from different sources and materials*.

Meanwhile, the interest in *The Travels of Ibn Battuta* in Oriental studies was increasing. In 1974 the book *Ibn Battuta* by G.V. Miloslavskiy was published, and, for the first time in the history of Russian literature, a story of the life and travels of the outstanding traveller was included. G.V. Miloslavskiy also wrote several articles about Ibn Battuta. In 1983 in a series entitled "The Life of Brilliant People", an article about the Moroccan traveller by I. Timofeyev was published. Also published were a number of articles belonging to the author of this very book.

The passages relating to the travels of Ibn Battuta to Africa are included in the anthology called *The History of Africa*. However, the full Russian translation of "The Travels" and its comprehensive study has not yet been carried out.

Concerning the separate data given in "The Travels" relating to Central Asia, this was fully used in the works of Russian scientists dealing with problems of the history and history of culture of Central Asia. V.V. Bartol'd was the first to apply the data given by the traveller. Together with the Arabic text he also made use of the above-mentioned translation by V. Tizengauzen. V.V. Bartol'd made quite substantial quotations from Ibn Battuta and referred to his data with full confidence. This very tendency exists in the works of the other scientists where they speak about "The Travels" as being of primary importance to explain the different phenomenons of the history and history of culture of Central Asia at the beginning of the fourteenth century.

I.P. Petrushevskiy made full use of the separate data of Ibn Battuta, mentioning that the stories of the medieval traveller comprised facts that it was impossible to find in other sources. A.Y. Yakubovskiy also frequently referred to the information in, and certain passages from, "The Travels".

"The Travels" of Ibn Battuta were used in such fundamental works on the history of Central Asia as *Tajiks* by B.G. Ghafurov, *The History of Irrigation of Khorezm* by Y.G. Ghulamov, *Bukhara Documents of Fourteenth century* by O.D. Chekhovich, and many others.

Besides, such famous scientists as S.P. Tolstov, M.Y. Masson, A.M. Belenitskiy, A.P. Smirnov and many others referred to the writing of

Ibn Battuta. The authors who worked on the history of Uzbekistan, Kazakhstan and Turkmenistan made full use of this work.

"The Travels" is becoming more valuable due to the fact that it is not just a collection of raw data taken from the original books but rather it is a live story from the witness. Ibn Battuta, the greatest among travellers of his time, was also one from the galaxy of pioneers, along with Marco Polo, Afanasiy Nikitin and others.

A thirst for knowledge that could not be exhausted, curiosity and persistence to see with one's own eyes "all the wonders of the world", were the characteristic features of the time and stipulated by the history. All the features of the epoch, with a human being striving to widen his impression of the world, were vividly reflected in the personality of Ibn Battuta. He was a greatly gifted and psychologically interesting figure. In particular, along with "faithfulness", he had a wide range of views, and combined strict observations and a desire to enlighten people with the "wonders of the saints", which he treated as real facts.

Ibn Battuta's method of description is different compared to that of other medieval authors. He is not concerned with the need to look scholastically scientific; indeed, he is not aware of it at all. His "Travels" read like the actual story of the witness. He does not give geographical co-ordinates of the cities that he is visiting, but simply tells us about his travel from one city to another, from one country to another (for example, from Saray Berke to Khorezm and further into Central Asia). Having been to the city he wrote about what he had seen with his own eyes. Very seldom did he write about the history of a certain city or a settlement that he had heard about from the local people. Largely, he recounted his own impressions about local rulers, spiritual figures and "sacred places".

In this context his stories remind us of Marco Polo, who had visited these places earlier. The latter, while speaking about the countries and cities, also focused on the "miracles". The only difference was that Marco Polo wrote about the orthodox saints, whereas Ibn Battuta told in quite some detail of the graves of "the saint shaykhs" and of miracles, which happened before his eyes or about which he had heard from other people.

Having visited Khorezm, the traveller focused his attention on the markets where "there were so many people that I could move neither ahead nor backward . . ." [25, III, 3]. We must bear in mind the fact that the traveller visited a great number of cities in the Middle East, including Cairo and Damascus. He described Urgench, the capital of Khorezm, using the same attributes as were used with these big cities ("the city is turbulent like the storming sea"). Thus, we may conclude that Urgench in 1333, when Ibn Battuta visited it, actually was a big and noisy city worthwhile of comparison with other famous cities.

The traveller did not have any intention of recounting details about Khorezm; he simply could not do it because he was not familiar with written documents. Added to that, the focus of his interest was different. The live picture of the city, the rush, the crowd in the bazaar: these were all more important for him. He writes about Urgench: "This is magnificent, the most beautiful and biggest city of the Turks with nice bazaars, wide streets, numerous buildings and impressive sights. Life in the city is seething due to its great number of citizens and reminds me of a storming sea" [25, III, 3].

The traveller does not, however, enumerate the products available in the bazaar of Urgench. Having mentioned briefly that in summer many ships sailed along Jayhun with wheat and barley supplied from Tirmith, he described with excitement the Khorezm melon which was his most favourite fruit. He also noted how melon was dried: "Neither in the East nor in the West are melons as delicious as in Khorezm, except for Bukhara and Isfahan. It is interesting to see how melons are cut into pieces, get dried in the sun and placed in the baskets, the same way as we do with dried figs, and then from Khorezm they take the fruit to the far distant cities in India and China . . ." [25, III, 15–16].

Ibn Battuta, in much detail, recalls the receptions and entertainments that were arranged in his honour by the Amir of Khorezm Qutludumur (Qutlugh Timur), the city *qadi* and other high-ranking officials. This story abounds in details of the richness of the premises of the amir and *qadi* – the carpets, plates and dishes, and food. We learn that the dinner table was weighed down with different fruits served in Iraqi glass vases, and that the rooms were decorated with cloth and gold-embroidered silk.

The description of the gifts received by Ibn Battuta is also very long and he recounts, without any embarrassment, regarding these gifts as a sign of respect regarding his personal and religious position. He advises about the money granted by the Amir of Khorezm and the wife of the *qadi*, underlining the "piety" of these people. He regards the gifts that were presented to him, the educated Muslim lawyer (he wanted to consider himself as such) and the person who visited "the sacred cities", as a testimony of this "piety".

From this very point of view Ibn Battuta writes about the construction of mosques, *madrasas*, "zawiyas" and hospitals.

As we see in other parts of the book, Ibn Battuta is very keen to describe the parties arranged in his honour. The detailed picture of the "zawiya" where he stays and information about his everyday life bring specific impact to his stories. His book cannot be described as a scientific geographic study but rather as a memoir of the course of his travels, where the subjective and private aspect is at the forefront – and it is for this reason that "The Travels" acquired the status of *belles-lettres.*

Ibn Battuta's interest in whether any of the rulers he encountered adopted Islam or not, was illustrated by other explorers – but this interest is not something peculiar to the Moroccans. This fact has been underlined by many historians who work largely on the aspects of the post-Mongolian period. Indeed, for the Muslim population of the territory conquered by Mongols it was extremely important to know if the ruler accepted the faith of the subjugated people – it was a matter to determine the question on taxes, rights of the citizens and the court system. This "vital" interest could not help but be reflected in literature. For example, Persian al-Juzjani, the author of the writing *Tabaqat-i Nasiri* and the witness of Mongol occupation, recounts in detail that Khan Jochi, the father of Berke, ordered that his son was brought up in the Muslim traditions and taught the Qur'an in Khujand at the house "of one of the faithful scientists of this city" [74, II, 16]. Continuing with the narration, the historian points out the friendly attitude of Berke to Muslims, the faithfulness of this ruler.

It is also significant for the Muslim authors of the thirteenth and fourteenth centuries to underline the respectful treatment of the Mongol rulers of *sufi* shaykhs, leaders of *sufi* orders. As the landowners and "spiritual leaders" of the peasants working largely on their lands, they played a large economic and ideological role [74, II, 16]. As an example of popularity and influence of the *sufi* shaykhs in the time of Ibn Battuta, it is sufficient to take an extract from the well-known *History of Wassaf,* distinguished by its periphrastic style which was common for both Persian and Arabic "official prose" of that time:

> The Prince Uzbek who was as handsome as a Muslim man could be with his candour neck decorated with pearls of pure faith sent the group of his confidential people (*inaq*) for pilgrimage and the old man of that time used to say: "With vagabonds the Khan and Qa'an behaved like vagabonds." Before the right and left regiments, the advance-guard (*manqila*) and the rear-guard (*kechka*) of the Army of Uzbek, which was as numerous as the ant-hill, could disembark, Saray Qutlugh, the brother of Qutlugh Timur put his hat of arrogance off his head of arbitrariness and power and humbly bowed before the threshold of humiliation and modesty.

Much of the information from the medieval *History of Wassaf* is fully in line with, at first sight, the seemingly exaggerated stories of Ibn Battuta about Sultan Uzbek, Tarmashirin, the ruler of Mawarannahr, Qutlugh Timur and the Amir of Khorezm, being extremely respectful towards Imam Husam al-Din al-Yaghi in Nakhshab, Shaykh hajj Nizam al-Din in Saray Berke and towards other shaykhs including Nu'man al-Din al-Khorezmi, who was "strict with the believers" [74, II, 87]. For example, Ibn Battuta says that Sultan Uzbek went to see Shaykh Nu'man al-Din every Friday, "but the latter does not even stand up to greet him" [25, II, 449].

"The Travels" of Ibn Battuta, who always stated exactly in which *sufi* "zawiya" he had stopped, how he was received and who fed him, indicated the number of *sufi* "zawiyas" in Central Asia (beginning with Khorezm). The enumeration of the "zawiyas" that he visited during his trip to Central Asia is quite important. He mentions the "zawiya" at the grave of Najm al-Din al-Kubra, where "the food for the visitors was prepared" [25, III, 6]. Mudarris Sayf al-Din ibn 'Asaba was the shaykh of that place. Ibn Battuta states that the "pious mujawir " Jalal al-Din al-Samarqandi, "one of the greatest pious men", was the shaykh of a neighbouring abode. Jalal al-Din also arranged a reception in honour of Ibn Battuta. Continuing, the traveller gives details about the grave site of the "educated *Imam* Abu-l-Qasim Mahmud ibn 'Umar al-Zamakhshari, where the mausoleum had been erected" [25, III, 6]. Although Ibn Battuta does not describe it in a detail, as a rule, with such mausoleums there was a "zawiya" and the grave site was usually a part of a *waqf*, which was the living source of the spiritual entity "taking care" of the mausoleum and the religious house attached to it.

Ibn Battuta also tells us about "a new *madrasa*" on the outskirts of Urgench where he spent a night so as not to enter the city during rush hour (before the close time of the city gates). In the *madrasa*, Ibn Battuta was visited by the *qadi* of Urgench and a number of religious figures; among them he mentions Shams al-Din al-Sinjari, the Imam of Amir of Khorezm.

Continuing on, Ibn Battuta describes the entertainment that was arranged in his honour by Turabek Khatun, the wife of the Amir of Khorezm inside the "zawiya" built on her order, where "they used to feed the visitors" [25,III,14]. However, these are the "zawiya" located only in Khorezm.

Going on with his trip, Ibn Battuta arrived to Fath'abad, on the outskirts of Bukhara, where the grave of "Sayf al-Din al-Bakharzi, the pious hermit and one of the greatest saints" was situated [25, III, 27]. The traveller says that the "zawiya" built at the mausoleum of Sayf al-Din al-Bakharzi exists at the expense of the numerous *waqfs*: "The zawiya, where we stopped, named after this shaykh was rather big and had a number of *waqfs* at the expense of which the visitors are fed."

The information about Yahya al-Bakharzi is very interesting. He made a pious pilgrimage and was one of the descendants of Sayf al-Din, was the shaykh of that "zawiya". We can suppose that at the time of Ibn Battuta the "*sufi* dynasties" existed where the title of shaykh was inherited.

The next important "zawiya" in Central Asia that was visited by Ibn Battuta was the abode attached to the mausoleum of Qutham ibn 'Abbas ibn 'Abd al-Muttalib, located in the vicinity of Samarqand. It was one of the most popular shrines in Central Asia at that time. Ibn Battuta tells us the following: "In the evening every Monday and Friday the citizens of Samarqand visit this grave. The Tatars also visit it; they make considerable donations and bring cows and sheep, they come with dirhams and dinars; it is used to treat the visitors and to cover the expenses of the people who serve in this zawiya with the blessed grave" [25, III, 52–53].

The significance of this shrine can be explained by the fact that Amir Ghiyath al-Din Muhammad ibn 'Abd al-Qadir ibn 'Abd al-'Aziz ibn Yusuf, the son of al-Mustansir, the 'Abbasid Caliph, was the one who took care of the grave and of all its surrounding land (that is, *waqfs* attached to this popular grave). According to Ibn Battuta, Tarmashirin, the Sultan of Mawarannahr, appointed him to this place when he returned from Iraq. Thus, appointing the descendant of Caliph al-Mustansir, the former leader of all Muslims, to be the keeper of the grave site, Tarmashirin wanted to emphasize "the dominating" role of his state in the system of Islam challenging the other Mongol sovereigns and his political rivals.

In Tirmith, Ibn Battuta lived in the "zawiya" of the "virtuous Shaykh-i 'Azizan, one of the major honourable shaykhs, the rich owner of many lands and orchards. He spends his earnings to feed the pilgrims" [25, III, 54].

Returning back to the writing of al-'Umari, the contemporary of Ibn Battuta, we notice that this author also focuses attention on the great number of "zawiyas" in Central Asia. Al-'Umari writes: "You can see how the rich people spend their money for their own pleasure and enjoyment, competing with each other. Meanwhile, in Mawarannahr, the rich and self-sufficient people use their money largely for building the *madrasas*, *ribats*, the roads and *waqf* in the name of Allah."

Thus, al-'Umari, as well as Ibn Battuta, emphasized the "piouty" and "faithful deeds" of the people of Mawarannahr and he especially pointed out the spread of "zawiya", which served as the centres of *sufism*, the significant religious trend of that epoch.

Ibn Battuta does not tell us anything about the charter and regulations of the *sufi* communities in "zawiyas", which probably suggests that they are well-known. However, we could restore these regulations in detail using documents dating from the time when Ibn Battuta lived and relating to one of the "zawiyas" he visited – the one that was built at the mausoleum of Shaykh Sayf al-Din al-Bakharzi [78, 19–20].

The document enumerates all the necessary facilities needed for everyday life in the "zawiya" and emphasizes the importance of keeping to the principals of "no wealth", "poverty" and "modesty", the inevitable elements of *sufi* "democracy" and darwish (vagabond) morality. (Of course, these principles were only formal because the Trustee of the *waqf*, Yahya al-Bakharzi, was an extremely rich person.) The document says: "Certainly, if any of the sons of the Trustee or the uncles of the Trustee who strives to earn wealth or seeks to occupy a high position, who dominates over the poor men or puts the dresses of the light-minded people on himself and wears the costly dresses, who denies and does not wear old coarse woollen clothes, torn and worn out rags, who forces one's wife and children to wear nice dresses and decorates his house with mundane wealth, let them not rule the *waqf* . . ." [78, 177].

The document clearly reads that the *waqf* is ruled on a hereditary basis with its leader appointed usually out of the descendants of the

Trustee. The latter must be "pious and far from mundane affairs, faithful and without adherence to earthly blessings, the appearance and soul of a darwish must prevail in him". "Mutawalli", the manager of the *waqf* was nominated (elected) by the *sufis* themselves: "It is important that he is nominated by the most anchoritic people, the most pious and wise *sufis* out of those who serve and live in khanaqah and the wandering darwishs" [78, 176].

One of the most detailed stories of "The Travels", relating to Central Asia, is the story of the "pious" Sultan Tarmashirin [25, III, 31]. Ibn Battuta gives him the features of the advocate of Muslims, quietly listening to the sharp words of the preachers. He reproduces the words of Tarmashirin: "When you are back in your country, tell the people how the poorest among the Persian-*sufis* treats the Sultan of Turks" [25, II, 31–36].

Ibn Battuta recounts a very long story about Tarmashirin but fails to notice the main features of his policy, which was pointed out by al-'Umari, who writes: "The sultans of this state adopted Islam just recently, after 725. The first among them was Tarmashirin, let Allah bless him. He was sincerely devoted to Allah, and supported and defended Islam as best as he could. He ordered his amirs and warriors to accept Islam: some of them had already become Muslim; the others adopted it following the order of him. Islam spread over and its banner was flying so high that hardly ten years passed before Islam was accepted by all the people: the noble and the common.The course was contributed to greatly by the intelligent *imams* and shaykhs blessed by Allah. They availed themselves of the opportunity to bring about the Turks to obedience and called to accept the right faith. It is well known to us that even now in matters concerning faith they [the Turk amirs] are the most jealous of the people and less than the others make mistakes in deciding what is allowed and what is prohibited" [75, 38–39].

Most probably Tarmashirin did very well out of the privileges of Islam and tried to attract the Muslim merchants to come to Mawarannahr. He treated with great honour all those coming from the other Muslim countries, trying to establish close contact with them. That was the reason for Tarmashirin to receive Ibn Battuta so cordially and to present such nice gifts. No wonder the stranger was so enthusiastic in speaking about his "piouty" (the thing that Tarmashirin was expecting to achieve in order to "advertise" himself). In this respect the information we get from al-'Umari proves more valuable and truthful because it leads us to understand the goal that Tarmashirin is going to achieve.

Al-'Umari continues: "We have already mentioned that the people in this state, the major population, the local people, belong to old Muslims who adopted Islam long ago. Despite their sultans being unfaithful, they honoured Islam and trouble avoided their faith, their way of life and property. When Tarmashirin came to power, as we have mentioned before, he adopted Islam, supported it and spread it over the territory of his kingdom. He followed the provisions of Shari'a and moved along the way determined by it.

"He received with honour the merchants arriving from different countries. Before him the merchants of Egypt and Syria were not allowed to enter his state and the strangers travelling all over the world could not even think of an idea to pass over this area. When Tarmashirin became the khan, quite a number of merchants made their way to reach his country and always came home gratified. So, his country turned out to become the beaten track leading to the aim. Sadr Badr al-Din Hasan al-Is'irdi, the merchant, told me how Tarmashirin treated the merchants and the coming travellers. He said about the hospitality and honour rendered to them, and about Tarmashirin trying to win their favour" [75, 41].

So, these two people who lived in one epoch describe the personality of Tarmashirin differently. Tarmashirin for Ibn Battuta was a faithful Muslim, who obeyed humbly his spiritual teacher and quietly bore humiliation "for the sake of the faith of Allah". He was devoted to Islam for the sake of Islam. With al-'Umari, Tarmashirin was a politician, patronizing merchants and travellers, taking care of the security of the travelling people and the development of trade. Probably, the picture depicted by al-'Umari was closer to reality; although he wrote it from the words of others and, unlike Ibn Battuta, had never been acquainted with that ruler.

With the prosperous development of *sufi* orders there appeared a phenomenon known in early Islam as "shirk" ("polytheism", "paganism") – the worship of the graves of the saints (wali, awliya'). The cult of the saints on the territory of Central Asia as well as in the other Muslim countries, first of all, brought about the tendency of revival of the ancient beliefs and cults that were forced out by Islam. As is clear from the stories of Ibn Battuta, the cult of saints in Central Asia, despite the negative attitude on the part of official theology and Sunna, become a real and concrete form of expression of religious consciousness of the people. The graves of the saints and the other places related to the cult of the saints became the centres of pilgrimage. At that time the cult of the saints was not considered to contradict the Qur'an, and received only "shirk", which was evidence of its deep penetration into the system of Islam. The denominations of the cult of the saints were quite different in essence and shape. Anybody could become a saint: a shaykh, religious hermit, a scholar and so on. According to Ibn Battuta, in each city there were a number of sacred graves. Each big settlement had its own saint and the inhabitants and pilgrims sought his help.

The wide spread of the cult of saints was encouraged by the remains of pre-Islamic beliefs. An interesting combination of the pre-Islamic and Muslim customs were observed. Ibn Battuta told us that at the tomb of Qutham ibn 'Abbas, located out of Samarqand, it was a custom with the pilgrims, local people and "tatars", to slaughter the sheep and bulls [25, III, 52–53].

Ibn Battuta also tells us about the "mazar" (grave) of Najm al-Din al-Kubra in the outskirts of Urgench, which was one of the most worshipped shrines in Central Asia. Without knowing the language, Ibn Battuta could not be aware of the legends that related to the name of that saint. Meanwhile, there is a legend preserved almost to the present day, which embraced the elements opposing Islam and proved the antiquity of the legend itself. It is known with Muslim people that the dog is considered to be an "unclean" animal. However, legend speaks about the wonderful dog of the saint "which could fly in the air". Near the "mazar" the pilgrims were shown the stone trough from which the dog would eat [124, 322]. Despite the fact that the inhabitants of Khorezm and the other pilgrims visiting the grave of Najm al-Din al-Kubra were Muslim ("old Muslim" as al-'Umari put it), they were not struck by the story of a dog in the legend. According to Ibn Battuta, similar shrines existed in all the cities and settlements of Mawarannahr.

The steadiness of the old customs and beliefs is proved by the fact related to the Turk tradition of giving the name to a child mentioned by Ibn Battuta [25, II, 396]. The ceremony of sacrifice was common for the ancient local cults, for Islam and for Mongols. The ritual of sacrificing horses, sheep and bulls at the graves of the saints was observed by both pagans and Muslims including those who were newly adopted (that is, the strangers, "tatars").

Belief in miracles performed by the living saints ("paganism" from the point of view of orthodox Islam) was also a very common phenomenon. Describing the cities he visited, Ibn Battuta used to recount this or that thaumaturge. He, as well as the local people, sincerely believed in what they showed. (In Maghrib, where Ibn Battuta was from, the cult of the saints was also quite popular.)

The authority of the saints, working "wonders", curing diseases and anticipating the events in the future, was very great. The Mongol khans as well as the local people worshiped them. In recounting the relations of Khan Uzbek and Shaykh Nu'man al-Din al-Khorezmi, praising the independence, piety and incorruptibility of the shaykh, Ibn Battuta does not fail to mention his "sacred ability" to work wonders: "He received me very tenderly – let Allah be kind to him – and sent me Turk 'ghulam'. I was the witness of the wonders he worked" [25, II, 449].

At this place, as it used to happen at the end of every description of a city and his saint, Ibn Battuta tells a story called "The Miracle of the shaykh", where modern people might not find anything miraculous. Similiar "miracles" are recounted in connection with Nur al-Din al-Kirmani, "hermit" Abu 'Abdallah al-Murshidi, Shaykh Shihab al-Din, Shaykh Qutb al-Din al-Naysaburi and many other saints. These are the characteristic features of the "The Travels" – bearing resemblance to books of an everyday life genre, which were quite popular at that time.

Information from Ibn Battuta on the custom of giving the name to a child highlights the ancient remnants of totemism that existed among Turks and Muslims. Although the Turks as a whole received Arabic-Muslim names (for example, Muhammad, Ibrahim, Fatima), there was still the custom of giving a child the name of the thing or animal the child's mother saw first after the birth. "The Turks, Ibn Battuta says, "call a child by the name of the person who is the first to enter the marquee" [25, II, 115]. Although this custom was largely common with paganists, Muslims did not deny it.

In another place Ibn Battuta says: "The name of the daughter of Sultan Uzbek is Itkujuk (Itkuchuk). This name means 'a puppy' because 'it' means 'dog' and 'kujuk' means puppy. We said above that the Turks used to receive the names 'on occasion' as it once was with Arabs" [25, II, 396].

There is a long range of names given "on occasion", substituting the Muslim names. Ibn Battuta compares it with the custom that was popular with Arabs. The totemic names were common largely in the names of the tribes (kalb – "a dog", kilab – "the dogs", kulayb – "a poppy", asad – "the lion", quraysh – "a shark" and so on).

Thus we can state, that the "interest in Islam" which one can observe in the writing of Ibn Battuta is characteristic not only for him but for many other authors of the thirteenth and fourteenth centuries. The question of belief, the adoption of Islam or its denial by the Mongol states was of great political and economic importance.

The stories of Ibn Battuta about the numerous *sufi* "zawiyas" in Central Asia correspond with other sources and reflect the vital realities of that period. The other side of this phenomenon is the wide spreading of the cult of saints in different spheres of life and the flourishing of the "eventual" (hagiographic) literature, which appeared in connection with the names of these saints.

The stories of Ibn Battuta about the preserved cult forms of the peoples of Central Asia are of great importance. The friendly and objective tone of Ibn Battuta's narration is evidence of a wide range of views.

والهند، وذلك في أوائل شهر يوليه. وتهب في هذه البرية ريح السموم القاتلة التي تعفن الجسوم، حتى ان الرجل، اذا مات، تتفسخ اعضاؤه. وقد ذكرنا ان هذه الريح تهب أيضاً في البرية بين هرمز وشيراز.

وكانت تقدمت أمامنا رفقة كبيرة فيها خداوند زاده قاضي ترمذ، فمات لهم جمال وخيل كثيرة، ووصلت رفقتنا سالمة بحمد الله تعالى الى بنج آب، وهو ماء السند، وبنج معناه خمسة وآب معناه الماء، فمعنى ذلك المياه الخمسة، وهي تصب في الهو الأعظم، وتسقي تلك النواحي، وسنذكرها ان شاء الله تعالى.

وكان وصولنا لهذا النهر سلخ ذي الحجة واستهل علينا تلك الليلة هلال المحرم من عام أربعة وثلاثين وسبعمائة. ومن هنالك كتب المخبرون بخبرنا إلى أرض الهند، وعرفوا ملكها بكيفية أحوالنا.

ثم سافرنا إلى قرية الجرخ، وهي كبيرة لها بساتين كثيرة وفواكهها طيبة، قدمناها في أيام الصيف، ووجدنا بها جماعة من الفقراء والطلب، وصلينا بها الجمعة، وأضافنا أميرها محمد الجرخي، ولقيته بعد ذلك بالهند، ثم سافرنا الى مدينة غزنة، وهي بلد السلطان المجاهد محمود بن سبكتكين الشهير الاسم، وكان من كبار السلاطين يلقب بيمين الدولة، وكان كثير الغزو، الى بلاد الهند، وفتح بها المدائن والحصون، وقبره بهذه المدينة عليه زاوية، وقد خرب معظم هذه البلدة، ولم يبق منها إلا يسير، وكانت كبيرة، وهي شديدة البرد والساكنون بها يخرجون عنها أيام البرد إلى مدينة القندهار، وهي كبيرة مخصبة، ولم أدخلها، وبينهما مسيرة ثلاث.

ونزلنا بخارج غزنة في قرية هنالك على نهر ماء تحت قلعتها، وأكرمنا أميرها مرذك أغا، ومرذك معناه الصغير، وأغا معناه كبير الأصل.

ثم سافرنا إلى كابل وكانت فيما سلف مدينة عظيمة، وبها الآن قرية يسكنها طائفة من الاعاجم يقال لهم الأفغان، ولهم جبال وشعاب، وشوكة قوية، وأكثرهم قطاع الطريق، وجبلهم الكبير يسمى كوه سليمان، ويذكر أن نبي الله سليمان، عليه السلام، صعد ذلك الجبل، فنظر الى أرض الهند، وهي مظلمة، فرجع ولم يدخلها، فسمي الجبل به، وفيه يسكن ملك الأفغان.

وبكابل زاوية الشيخ اسماعيل الأفغاني تلميذ الشيخ عباس من كبار الأولياء، ومنها رحلنا الى كرماش، وهي حصن بين جبلين تقع به الأفغان، وكنا حين جوازنا عليه نقاتلهم، وهم بسفح الجبل، ونرميهم بالنشاب، فيفرون. وكانت رفقتنا مخفة، ومعهم نحو أربعة آلاف فرس، وكانت لي جمال انقطعت عن القافلة لأجلها، ومعي جماعة بعضهم من الأفغان، وطرحنا بعض الزاد، وتركنا أحمال الجمال التي أعيت بالطريق، وعادت إليها خيلنا بالغد فاحتملتها.

ووصلنا إلى القافلة بعد صلاة العشاء الآخرة فبتنا بمنزل ششنغار، وهي آخر العمارة مما يلي بلاد الترك، ومن هناك دخلنا البرية الكبرى، وهي مسيرة خمس عشرة لا تدخل إلا في فصل واحد، وهو بعد نزول المطر بأرض السند

وأقمنا حتى تمكن دخول الحر، وقطعنا ذلك الجبل من آخر اليل وسلكنا به جميع نهارنا الى الغروب، وكنا نضع اللبود بين أيدي الجمال تطأ عليها لئلا تغرق في الثلج.

ثم سافرنا إلى موضع يعرف بأندر، وكانت هنالك فيما تقدم مدينة عفي رسمها، ونزلنا بقرية عظيمة فيها زاوية لأحد الفضلاء، ويسمى بمحمد المهروي، ونزلنا عنده وأكرمنا، وكان متى غسلنا أيدينا من الطعام يشرب الماء الذي غسلناها به لحسن اعتقاده وفضله، وسافر معنا الى ان صعدنا جبل هند كوش المذكور، ووجدنا بهذا الجبل عين ماء حارة فغسلنا منها وجوهنا فتقشرت، وتألمنا لذلك.

ثم نزلنا بموضع يعرف ببنج هير، معنى بنج خمسة، وهير الجبل، فمعناه خمسة جبال، وكانت هناك مدينة حسنة كثيرة العمارة على نهر عظيم أزرق كأنه بحر ينزل من جبال بدخشان، وبهذه الجبال يوجد الياقوت الذي يعرفه الناس بالبلخش. وخرب هذه البلاد تنكيز ملك التتر، فلم تعمر بعد. وبهذه المدينة مزار الشيخ سعيد المكي، وهو معظم عندهم.

ووصلنا إلى جبل بشاي، وبه زاوية الشيخ الصالح أطا أولياء، وأطا معناه بالتركية الأب، وأولياء باللسان العربي، فمعناه أبو الأولياء، ويسمى أيضاً سيصد صاله، وسيصد معناه بالفارسية ثلاثمائة، وصاله (ساله) معناه عام، وهم يذكرون أن عمره ثلاثمائة وخمسون عاماً، ولهم فيه اعتقاد حسن، ويأتون لزيارته من البلاد والقرى، ويقصده السلاطين والخواتين، وأكرمنا وأضافنا، ونزلنا على نهر عند زاويته ودخلنا إليه، فسلمت عليه وعانقني، وجسمه رطب لم أر ألين منه، ويظن رائيه ان عمره خمسون سنة، وذكر لي أنه في كل مائة سنة ينبت له الشعر والأسنان، وانه رأى أبارهم الذي قبره بملتان من السند. وسألته عن راوية حديث فأخبرني بحكايات وشككت في حاله، والله أعلم بصدقه.

ثم سافرنا إلى برون، وفيها لقيت الأمير برنطيه، وأحسن إلي وأكرمني، وكتب إلى نوابه بمدينة غزنه في اكرامي، وقد تقدم ذكره وذكر ما أعطي من البسطة في الجسم. وكان عنده جماعة من المشايخ والفقراء أهل الزوايا.

التجار، وودعت الشيخ وانصرفت، فلما حللت بمدينة بسطام كتب إلى بعض أصحابي من نيسابور، وذكر أن الغلام المذكور قتل بعض أولاد الأتراك، وقتل به، وهذه كرامة واضحة لهذا الشيخ، رضي الله عنه.

وسافرت من نيسابور إلى مدينة بسطام التي ينسب إليها الشيخ العارف أبو يزيد البسطامي الشهير، رضي الله عنه، وبهذه المدينة قبره، ومعه في قبة واحدة احد أولاد جعفر الصادق، رضي الله عنه، وببسطام أيضاً قبر الشيخ الصالح الولي الحسن الخرقاني.

وكان نزولي من هذه المدينة بزاوية الشيخ أبي يزيد البسطامي، رضي الله عنه، ثم سافرت من هذه المدينة على طريق هند خير إلى قندوس وبغلان، وهي قرى فيها مشائخ وصالحون، وبها البساتين والأنهار فنزلنا بقندوس على نهر ماء به زاوية لأحد شيوخ الفقراء من أهل مصر يسمى بشير سياه، معنى ذلك الأسد الأسود، وأضافنا بها والي تلك الأرض، وهو من أهل الموصل، وسكناه ببستان عظيم هنالك، وأقمنا بخارج هذه القرية نحو أربعين يوماً لرعي الجمال والخيل، وبها مراع طيبة وأعشاب كثيرة، والأمن بها شامل بسبب شدة أحكام الأمير برنطيه. وقد قدمنا ان أحكام الترك في من سرق فرساً أن يعطي معه تسعة مثله، فان لم يجد ذلك أخذ فيها أولاده، فان لم يكن له أولاد ذبح ذبح الشاة. والناس يتركون دوابهم مهملة دون راع بعد أن يسم كل واحد دوابه في أفخاذها وكذلك فعلنا في هذه البلاد.

واتفق أن تفقدنا خيلنا بعد عشر من نزولنا بها، ففقدنا منها ثلاثة أفراس ولما كان بعد نصف شهر جاءنا التتر بها إلى منزلنا خوفاً على أنفسهم من الاحكام، وكنا نربط في كل ليلة إزاء أخبيتنا فرسين لما عسى ان يقع باليل، ففقدنا الفرسين ذات ليلة، وسافرنا من هناك، وبعد اثنتين وعشرين ليلة جاؤوا بهما إلينا في أثناء طريقنا.

وكان أيضاً من أسباب اقامتنا خوف الثلج، فان بأثناء الطريق جبلاً يقال له هند كوش، ومعناه قاتل الهنود، لأن العبيد والجواري الذين يؤتى بهم من بلاد الهند يموت هنالك الكثير منهم لشدة البرد، وكثرة الثلج، وهو مسيرة يوم كامل.

وإزاء هذا القبر قبر هارون الرشيد أمير المؤمنين، رضي الله عنه، وعليه دكانة يضعون عليها الشمعدانات التي يعرفها أهل المغرب بالحسك، والمنائر، وإذا دخل الرافضي للزيارة ضرب قبر الرشيد برجله وسلم على الرضا.

ثم سافرنا إلى مدينة سرخس وإليها ينسب الشيخ الصالح لقمان السرخسي، رضي الله عنه، ثم سافرنا منها إلى مدينة زاوة، وهي مدينة الشيخ الصالح قطب الدين حيدر، وإليه تنتسب طائفة الحيدرية من الفقراء، وهم الذين يجعلون حلق الحديد في أيديهم وأعناقهم وآذانهم، ويجعلونها أيضاً في ذكورهم حتى لا يتأتى لهم النكاح.

ثم رحلنا منها فوصلنا إلى مدينة نيسابور، وهي إحدى المدن الأربع التي هي قواعد خراسان، ويقال لها دمشق الصغيرة لكثرة فواكهها وبساتينها ومياهها وحسنها. وتخترقها أربعة من الأنهار، وأسواقها حسنة متسعة، مسجدها بديع، وهو في وسط السوق، ويليه أربع من المدارس يجري بها الماء الغزير. وفيها من الطلبة خلق كثير يقرأون القرآن والفقه، وهي من حسان مدارس تلك البلاد، ومدارس خراسان والعراقين ودمشق وبغداد ومصر، وإن بلغت الغاية من الاتقان والحسن، فكلها تقصر عن المدرسة التي عمرها مولانا أمير المؤمنين المتوكل على الله المجاهد في سبيل الله، عالم الملوك، واسطة عقد الخلفاء العادلين، أبو عنان وصل الله سعده ونصر جنده، وهي التي عند القصبة من حضرة فاس، حرسها الله تعالى، فإنها لا نظير لها سعة وارتفاعاً، ونقش الجص بها لا قدرة لأهل المشرق عليه.

ويصنع بنيسابور ثياب الحرير من النخ والكمخا وغيرها، وتحمل منها إلى الهند، وفي هذه المدينة زاوية الشيخ الامام العالم القطب العابد قطب الدين النيسابوري أحد الوعاظ العلماء الصالحين، نزلت عنده فأحسن القرى وأكرم، ورأيت له البراهين والكرامات العجيبة.

ذكر كرامة

كنت قد اشتريت بنيسابور غلاماً تركياً فرآه معي، فقال لي: هذا الغلام لا يصلح لك، فبعه! فقلت له: نعم! وبعت الغلام في غد ذلك اليوم، واشتراه بعض

الشيخ شهاب الدين ومدينة الجام التي تنسب إليه

يذكر أنه كان صاحب راحة مكثراً من الشرب، وكان له من الندماء نحو ستين، وكانت لهم عادة أن يجتمعوا يوماً في منزل كل واحد منهم، فتدور النوبة على أحدهم بعد شهرين، وبقوا على ذلك مدة. ثم ان النوبة وصلت يوماً إلى الشيخ شهاب الدين، فعقد التوبة ليلة النوبة، وعزم على إصلاح حاله مع ربه، وقال في نفسه: إن قلت لأصحابي إني قد تبت قبل اجتماعهم عندي ظنوا ذلك عجزاً عن مؤونتهم، فأحضر ما كان يحضر مثله قبل من مأكول ومشروب، وجعل الخمر في الزقاق، وحضر أصحابه، فلما أرادوا الشرب، فتحوا زقاً فذاقه أحدهم فوجده حلواً، ثم فتحوا ثانياً فوجدوه كذلك، ثم ثالثاً فوجدوه كذلك، فكلموا الشيخ في ذلك، فخرج لهم عن حقيقة أمره، وصدقهم سن بكره، وعرفهم بتوبته، وقال لهم: والله ما هذا إلا الشراب الذي كنتم تشربونه فيما تقدم، فتابوا جميعاً إلى الله تعالى، وبنوا تلك الزاوية وانقطعوا بها لعبادة الله تعالى، وظهر لهذا الشيخ كثير من الكرامات والمكاشفات.

ثم سافرنا من الجام إلى مدينة طوس، وهي من أكبر بلاد خراسان وأعظمها، بلد الإمام الشهير أبي حامد الغزالي، رضي الله عنه، وبها قبره، ورحلنا منها إلى مدينة مشهد الرضا، وهو علي بن موسى الكاظم بن جعفر الصادق بن محمد الباقر بن علي زين العابدين بن الحسين الشهيد أبن أمير المؤمنين علي بن أبي طالب، رضي الله عنهم، وهي أيضاً مدينة كبيرة ضخمة، كثيرة الفواكه والمياه والأرحاء الطاحنة، وكان بها الطاهر محمد شاه، والطاهر عندهم بمعنى النقيب عند أهل مصر والشام والعراق، وأهل الهند والسند وتركستان يقولون: السيد الأجل.

وكان أيضاً بهذا المشهد القاضي الشريف جلال الدين لقيته بأرض الهند، والشريف علي وولداه أمير هندو، ودولة شاه، وصحبوني من ترمذ إلى بلاد الهند، وكانوا من الفضلاء.

والمشهد المكرم عليه قبة عظيمة في داخل زاوية وتجاورها مدرسة ومسجد، وجميعها مليح البناء مصنوع الحيطان بالقاشاني. وعلى القبر دكانة خشب ملبسة بصفائح الفضة، وعليه قناديل فضة معلقة، وعتبة باب القبة فضة، وعلى بابها ستر حرير مذهب، وهي مبسوطة بأنواع البسط.

فقال: أنا أحمل الفقيه نظام الدين معي إلى الترك ليرضوا بذلك ثم أرده، فمال الناس إلى قوله، ورأى الفقيه نظام الدين اتفاقهم على ذلك، فركب مع الشيخ أبي أحمد ووصل إلى الترك، فقام إليه الأمير تمور الطي وقال له: أنت أخذت امرأتي مني، وضربه بدبوسه فكسر دماغه، فخر ميتاً، فسقط في يد الشيخ أبي أحمد، وانصرف من هنالك إلى بلده، ورد الترك ما كانوا أخذوه من الخيل والماشية.

وبعد مدة قدم ذلك التركي الذي قتل الفقيه على مدينة هراة، فلقيه جماعة من أصحاب الفقيه، فتقدموا إليه كأنهم مسلمون عليه وتحت ثيابهم السيوف فقتلوه، وفر أصحابه، ولما كان بعد هذا بعث الملك حسين ابن عمه ملك ورنا، الذي كان رفيق الفقيه نظام الدين في تغيير المنكر، رسولاً إلى ملك سجستان، فلما حصل بها بعث إليه أن يقيم هنالك، ولا يعود إليه، فقصد بلاد الهند، ولقيته وأنا خارج منها بمدينة سيوستان من السند، وهو أحد الفضلاء، وفي طبعه حب الرياسة والصيد والبزاة والخيل والمماليك والأصحاب واللباس الملوكي الفاخر، ومن كان على هذا الترتيب فإنه لا يصلح حاله بأرض الهند، فكان من أمره أن ملك الهند ولاه بلداً صغيراً، وقتله به بعض أهل هراة المقيمين بالهند بسبب جارية. وقيل إن ملك الهند دس عليه من قتله بسعي الملك حسين في ذلك، ولأجله خدم الملك حسين ملك الهند بعد موت ملك ورنا المذكور، وهاداه ملك الهند، وأعطاه مدينة بكار من بلاد السند، ومجباها خمسون ألفاً من دنانير الذهب في كل سنة.

ولنعد إلى ما كنا بسبيله فنقول: سافرنا من هراة إلى مدينة الجام، وهي متوسطة حسنة، ذات بساتين وأشجار وعيون كثيرة وأنهار، وأكثر شجرها التوت، والحرير بها كثير، وهي تنسب إلى الولي العابد الزاهد شهاب الدين أحمد الجامي، وسنذكر حكايته، وحفيده الشيخ أحمد المعروف بزاده الذي قتله ملك الهند، والمدينة الآن لأولاده، وهي محررة من قبل السلطان؛ ولهم بها نعمة وثروة.

وذكر لي من أثق به أن السلطان أبا سعيد ملك العراق قدم خراسان مرة ونزل على هذه المدينة، وبها زاوية الشيخ، فاضافه ضيافة عظيمة وأعطى لكل خباء بمحلته رأس غنم، ولكل أربعة رجال رأس غنم، ولكل دابة بالمحلة من فرس وبغل وحمار علف ليلة، فلم يبق في المحلة حيوان إلا وصلته ضيافته.

حكاية منكر بدار الملك

ذكر لي أنهم تعرفوا يوماً أن بدار الملك حسين منكراً فاجتمعوا لتغييره وتحصن منهم بداخل داره، فاجتمعوا على الباب في ستة آلاف رجل، فخاف منهم، فاستحضر الفقيه كبار البلد، وكان قد شرب الخمر، فأقاموا عليه الحد بداخل قصره وانصرفوا عنه.

سبب قتل الفقيه نظام الدين المذكور

كان الأتراك المجاورون لمدينة هراة الساكنون بالصحراء، وملكهم طغيتمور الذي مر ذكره، وهم نحو خمسين ألفاً يخافهم الملك حسين، ويهدي لهم الهدايا في كل سنة ويداريهم، وذلك قبل هزيمته للرافضة، وأما بعد هزيمته للرافضة، فتغلب عليهم، ومن عادة هؤلاء الأتراك التردد إلى مدينة هراة، وربما شربوا بها الخمر، وأتاها بعضهم وهو سكران فكان نظام الدين يحد من وجد منهم سكران.

وهؤلاء الأتراك أهل نجد وبأس، ولا يزالون يضربون على بلاد الهند، فيسبون ويقتلون، وربما سبوا بعض المسلمات اللاتي يكن بأرض الهند ما بين الكفار، فإذا خرجوا بهن إلى خراسان يطلق نظام الدين المسلمات من أيدي الترك. وعلامة النسوة المسلمات بأرض الهند ترك ثقب الأذن، والكافرات آذانهن مثقوبات، فاتفق مرة أن أميراً من أمراء الترك يسمى تمور الطي سبى امرأة، وكلف بها كلفاً شديداً، فذكرت أنها مسلمة فانتزعها الفقيه من يده، فبلغ ذلك من التركي مبلغاً عظيماً وركب في آلاف من أصحابه وأغار على خيل هراة، وهي من مرعاها بصحراء مرغيس (بدغيس) واحتملوها، فلم يتركوا لأهل هراة ما يركبون ولا يحلبون، وصعدوا بها إلى جبل هنالك لا يقدر عليهم فيه، ولم يجد السلطان ولا جنده خيلاً يتبعونهم بها، فبعث إليهم رسولاً يطلب منهم رد ما أخذوه من الماشية والخيل، ويذكرهم العهد الذي بينهم، فأجابوا بأنهم لا يردون ذلك حتى يمكنوا من الفقيه نظام الدين، فقال السلطان: لا سبيل إلى هذا.

وكان الشيخ أبو أحمد الجستي حفيد الشيخ مودود الجستي له بخراسان شأن عظيم، وقوله معتبر لديهم، فركب في جماعة خيل من أصحابه ومماليكه،

أرغون شاه فهزموه وأسروه ومنوا عليه، ثم غزاهم طغيتمور بنفسه في خمسين ألفاً من التتر، فهزموه، وملكوا البلاد، وتغلبوا على سرخس والزاوه وطوس، وهي من أعظم بلاد خراسان، وجعلوا خليفتهم بمشهد علي بن موسى الرضى، وتغلبوا على مدينة الجام، ونزلوا بخارجها، وهم قاصدون مدينة هراة وبينها وبينهم مسيرة ست.

فلما بلغ ذلك الملك حسيناً جمع الأمراء والعساكر وأهل المدينة واستشارهم هل يقيمون حتى يأتي القوم أو يمضون إليهم فيناجزونهم، فوقع إجماعهم على الخروج إليهم، وهم قبيلة واحدة يسمون الغورية، ويقال انهم منسوبون إلى غور الشام، وإن أصلهم منه، فتجهزوا أجمعون، واجتمعوا من أطراف البلاد، وهم ساكنون بالقرى وبصحراء مرغيس (بدغيس) وهي مسيرة أربع لا يزال عشبها أخضر ترعى منه ماشيتهم وخيلهم، وأكثر شجرهم الفستق، ومنها يحمل إلى أرض العراق، وعضدهم أهل مدينة سمنان، ونفروا جميعاً إلى الرافضة، وهم مائة وعشرون ألفاً ما بين رجالة وفرسان يقودهم الملك حسين، واجتمعت الرافضة في مائة وخمسين ألفاً من الفرسان، وكانت الملاقاة بصحراء بوشنج، وصبر الفريقان معاً ثم كانت الدائرة على الرافضة، وفر سلطانهم مسعود، وثبت خليفتهم حسن في عشرين ألفاً حتى قتل وقتل أكثرهم وأسر منهم نحو أربعة آلاف.

وذكر لي بعض من حضر هذه الوقيعة أن ابتداء القتال كان في وقت الضحى، وكانت الهزيمة عند الزوال. ونزل الملك حسين بعد الظهر فصلى وأتى بالطعام، فكان هو وكبار أصحابه يأكلون، وسائرهم يضربون أعناق الأسرى. وعاد الى حضرته بعد هذا الفتح العظيم، وقد نصر الله السنة على يديه وأطفأ نار الفتنة. وكانت هذه الوقيعة بعد خروجي من الهند عام ثمانية وأربعين.

ونشأ بهراة رجل من الزهاد والصلحاء الفضلاء واسمه نظام الدين مولانا، وكان أهل هراة يحبونه ويرجعون إلى قوله، وكان يعظمهم ويذكرهم، وتوافقوا معه على تغيير المنكر، وتعاقد معهم على ذلك خطيب المدينة المعروف بملك ورنا، وهو ابن عم الملك حسين ومتزوج بزوجة والده، وهو من أحسن الناس صورة وسيرة، والملك يخافه على نفسه، وسنذكر خبره، وكانوا متى علموا بمنكر، ولو كان عند الملك، غيروه.

الشجاعة المأثورة، والتأييد والسعادة، ظهر له من إنجاد الله تعالى وتأييده في موطنين اثنين ما يقضي منه العجب: أحدهما عند ملاقاة جيشه للسلطان خليل الذي بغى عليه، وكان منتهى أمره حصوله أسيراً في يديه، والموطن الثاني عند ملاقاته بنفسه لمسعود سلطان الرافضة، وكان منتهى أمره تبديده وفراره وذهاب ملكه. وولي السلطان حسين الملك بعد أخيه المعروف بالحافظ، وولي أخوه بعد أبيه غياث الدين.

حكاية الرافضة

كان بخراسان رجلان أحدهما يسمى بمسعود والآخر يسمى بمحمد، وكان لهما خمسة من الأصحاب، وهم من الفتاك، ويعرفون بالعراق بالشطار، ويعرفون بخراسان بسرا بداران (سر بداران)، ويعرفون بالنغرب بالصقورة، فاتفق سبعتهم على الفساد، وقطع الطرق وسلب الأموال، وشاع خبرهم، وسكنوا جبلاً منيعاً بمقربة من مدينة بهيق، وتسمى أيضاً مدينة سيزار (سيزوار)، وكانوا يكمنون بالنهار، ويخرجون بالليل والعشي، فيضربون على القرى، ويقطعوق الطرق، ويأخذون الأموال، وانثال عليهم أشباههم من أهل الشر والفساد، فكثر عددهم واشتدت شكواهم، وهابهم الناس، وضربوا على مدينة بيهق، فملكوها ثم ملكوا سواها من المدن واكتسبوا الأموال، وجندوا الجنود، وركبوا الخيل، وتسمى مسعود بالسلطان وصار العبيد يفرون عن مواليهم إليه، فكل عبد فر منهم يعطيه الفرس والمال، وإن ظهرت له شجاعة أمره على جماعة، فعظم جيشه واستفحل أمره، وتمذهب جميعهم بمذهب الرفض، وطمحوا إلى استئصال أهل السنة بخراسان، وان يجعلوها كلمة واحدة رافضية.

وكان بمشهد طوس شيخ من الرافضة يسمى بحسن، وهو عندهم من الصلحاء، فوافقهم على ذلك وسموه بالخليفة، وأمرهم بالعدل، فأظهروه حتى كانت الدراهم والدنانير تسقط من معسكرهم، فلا يلتقطها أحد حتى يأتي ربها فيأخذها، وغلوا على نيسابور.

وبعث إليهم السلطان طغيتمور بالعساكر فهزموها، ثم بعث ابيهم نائبه

ورد عليها الثوب، فقالت له: أوقع بصر الخليفة على هذا الثوب؟ قال: نعم! قالت: لا ألبس ثوباً وقع عليه بصر غير ذي محرم مني، وأمرت ببيعه، فبني منه المسجد والزاوية ورباط في مقابلته مبني بالكذان، وهو عامر حتى الآن، وفضل من ثمن الثوب مقدار ثلثه، فذكر أنها أمرت بدفنه تحت بعض سواري المسجد ليكون هنالك متيسراً إن احتيج إليه أخرج، فأخبر تنكيز بهذه الحكاية فأمر بهدم سواري المسجد فهدم منها نحو الثلث ولم يجد شيئاً، فترك الباقي على حاله.

وبخارج بلخ قبر يذكر أنه قبر عكاشة بن محصن الأسدي صاحب رسول الله، صلى الله عليه وسلم تسليماً، الذي يدخل الجنة بلا حساب، وعليه زاوية معظمة بها كان نزولنا، وبخارجها بركة ماء عجيبة عليها شجرة جوز عظيمة، ينزل الواردون في الصيف تحت ظلالها.

وشيخ هذه الزاوية يعرف بالحاج خرد، وهو الصغير من الفضلاء، وركب معنا وأرانا مزارات هذه المدينة، منها قبر حزقيل النبي، عليه السلام، وعليه قبة حسنة، وزرنا بها أيضاً قبوراً كثيرة من قبور الصالحين لا أذكرها الآن، ووقفنا على دار ابراهيم بن أدهم، رضي الله عنه، وهي دار ضخمة مبنية بالصخر الأبيض الذي يشبه الكذان، وكان زرع الزاوية مقترناً بها، وقد سدت عليه، فلم ندخلها، وهي بمقربة من المسجد الجامع.

ثم سافرنا من مدينة بلخ فسرنا في جبال قوة استان (قهستان) سبعة أيام، وهي قرى كثيرة عامرة بها المياه الجارية والأشجار المورقة وأكثرها شجر التين، وبها زوايا كثيرة فيها الصالحون المنقطعون إلى الله تعالى. وبعد ذلك كان وصولنا إلى مدينة هراة، وهي أكبر المدن العامرة بخراسان، ومدن خراسان العظيمة أربع، اثنتان عامرتان وهما هراة ونيسابور، واثنتان خربتان وهما بلخ ومرو. ومدينة هراة كبيرة عظيمة، كثيرة العمارة، ولأهلها صلاح وعفاف وديانة، وهم على مذهب الإمام أبي حنيفة، رضي الله عنه، وبلدهم طاهر من الفساد.

سلطان هراة

وهو السلطان المعظم حسين ابن السلطان غياث الدين الغوري صاحب

وبرهان الدين، بملتان وسفرنا جميعاً إلى الهند، وذكر أخويه الآخرين عماد الدين وسيف الدين ولقائي لهما بحضرة ملك الهند، وذكر ولديه وقدومهما على ملك الهند، بعد قتل أبيهما، وتزويجهما بنتي الوزير خواجة جهان، وما جرى في ذلك كله إن شاء الله تعالى.

ثم أجزنا نهر جيحون إلى بلاد خراسان وسرنا، بعد انصرافنا من ترمذ وإجازة الوادي، يوماً ونصف يوم في صحراء ورمال لا عمارة بها إلى مدينة بلخ، وهي خاوية على عروشها، غير عامرة، ومن رآها ظنها عامرة لإتقان بنائها، وكانت ضخمة فسيحة، ومساجدها ومدارسها باقية الرسم حتى الآن، ونقوش مبانيها مدخلة بأصبغة اللازورد، والناس ينسبون اللازورد إلى خراسان، وإنما يجلب من جبال بدخشان التي ينسب إليها الياقوت البدخشي، والعامة يقولون البلخش وسيأتي ذكرها إن شاء الله تعالى، وخرب هذه المدينة تنكيز اللعين وهدم من مسجدها نحو الثلث بسبب كنز ذكر له أنه تحت سارية من سواريه، وهو من أحسن مساجد الدنيا وأفسحها، ومسجد رباط الفتح بالمغرب يشبهه في عظم سواريه، ومسجد بلخ أجمل منه في سوى ذلك.

أميرة تبني مسجداً

ذكر لي بعض أهل التاريخ أن مسجد بلخ بنته امرأة كان زوجها أميراً ببلخ لبني العباس يسمى داود بن علي، فاتفق أن الخليفة غضب مرة على أهل بلخ لحادث أحدثوه، فبعث إليهم من يغرمهم مغرماً فادحاً، فلما بلغ إلى بلخ أتى نساؤها وصبيانها إلى تلك المرأة التي بنت المسجد، وهي زوج أميرهم، وشكوا حالهم وما لحقهم من هذا المغرم، فبعثت إلى الأمير الذي قدم برسم تغريمهم بثوب لها مرصع بالجوهر، قيمته أكثر مما أمر بتغريمه، فقاله له: اذهب بهذا الثوب إلى الخليفة، فقد أعطيته صدقة عن أهل بلخ لضعف حالهم. فذهب به إلى الخليفة وألقى الثوب بين يديه، وقص عليه القصة، فخجل الخليفة وقال: أتكون المرأة أكرم منا؟ وأمره برفع المغرم عن أهل بلخ، وبالعودة إليها ليرد للمرأة ثوبها. وأسقط عن أهل بلخ خراج سنة، فعاد الأمير إلى بلخ، وأتى منزل المرأة، وقص عليها مقالة الخليفة،

وللملك الهند في كل بلد من بلاده صاحب الخبر يكتب له بكل ما يجري في ذلك البلد من الأمور وبمن يرد عليه من الواردين، وإذا أتى الوارد كتبوا من أي البلاد ورد، وكتبوا اسمه ونعته وثيابه وأصحابه وخيله وخدامه وهيئته من الجلوس والمأكل وجميع شؤونه وتصرفاته، وما يظهر منه من فضيلة أو ضدها، فلا يصل الوارد إلى الملك إلا وهو عارف بجميع حاله، فتكون كرامته على مقدار ما يستحقه.

وسافرنا من سمرقند فاجتزنا ببلدة نسف، وإليها ينسب أبو حفص عمر النسفي مؤلف كتاب المنظومة في المسائل الخلافية بين الفقهاء الأربعة، رضي الله عنهم، ثم وصلنا إلى مدينة ترمذ التي ينسب إليها الإمام أبو عيسى محمد بن عيسى ابن سورة الترمذي، مؤلف الجامع الكبير في السنن، وهي مدينة كبيرة حسنة العمارة والأسواق، تخترقها الأنهار، وبها البساتين الكثيرة والعنب، والسفرجل بها كثير متناهي الطيب، واللحوم بها كثيرة، وكذلك الألبان، وأهلها يغسلون رؤوسهم في الحمام باللبن عوضاً عن الطفل، ويكون عند كل صاحب حمام أوعية كبار مملوءة لبناً فإذا دخل الرجل الحمام أخذ منها في إناء صغير، فغسل رأسه، وهو يرطب الشعر ويصقله.

وأهل الهند يجعلون في رؤوسهم زيت السمسم، ويسمونه الشيرج، ويغسلون الشعر بعده بالطفل فينعم الجسم، ويصقل الشعر ويطيله، وبذلك طالت لحى أهل الهند ومن سكن معهم.

وكانت مدينة ترمذ القديمة مبنية على شاطئ جيحون، فلما خربها تنكيز بنيت هذه الحديثة على ميلين من النهر، وكان نزولنا بزاوية الشيخ الصالح عزيزان من كبار المشائخ وكرامائهم، كثير المال والرباع والبساتين، ينفق على الصادر والوارد من ماله.

واجتمعت قبل وصولي إلى هذه المدينة بصاحبها علاء الدين خداوند زاده، وكتب لي إليها بالضيافة، فكانت تحمل إلينا أيام مقامنا بها في كل يوم، ولقيت أيضاً قاضيها قوام الدين، وهو متوجه لرؤية السلطان طرمشيرين، وطالب للإذن له في السفر إلى بلاد الهند، وسيأتي ذكر لقائي له بعد ذلك، ولأخويه ضياء الدين

وأهل سمرقند لهم مكارم أخلاق ومحبة في الغريب، وهم خير من أهل بخارى. وبخارج سمرقند قبر قثم بن العباس بن عبد المطلب، رضي الله عن العباس وعن ابنه، وهو المستشهد حين فتحها. ويخرج أهل سمرقند كل ليلة اثنين وجمعة إلى زيارته، والتتر يأتون لزيارته، وينذرون له النذور العظيمة، ويأتون إليه بالبقر والغنم والدراهم والدنانير، فيصرف ذلك في النفقة على الوارد والصادر ولخدام الزاوية والقبر المبارك وعليه قبة قائمة على أربع أرجل، وحيطان ومع كل رجل ساريتان من الرخام منها الخضر والسود والبيض والحمر، وحيطان القبة بالرخام المجزع المنقوش بالذهب، وسقفها مصنوع بالرصاص، وعلى القبر خشب الآبنوس المرصع مكسو الأركان بالفضة، وفوقه ثلاثة من قناديل الفضة. وفرش القبة بالصوف والقطن، خارجها نهر كبير يشق الزاوية التي هنالك، وعلى حافتيه الأشجار ودوالي العنب والياسمين.

وبالزاوية مساكن يسكنها الوارد والصادر، ولم يغير التتر أيام كفرهم شيئاً من حال هذا الموضع المبارك بل كانوا يتبركون به لما يرون له من الآيات. وكان الناظر في كل حال هذا الضريح المبارك وما يليه، حين نزولنا به، الأمير غياث الدين محمد بن عبد القادر بن عبد العزيز بن يوسف ابن الخليفة المستنصر بالله العباسي، قدمه لذلك السلطان طرمشرين لما قدم عليه من العراق، وهو الآن عند ملك الهند، وسيأتي ذكره.

ولقيت بسمرقند قاضيها المسمى عندهم صدر الجهان، وهو من الفضلاء ذوي المكارم، وسافر إلى بلاد الهند بعد سفري إليها فأدركته منيته بمدينة ملتان قاعدة بلاد السند.

حكاية ملك الهند

لما مات هذا القاضي بملتان كتب صاحب الخبر بأمره إلى ملك الهند، وأنه قدم برسم بابه فاخترم دون ذلك، فلما بلغ الخبر إلى الملك أمر أن يبعث إلى أولاده عدد من آلاف الدنانير، لا أذكره الآن، وأمر أن يعطى لأصحابه ما كان يعطى لهم لو وصلوا معه وهو بقيد الحياة.

حملة لم يثبت لها التتر، فانهزموا واشتد فيهم القتل. وأقام خليل بالمالق ثلاثاً، وخرج إلى استئصال من بقي من التتر، فأذعنوا له بالطاعة، وجاز إلى تخوم الخطا والصين، وفتح مدينة قراقرم ومدينة بش بالغ، وبعث إليه سلطان الخطا بالعساكر ثم وقع بينهما الصلح.

وعظم أمر خليل وهابته الملوك وأظهر العدل ورتب العساكر بالمالق، وترك بها وزيره خداوند زاده، وانصرف إلى سمرقند وبخارى.

ثم ان الترك أرادوا الفتنة فسعوا إلى خليل بوزيره المذكور، وزعموا أنه يريد الثورة، ويقول انه أحق بالملك لقرابته من النبي، صلى الله عليه وسلم، وكرمه وشجاعته، فبعث والياً إلى المالق عوضاً عنه، وأمره أن يقدم عليه في نفر يسير من أصحابه، فلما قدم عليه قتله عند وصوله، من غير تثبت، فكان ذلك سبب خراب ملكه.

وكان خليل لما عظم أمره بغى على صاحب هراة الذي أورثه الملك وجهزه بالعساكر والمال، فكتب إليه أن يخطب في بلاده باسمه ويضرب الدنانير والدراهم على سكته، فغاظ ذلك الملك حسيناً، وأنف منه، وأجابه بأقبح جواب، فجهز خليل لقتاله، فلم توافقه عساكر الاسلام ورأوه باغياً عليه، وبلغ خبره إلى الملك حسين، فجهز العساكر مع ابن عمه ملك ورنا، والتقى الجمعان، فانهزم خليل وأتي به إلى الملك حسين أسيراً فمن عليه بالبقاء، وجعله في دار وأعطاه جارية وأجرى عليه النفقة. وعلى هذا الحال تركته عنده في أواخر سنة سبع وأربعين عند خروجي من الهند.

(ولنعد إلى ما كان بسبيله) ولما ودعت السلطان طرمشيرين سافرت إلى مدينة سمرقند، وهي من أكبر المدن وأحسنها وأتمها جمالاً، مبنية على شاطئ واد يعرف بوادي القصارين، عليه النواعير تسقي البساتين، وعنده يجتمع أهل البلد بعد صلاة العصر للنزهة والتفرج، ولهم عليه مساطب ومجالس يقعدون عليها، ودكاكين تباع بها الفاكهة وسائر المأكولات.

وكانت على شاطئه قصور عظيمة وعمارة تنبئ عن علو همم أهلها، فدثر أكثر ذلك، وكذلك المدينة خرب كثير منها، ولا سور لها ولا أبواب عليها، وفي داخلها البساتين.

لو لا المعرة لقتلتك، ولكن أعطوه خمسة آلاف دينار، واذهبوا به إلى دار بشاي أغل وأخته ولدي طرمشيرين، وقالوا لهم: ان هذا الكاذب يزعم أنه والدكم، فدخل عليهم فعرفوه وبات عندهم والحراس يحرسونه، وأخرج بالغد، وخافوا أن يهلكوا بسببه، فأنكروه ونفي عن بلاد الهند والسند، فسلك طريق كيج ومكران، وأهل البلاد يكرمونه ويضيفونه ويهادونه، ووصل إلى شيراز فأكرمه سلطانها أبو إسحاق وأجرى له كفايته.

ولما دخلت عند وصولي من الهند إلى مدينة شيراز ذكر لي أنه باق بها، وأردت لقاءه ولم أفعل لأنه كان في دار لا يدخل إليه أحد إلا بإذن من السلطان أبي اسحاق، فخفت مما يتوقع بسبب ذلك، ثم ندمت على عدم لقائه.

(رجع الحديث إلى بوزن) وذلك أنه لما ملك ضيق على المسلمين وظلم الرعية وأباح للنصارى واليهود عمارة كنائسهم، فضج المسلمون من ذلك، وتربصوا به الدوائر، واتصل خبره بخليل ابن السلطان اليسور المهزوم على خراسان، فقصد ملك هراة، وهو السلطان حسين ابن السلطان غياث الدين الغوري، فأعلمه بما كان في نفسه وسأل منه الإعانة بالعساكر والمال على أن يشاطره الملك إذا استقام له، فبعث معه الملك حسين عسكراً عظيماً، وبين هراة وترمذ تسعة أيام، فلما سمع أمراء الإسلام بقدوم خليل تلقوه بالسمع والطاعة والرغبة في جهاد العدو.

وكان أول قادم عليه علاء الملك خداوند زاده صاحب ترمذ، وهو أمير كبير شريف حسيني النسب، فأتاه في أربعة آلاف من المسلمين، فسر به وولاه وزارته، وفوض إليه أمره، وكان من الأبطال؛ وجاء الأمراء من كل ناحية واجتمعوا على خليل والتقى مع بوزن، فمالت العساكر إلى خليل وأسلموا بوزن، وأتوا به أسيراً، فقتله خنقاً بأوتار القسي، وتلك عادة لهم أنهم لا يقتلون من كان من أبناء الملوك إلا خنقاً، واستقام الملك لخليل.

وعرض عساكره بسمرقند فكانوا ثمانين ألفاً عليهم وعلى الدروع، فصرف العسكر الذي جاء به من هراة، وقصد بلاد المالق، فقدم التتر على أنفسهم واحداً منهم، ولقوه على مسيرة ثلاث من المالق بمقربة من أطراز (طراز) وحمي القتال وصبر الفريقان، فحمل الأمير خداوند زاده وزيره في عشرين ألفاً من المسلمين

انه لم يقتل كما سنذكره، وكردن معناه العنق، وبريدا معناه المقطوع، ويسمى بذلك لضربة كانت في عنقه. وقد رأيته بأرض الهند، ويقع ذكره فيما بعد.

ولما ملك بوزن هرب ابن السلطان طرمشيرين، وهو بشاي أغل (أغلي)، وأخته وزوجها فيروز إلى ملك الهند، فعظمهم وأنزلهم منزلة عليه بسبب ما كان بينه وبين طرمشيرين من الود والمكاتبة والمهاداة، وكان يخاطبه بالأخ. ثم بعد ذلك أتى رجل من أرض السند وادعى أنه هو طرمشيرين، واختلف الناس فيه، فسمع بذلك عماد الملك سرتيز غلام ملك الهند ووالي بلاد السند، ويسمى ملك عرض، وهو الذي تعرض بين يديه عساكر الهند وإليه أمرها، ومقره بملتان قاعدة السند، فبعث إليه بعض الأتراك العارفين به، فعادوا إليه وأخبروه أنه هو طرمشيرين حقاً، فأمر له بالسراجة، وهي افراج، فضرب خارج المدينة، ورتب له ما يترتب لمثله، وخرج لاستقباله، وترجل له وسلم عليه، وأتى في خدمته إلى السراجة، فدخلها راكباً كعادة الملوك، ولم يشك أحد أنه هو، وبعث إلى ملك الهند بخبره فبعث إليه الأمراء يستقبلونه بالضيافات.

وكان في خدمة ملك الهند حكيم ممن خدم طرمشيرين فيما تقدم، وهو كبير الحكماء بالهند، فقال للملك: أنا أتوجه إليه، وأعرف حقيقة أمره، فإني كنت عالجت له دملاً تحت ركبته، وبقي أثره، وبه أعرفه. فأتى إليه ذلك الحكيم واستقبله مع الأمراء، ودخل عليه ولازمه لسابقته عنده، وأخذ يغمز رجليه وكشف عن الأثر فشتمه، وقال له: تريد أن تنظر الى الدمل الذي عالجته؟ ها هوذا، أراه أثره، فتحقق أنه هو وعاد إلى ملك الهند فأعلمه بذلك.

ثم ان الوزير خواجة جهان أحمد بن أياس، وكبير الأمراء قطلوخان معلم السلطان أيام صغره، دخلا على ملك الهند، وقالا له: يا خوند عالم! هذا السلطان طرمشيرين قد وصل، وصح أنه هو، وهاهنا من قومه نحو أربعين ألفاً، وولده وصهره، أرأيت إن اجتمعوا عليه ما يكون من العمل؟ فوقع هذا الكلام بموقع منه عظيم وأمر أن يؤتى بطرمشيرين معجلاً، فلما دخل عليه أمر بالخدمة كسائر الواردين، ولم يعظم، وقال له السلطان: ياماذركاني، وهي شتمة قبيحة، كيف تكذب وتقول إنك طرمشيرين، وطرمشيرين قد قتل، وهذا خادم تربته عندنا؟ والله

ابن عم له اسمه بوزن أغلي. وكل من كان من أبناء الملوك فهم يسمونه أغلي، وكان مسلماً إلا أنه فاسد الدين سيء السيرة. وسبب بيعتهم له وخلعهم لطرمشيرين أن طرمشيرين خالف أحكام جدهم تنكيز اللعين الذي خرب بلاد الإسلام، وقد تقدم ذكره، وكان تنكيز ألف كتاباً في أحكامه يسمى عندهم اليساق، وعندهم أنه من خالف أحكام هذا الكتاب، فخلعه واجب، ومن جملة أحكامه أنهم يجتمعون يوماً في السنة يسمونه الطوى، ومعناهُ يوم الضيافة، ويأتي أولاد تنكيز والأمراء من أطراف البلاد ويحضر الخواتين وكبار الأجناد، وان كان سلطانهم قد غير شيئاً من تلك الأحكام يقوم إليه كبراؤهم فيقولون له: غيرت كذا وغيرت كذا، وفعلت كذا، وقد وجب خلعك، ويأخذون بيده ويقيمونه عن سرير الملك، ويقعدون غيره من أبناء تنكيز. وإن كان أحد الأمراء الكبار أذنب ذنباً في بلاده حكموا عليه بما يستحقه.

وكان السلطان طرمشيرين قد أبطل حكم هذا اليوم ومحا رسمه، فأنكروه عليه أشد الانكار، وأنكروا عليه أيضاً كونه أقام أربع سنين فيما يلي خراسان من بلاده، ولم يصل إلى الجهة التي توالي الصين، والعادة أن الملك يقصد تلك الجهة في كل سنة فيختبر أحوالها وحال الجند بها لأن أصل ملكهم منها، ودار الملك هي مدينة المالق، فلما بايعوا بوزن أتى في عسكر عظيم، وخاف طرمشيرين على نفسه من أمرائه، ولم يأمنهم، فركب في خمسة عشر فارساً يريد بلاد غزنة، وهي من عمالته، وواليها كبير أمرائه، وصاحب سره برنطية، وهذا الأمير محب في الإسلام والمسلمين قد عمر في عمالته نحو أربعين زاوية فيها الطعام للوارد والصادر، وتحت يده العساكر العظيمة، ولم أر قط فيمن رأيته في الادميين بجميع بلاد الدنيا أعظم خلقة منه، فلما عبر جيحون وقصد طريق بلخ رآه بعض الأتراك من أصحاب ينقي ابن أخيه كبك. وكان السلطان طرمشيرين المذكور قتل أخاه كبك المذكور وبقي ابنه ينقي ببلخ، فلما أعلمه التركي بخبره قال: ما فر إلا لأمر حدث عليه، فركب في أصحابه وقبض عليه وسجنه، ووصل بوزن إلى سمرقند وبخارى فبايعه الناس، وجاءه ينقي بطرمشيرين، فيذكر أنه لما وصل إلى نسف بخارج سمرقند قتل هنالك، ودفن بها، وخدم تربته الشيخ شمس الدين كردن بريدا، وقيل

فجاء أحد فتيانه بسجادة ووضعها قبالة المحراب، حيث جرت عادته أن يصلي، وقال للامام حسام الدين الياغي: إن مولانا يريد أن تنتظره بالصلاة قليلاً ريثما يتوضأ، فقام الإمام المذكور وقال: نماز، ومعناه الصلاة، براي خداو وبراي طرمشيرين، أي الصلاة لله أو لطرمشيرين، ثم أمر المؤذن بإقامة الصلاة، وجاء السلطان وقد صلي منها ركعتان، فصلى الركعتين الأخريين حيث انتهى به القيام، وذلك في الموضع الذي تكون فيه أنعلة الناس عند باب المسجد، وقضى ما فاته، وقام إلى الامام ليصافحه، وهو يضحك، وجلس قبالة المحراب، والشيخ الامام إلى جانبه، وأنا إلى جانب الإمام، فقال لي: إذا مشيت إلى بلادك فحدث أن فقيراً من فقراء الأعاجم يفعل هكذا مع سلطان الترك.

وكان هذا الشيخ يعظ الناس في كل جمعة ويأمر السلطان بالمعروف وينهاه عن المنكر وعن الظلم، ويغلظ عليه القول، والسلطان ينصت لكلامه، ويبكي؛ وكان لا يقبل من عطاء السلطان شيئاً، ولم يأكل قط من طعامه، ولا لبس من ثيابه.

وكان هذا الشيخ من عباد الله الصالحين، وكنت كثيراً ما أرى عليه قباء قطن مبطناً بالقطن محشواً به، وقد بلي وتمزق، وعلى رأسه قلنسوة لبد يساوي مثلها قيراطاً، ولا عمامة عليه. فقلت له في بعض الأيام: يا سيدي، ما هذا القباء الذي أنت لابسه؟ إنه ليس بجيد. فقال لي: يا ولدي ليس هذا القباء لي وإنما هو لابنتي. فرغبت منه أن يأخذ بعض ثيابي، فقال لي: عاهدت الله منذ خمسين سنة أن لا أقبل من أحد شيئاً، ولو كنت أقبل من أحد لقبلت منك.

ولما عزمت على السفر بعد مقامي عند هذا السلطان أربعة وخمسين يوماً أعطاني السلطان سبعمائة دينار دراهم وفروة سمور تساوي مائة دينار، طلبتها منه لأجل البرد، ولما ذكرتها له أخذ أكمامي وجعل يقبلها بيده تواضعاً منه وفضلاً وحسن خلق، وأعطاني فرسين وجملين. ولما أردت وداعه أدركته في أثناء طريقه الي متصيده، وكان اليوم شديد البرد جداً، فوالله ما قدرت على أن أنطق بكلمة لشدة البرد، ففهم ذلك وضحك وأعطاني يده وانصرفت.

وبعد سنتين من وصولي إلى أرض الهند بلغنا الخبر بأن الملأ من قومه وأمرائه اجتمعوا بأقصى بلاده المجاورة للصين، وهنالك معظم عساكره، وبايعوا

الحين قباء قدسي أخضر، وعلى رأسه شاشية مثله، ثم انصرف إلى مجلسه راجلاً، والناس يتعرضون له بالشكايات، فيقف لكل مشتك منهم صغيراً أو كبيراً، ذكراً أو أنثى.

ثم بحث عني فوصلت إليه وهو في خرقة، والناس خارجها ميمنة وميسرة، والأمراء منهم على الكراسي، وأصحابهم وقوف على رؤوسهم وبين أيديهم، وسائر الجند قد جلسوا صفوفاً، وأمام كل واحد منهم سلاحه، وهم أهل النوبة، يقعدون هنالك إلى العصر، ويأتي آخرون فيقعدون الى آخر الليل. وقد صنعت هنالك سقائف من ثياب القطن يكونون بها.

ولما دخلت إلى الملك بداخل الخرقة وجدته جالساً على كرسي شبه المنبر مكسو بالحرير المزركش بالذهب، وداخل الخرقة ملبس بثياب الحرير المذهب، والتاج المرصع بالجوهر واليواقيت معلق فوق رأس السلطان، بينه وبين رأسه قدر ذراع، والأمراء الكبار على الكراسي عن يمينه ويساره، وأولاد الملوك بأيديهم المذاب بين يديه. وعند باب الخرقة النائب والوزير والحاجب وصاحب العلامة وهم يسمون أل طمغي، وأل معناه الأحمر وطمغي معناه العلامة.

وقام إلي أربعتهم، حين دخولي، ودخلوا معي فسلمت عليه، وسألني، وصاحب العلامة يترجم بيني وبينه، عن مكة والمدينة والقدس، شرفها الله، وعن مدينة الخليل، عليه السلام، وعن دمشق ومصر والملك الناصر، وعن العراقين وملكهما وبلاد الأعاجم، ثم أذن المؤذن بالظهر، فانصرفنا، وكنا نحضر معه الصلوات وذلك أيام البرد الشديد المهلك، فكان لا يترك صلاة الصبح والعشاء في الجماعة، ويقعد للذكر بالتركية بعد صلاة الصبح إلى طلوع الشمس، ويأتي إليه كل من في المسجد فيصافحه ويشد بيده على يده، وكذلك يفعلون في صلاة العصر. وكان إذا أُتي بهدية من زبيب أو تمر، والتمر عزيز عندهم، وهم يتبركون به، يعطي منها بيده لكل من في المسجد.

حكاية فضائل السلطان طرمشيرين

ومن فضائل هذا الملك أنه حضرت صلاة العصر يوماً ولم يحضر السلطان،

سلطان ما وراء النهر

وهو السلطان المعظم علاء الدين طرمشيرين، وهو عظيم المقدار كثير الجيوش والعساكر ضخم المملكة، شديد القوة عادل الحكم.

وبلاده متوسطة بين أربعة من ملوك الدنيا الكبار، وهم ملك الصين، وملك الهند، وملك العراق وملك اوزبك، وكلهم يهابونه ويعظمونه ويكرمونه وولي الملك بعد أخيه الجكطي، وكان الجكطي هذا كافراً، وولي بعد أخيه الأكبر كبك. وكان كبك هذا كافراً أيضاً لكنه كان عادل الحكم، منصفاً للمظلومين، يكرم المسلمين ويعظمهم.

الملك كبك والواعظ

يذكر ان هذا الملك كبك تكلم يوماً مع الفقيه الواعظ المذكر بدر الدين الميداني فقال له: أنت تقول ان الله ذكر كل شيء في كتابه العزيز؟ قال: نعم! فقال: أين اسمي فيه؟ فقال: هو في قوله تعالى: في أي صورة ما شاء ركبك. فأعجبه ذلك، وقال: يخشي، ومعناه بالتركية جيد، فأكرمه اكراماً كثيراً وزاد في تعظيم المسلمين.

عدل كبك

ومن أحكام كبك ما ذكر أن امرأة شكت له بأحد الأمراء، وذكرت أنها فقيرة ذات أولاد، وكان لها لبن تقوتهم بثمنه، فاغتصبه ذلك الأمير وشربه، فقال لها أنا اوسطه فإن خرج اللبن من جوفه مضى لسبيله، وإلا وسطتك بعده. فقالت المرأة: قد حللته ولا أطلبه بشيء. فأمر به فوسط فخرج اللبن من بطنه.

ولنعد لذكر السلطان طرمشيرين: ولما أقمت بالمحلة، وهم يسمونها الأردوايا، ذهبت يوماً لصلاة الصبح بالمسجد على عادتي، فلما صليت ذكر لي بعض الناس أن السلطان بالمسجد، فلما قام عن الصلاة تقدمت للسلام عليه، وقام الشيخ حسن والفقيه حسام الدين الياغي، وأعلماه بحالي وقدومي منذ أيام، فقال لي بالتركية: خش ميسن يخشي ميسن قطلو أيوسن، معنى خش ميسن: في عافية أنت، ومعنى يخشي ميسن: جيد أنت، ومعنى قطلو أيوسن: مبارك قدومك. وكان عليه في ذلك

ولقيت بها الفقيه العالم الفاضل صدر الشريعة، وكان قد قدم من هراة، وهو من الصلحاء الفضلاء، وزرت ببخارى قبر الإمام أبي عبد الله البخاري مصنف الجامع الصحيح، شيخ المسلمين، رضي الله عنه، وعليه مكتوب: هذا قبر محمد بن إسماعيل البخاري، وقد صنف من الكتب كذا وكذا؛ وأيضاً على قبور علماء بخارى أسماؤهم وأسماء تصانيفهم، وكنت قيدت من ذلك كثيراً وضاع مني في جملة ما ضاع لي لما سلبني كفار الهند في البحر.

ثم سافرنا من بخارى قاصدين معسكر السلطان الصالح المعظم علاء الدين طرمشيرين، وسنذكره، فمررنا على نخشب البلدة التي ينسب اليها الشيخ أبو تراب النخشبي، وهي صغيرة تحف بها البساتين والمياه، فنزلنا بخارجها بدار لأميرها، وكان عندي جارية قد قاربت الولادة وكنت أردت حملها الى سمرقند لتلد بها، فاتفق انها كانت في المحمل فوضع المحمل على الجمل، وسافر أصحابنا من الليل، وهي معهم والزاد وغيره من أسبابي، وأقمت أنا حتى ارتحل نهاراً مع بعض من معي، فسلكوا طريقاً وسلكت طريقاً سواها، فوصلنا عشية النهار إلى محلة السلطان المذكور، وقد جعنا، فنزلنا على بعد من السوق واشترى بعض أصحابنا ما سد جوعتنا، وأعارنا بعض التجار خباء بتنا به تلك الليلة.

ومضى أصحابنا من الغد في البحث عن الجمال وباقي الأصحاب، فوجدوهم عشياً وجاؤوا بهم، وكان السلطان غائباً عن المحلة في الصيد فاجتمعت بنائبه الأمير تقبغا، فأنزلني بقرب مسجده وأعطاني خرقة (خركاه) وهي شبه الخباء، وقد ذكرنا صفتها فيما تقدم، فجعلت الجارية في تلك الخرقة، فولدت تلك الليلة مولوداً، وأخبروني أنه ولد ذكر، ولم يكن كذلك فلما كان بعد العقيقة أخبرني بعض الأصحاب أن المولود بنت، فاستحضرت الجواري، فسألتهن، فأخبرنني بذلك، وكانت هذه البنت مولودة في طالع سعد، فرأيت كل ما يسرني ويرضيني منذ ولدت، وتوفيت بعد وصولي الى الهند بشهرين، وسيذكر ذلك، واجتمعت بهذه المحلة بالشيخ الفقيه العابد مولانا حسام الدين الياغي، ومعناه بالتركية الثائر، وهو من أهل أطرار، وبالشيخ حسن صهر السلطان.

ولا أطعمه شيئاً، فلما أمسى أخرج يابسة عنده، فبلها بالماء وفصد فرسه وملأها بدمه وعقدها وشواها بالنار، فكانت طعامه، فعاد إلى اطرار فأخبر عاملها بأمرهم وأعلمه أن لا طاقة لأحد بقتالهم، فاستمد مليكه جلال الدين فأمده بستين ألفاً زيادة على من كان عنده من العساكر، فلما وقع القتال هزمهم تنكيز ودخل مدينة أطرار بالسيف فقتل الرجال وسبى الذراري.

وأتى جلال الدين بنفسه لمحاربته، فكانت بينهم وقائع لا يعلم في الإسلام مثلها، وآل الأمر الى أن تملك تنكيز ما وراء النهر وخرب بخارى وسمرقند وترمذ، وعبر النهر، وهو نهر جيحون، الى مدينة بلخ فتملكها، ثم الى الياميان (الباميان) فتملكها، وأوغل في بلاد خراسان وعراق العجم، فثار عليه المسلمون في بلخ وفي ما وراء النهر فكر عليهم ودخل بلخ بالسيف وتركها خاوية على عروشها، ثم فعل مثل ذلك في ترمذ فخربت ولم تعمر بعد، لكنها بنيت مدينة على ميلين منها، هي التي تسمى اليوم ترمذ، وقتل أهل الياميان (الباميان) وهدمها بأسرها الا صومعة جامعها، وعفا عن أهل بخارى وسمرقند، ثم عاد بعد ذلك الى العراق وانتهى أمر التتر حتى دخلوا حضرة الإسلام ودار الخلافة بغداد بالسيف؛ وذبحوا الخليفة المستعصم بالله العباسي، رحمه الله.

قال ابن جزي: أخبرنا شيخنا قاضي القضاة أبو البركات بن الحاج أعزه الله، قال: سمعت الخطيب أبا عبد الله بن رشيد يقول: لقيت بمكة نور الدين ابن الزجاج من علماء العراق، ومعه ابن أخ له، فتفاوضنا الحديث فقال لي: هلك في فتنة التتر بالعراق أربعة وعشرون ألف رجل من أهل العلم، ولم يبق منهم غيري وغير ذلك، وأشار الى ابن أخيه.

قال: ونزلنا من بخارى بربضها المعروف بفتح أباد، حيث قبر الشيخ العالم العابد الزاهد سيف الدين الباخرزي، وكان من كبار الأولياء. وهذه الزاوية المنسوبة لهذا الشيخ، حيث نزلنا، عظيمة لها وقاف ضخمة يطعم منها الوارد والصادر، وشيخها من ذريته، وهو الحاج السياخ يحيى الباخرزي، وأضافني هذا الشيخ بداره وجمع وجوه أهل المدينة وقرأ القراء بالأصوات الحسان، ووعظ الواعظ، وغنوا بالتركي والفارسي على طريقة حسنة، ومرت لنا هنالك ليلة بديعة من أعجب الليالي.

فاكهة يسمونها العلو (الآلو)، فييبسونه ويجلبه الناس الى الهند والصين، ويجعل عليه الماء ويشرب ماؤه، وهو، أيام كونه أخضر، حلو، فإذا يبس صار فيه يسير حموضة. ولحميته كثيرة ولم أر مثله بالأندلس ولا بالمغرب ولا بالشام.

ثم سرنا في بساتين متصلة وأنهار وأشجار وعمارة يوماً كاملاً، ووصلنا إلى مدينة بخارى التي ينسب اليها إمام المحدثين أبو عبد الله محمد بن إسماعيل البخاري، وهذه المدينة كانت قاعدة ما وراء نهر جيحون من البلاد، وخربها اللعين تنكيز التتري جد ملوك العراق، فمساجدها الآن ومدارسها وأسواقها خربة الا القليل، وأهلها أذلاء، وشهادتهم لا تقبل بخوارزم وغيرها لاشتهارهم بالتعصب ودعوى الباطل، وانكار الحق. وليس بها اليوم من الناس من يعلم شيئاً من العلم ولا من له عناية به.

أولية التتر وتخريبهم بخارى وسواها

كان تنكيز خان حداداً بأرض الخطا، وكان له كرم نفس وقوة وبسطة في الجسم، وكان يجمع الناس ويطعمهم، ثم صارت له جماعة فقدموه على أنفسهم وغلب على بلده وقوي واشتدت شوكته واستفحل أمره فغلب على ملك الخطا، ثم على ملك الصين. وعظمت جيوشه وتغلب على بلاد الختن وكاشغر والمالق.

وكان جلال الدين سنجر بن خوارزم شاه ملك خوارزم وخراسان وماوراء النهر، له قوة عظيمة وشوكة، فهابه تنكيز وأحجم عنه ولم يتعرض له، فاتفق أن بعث تنكيز تجاراً بأمتعة الصين والخطا من الثياب الحريرية وسواها الى بلدة أطرار، وهي آخر عمالة جلال الدين، فبعث اليه عامله عليها معلماً بذلك، واستأذنه ما يفعل في أمرهم، فكتب اليه يأمره أن يأخذ أموالهم ويمثل بهم، ويقطع أعضاءهم ويردهم الى بلادهم لما أراد الله تعالى من شقاء أهل بلاد المشرق ومحنتهم رأياً فائلاً، وتدبيراً سيئاً مشؤوماً، فلما فعل ذلك تجهز تنكيز بنفسه في عساكر لا تحصى كثرة برسم غزو بلاد الاسلام، فلما سمع عامل أطرار بحركته بعث الجواسيس ليأتوه بخبره، فذكر أن أحدهم دخل محلة بعض أمراء تنكيز في صورة سائل، فلم يجد من يطعمه، ونزل الى جانب رجل منهم، فلم ير عنده زاداً،

بأن أراد الزيادة عليه في المسكن الذي كان له في الفندق، فبلغ ذلك الشريف، فاغتم منه، ودخل الى بيته فذبح نفسه، فأدرك وبه رمق، واتهموا غلاماً كان له بقتله، فقال لهم: لا تظلموه فإني أنا فعلت ذلك بنفسي. ومات من يومه، غفر الله له.

وكان قد حكى لي عن نفسه أنه أخذ مرة من بعض تجار دمشق ستة آلاف درهم قراضاً، فلقيه ذلك التاجر بمدينة حماة من أرض الشام فطالبه بالمال، وكان قد باع ما اشترى به من المتاع بالدين، فاستحيا من صاحب المال، ودخل إلى بيته وربط عمامته بسقف البيت، وأراد أن يخنق نفسه. وكان في أجله تأخير، فتذكر صاحباً له من الصيارفة، فقصده وذكر له القضية، فسلفه مالاً دفعه للتاجر.

ولما أردت السفر من خوارزم اكتريت جمالاً واشتريت محارة، وكان عديلي بها عفيف الدين التوزري، وركب الخدام بعض الخيل، وجللنا باقيها لأجل البرد، ودخلنا البرية التي بين خوارزم وبخارى، وهي مسيرة ثمانية عشر يوماً في رمال لا عمارة بها الا بلدة واحدة، فودعت الأمير قطلودمور، وخلع لي خلعة، وخلع علي القاضي أخرى، وخرج مع الفقهاء لوداعي وسرنا أربعة أيام ووصلنا إلى مدينة الكات.

وليس بهذه الطريق عمارة سواها، وهي صغيرة حسنة، نزلنا خارجها على بركة ماء قد جمدت من البرد، فكان الصبيان يلعبون فوقها ويزلقون عليها.

وسمع بقدومي قاضي الكات ويسمى صدر الشريعة، وكنت قد لقيته بدار قاضي خوارزم، فجاء الي مسلماً مع الطلبة وشيخ المدينة الصالح العابد محمود الخيوقي، ثم عرض علي القاضي الوصول الى أمير تلك المدينة، فقال له الشيخ محمود: القادم ينبغي له أن يزار، وإن كانت لنا همة نذهب إلى أمير المدينة ونأتي به، ففعلوا ذلك، وأتى الأمير بعد ساعة في أصحابه وخدامه، فسلمنا عليه، وكان غرضنا تعجيل السفر، فطلب منا الإقامة، وصنع دعوة جمع لها الفقهاء ووجوه العساكر وسواهم، ووقف الشعراء يمدحونه، وأعطاني كسوة وفرساً جيداً، وسرنا على الطريق المعروفة بسيباية في تلك الصحراء، مسيرة ست دون ماء.

ووصلنا بعد ذلك الى بلدة وبكنة، وهي على مسيرة يوم واحد من بخارى، بلدة حسنة ذات أنهار وبساتين، وهم يدخرون العنب من سنة الى سنة، وعندهم

ومن العجائب أنه يقدد وييبس في الشمس ويجعل في القواصر كما يصنع عندنا بالشريحة وبالتين المالقي، ويحمل في خوارزم إلى أقصى بلاد الهند والصين، وليس في جميع الفواكه اليابسة أطيب منه.

وكنت أيام إقامتي بدهلي من بلاد الهند، متى قدم المسافرون بعثت من يشتري لي منهم قديد البطيخ، وكان ملك الهند إذا أتي إليه بشيء منه بعث إلي به لما يعلم من محبتي فيه. ومن عادته أنه يطرف الغرباء بفواكه بلادهم، ويتفقدهم بذلك.

التاجر الكريم

كان قد صحبني من مدينة السرا في خوارزم شريف من أهل كربلاء يسمى علي بن منصور، وكان من التجار، فكنت أكلفه أن يشتري لي الثياب وسواها، فكان يشتري لي الثوب بعشرة دنانير، ويقول اشتريته بثمانية، ويحاسبني بالثمانية، ويدفع الدينارين من ماله، وأنا لا علم لي بفعله، إلى أن تعرفت ذلك على ألسنة الناس؛ وكان من ذلك قد أسلفني دنانير، فلما وصل إلي احسان أمير خوارزم رددت إليه ما أسلفنيه، وأردت أن أحسن بعده إليه مكافأة لأفعاله الحسنة، فأبى ذلك، وحلف أن لا أفعل، وأردت أن أحسن إلى فتى كان له اسمه كافور، فحلف أن لا أفعل، وكان أكرم من لقيته من العراقيين.

وعزم على السفر معي إلى بلاد الهند، ثم ان جماعة من أهل بلده وصلوا إلى خوارزم برسم السفر إلى الصين، فأخذ في السفر معهم، فقلت له في ذلك فقال: هؤلاء أهل بلدي يعودون الى أهلي وأقاربي ويذكرون اني سافرت الى أرض الهند برسم الكدية، فيكون سبة علي، لا أفعل ذلك.

وسافر معهم الى الصين، فبلغني بعد، وأنا بأرض الهند، انه لما بلغ الى مدينة المالق، وهي آخر البلاد التي من عمالة ما وراء النهر وأول بلاد الصين، أقام بها وبعث فتى له بما كان عنده من المتاع، فأبطأ الفتى عليه وفي أثناء ذلك وصل من بلاده بعض التجار ونزل معه في فندق واحد، فطلب منه الشريف ان يسلفه شيئاً بخلال ما يصل فتاه، فلم يفعل. ثم أكد قبح ما صنع في عدم التوسعة على الشريف

درهم أخرى، يحضرها المشائخ والفقهاء والوجوه، فلما أمر بذلك قلت له: أيها الأمير تصنع دعوة يأكل من حضرها لقمة أو لقمتين، ولو جعلت له جميع المال كان أحسن له للنفع، فقال: افعل ذلك. رقد أمر لك بالألف كاملة، ثم بعثها الأمير امامه شمس الدين السنجري في خريطة يحملها غلامه، وصرفها من الذهب المغربي ثلاثمائة دينار.

وكنت قد اشتريت ذلك اليوم فرسا أدهم اللون بخمسة وثلاثين ديناراً دراهم، وركبته في ذهابي إلى المسجد، فما أعطيت ثمنه إلا من تلك الألف. وتكاثرت عندي الخيل بعد ذلك حتى انتهت إلى عدد لا أذكره خيفة مكذب يكذب به، ولم تزل حالي في الزيادة حتى دخلت أرض الهند، وكانت عندي خيل كثيرة لكني كنت أفضل هذا الفرس وأوثره وأربطه أمام الخيل؛ وبقي عندي إلى انقضاء ثلاث سنين. ولما هلك تغيرت حالي، بعثت إلى الخاتون جيجا آغا امرأة القاضي مائة دينار دراهم، وصنعت لي أختها ترابك زوجة الأمير دعوة جمعت لها الفقهاء ووجوه المدينة بزاويتها التي بنتها، وفيها الطعام للوارد والصادر، وبعثت إلي بفروة سمور وفرس جيد، وهي من أفضل النساء وأصلحهن وأكرمهن جزاها الله خيراً.

الخاتون المتقشفة

ولما انفصلت من الدعوة التي صنعت لي هذه الخاتون وخرجت عن الزاوية تعرضت لي بالباب امرأة عليها ثياب دنسة، وعلى رأسها مقنعة ومعها نسوة لا أذكر عددهن، فسلمت علي فرددت عليها السلام ولم أقف معها، ولا التفت إليها. فلما خرجت أدركني بعض الناس، وقالي لي: ان المرأة التي سلمت عليك هي الخاتون، فخجلت عند ذلك، وأردت الرجوع إليها؛ فوجدتها قد انصرفت، فأبلغت إليها السلام مع بعض خدامها، واعتذرت عما كان مني لعدم معرفتي بها.

بطيخ خوارزم

وبطيخ خوارزم لا نظير له في بلاد الدنيا شرقاً ولا غرباً إلا ما كان من بطيخ بخارى، ويليه بطيخ أصفهان، وقشره أخضر، وباطنه أحمر، وهو صادق الحلاوة، وفيه صلابة.

ولما أتاني القاضي مسلماً علي كما ذكرته قال لي: إن الأمير قد علم بقدومك، وبه بقية مرض يمنع من الاتيان إليك، فركبت مع القاضي إلى زيارته، وأتينا داره، فدخلنا مشوراً كبيراً أكثر بيوته خشب، ثم دخلنا مشوراً صغيراً فيه قبة خشب مزخرفة قد كسيت حيطانها بالملف الملون، وسقفها بالحرير المذهب، والأمير على فرش له من الحرير، وقد غطى رجليه لما بهما من النقرس، وهي علة فاشية في الترك، فسلمت عليه وأجلسني إلى جانبه، وقعد القاضي والفقهاء، وسألني عن سلطانه الملك محمد أوزبك وعن الخاتون بيلون وعن أبيها، وعن مدينة القسطنطينية، فأعلمته بذلك كله، ثم أتي بالموائد فيها الطعام من الدجاج المشوية والكراكي وأفراخ الحمام، وخبز معجون بالسمن، يسمونه الكليجا، والكعك والحلوى، ثم أتي بموائد أخرى فيها الفواكه من الرمان المحبب في أواني الذهب والفضة، ومعه ملاعق الذهب، وبعضه في أواني الزجاج العراقي ومعه ملاعق الخشب، ومن العنب والبطيخ العجيب.

ومن عوائد هذا الأمير أن يأتي القاضي في كل يوم إلى مشوره فيجلس بمجلس معد له، ومعه الفقهاء وكتابه، ويجلس في مقابلته أحد الأمراء الكبراء ومعه ثمانية من كبراء أمراء الترك وشيوخهم، يسمون الأرغجية (يارغوجي) ويتحاكم الناس إليهم، فما كان من القضايا الشرعية حكم فيها القاضي، وما كان من سواها حكم فيها أولئك الأمراء. وأحكامهم مضبوطة عادلة لأنهم لا يتهمون بميل، ولا يقبلون رشوة.

ولما عدنا إلى المدرسة بعد الجلوس مع الأمير بعث إلينا الأرز والدقيق والغنم والسمن والأبزار وأحمال الحطب وتلك البلاد كلها لا يعرف بها الفحم، وكذلك الهند وخراسان وبلاد العجم، وأما الصين فيوقدون فيها حجارة تشتعل فيها النار كما تشتعل في الفحم، ثم إذا صارت رماداً عجنوه بالماء وجففوه بالشمس، وطبخوا به حتى يتلاشى.

حكاية مكرمة لهذا القاضي والأمير

صليت في بعض أيام الجمع على عادتي بمسجد القاضي أبي حفص فقال لي: ان الأمير أمر لك بخمسمائة درهم، وأمر أن يصنع لك دعوة ينفق فيها خمسمائة

المذكور، والآخر نور الدين الكرماني من كبار الفقهاء، وهو الشديد في أحكامه القوي في ذات الله تعالى.

ولما حصل الاجتماع بالقاضي قال لي: إن هذه المدينة كثيرة الزحام ودخولكم نهاراً لا يتأتى، وسيأتي إليكم نور الإسلام لتدخلوا معه في آخر الليل، ففعلنا ذلك، ونزلنا بمدرسة جديدة ليس بها أحد. ولما كان بعد صلاة الصبح أتى إلينا القاضي المذكور، ومعه من كبار المدينة جماعة منهم: مولانا همام الدين، ومولانا زين الدين المقدسي، ومولانا رضي الدين يحيى، ومولانا فضل الله الرضوي، ومولانا جلال الدين العمادي، ومولانا شمس الدين السنجري إمام أميرها، وهم أهل مكارم وفضائل. والغالب على مذهبهم الاعتزال لكنهم لا يظهرونه لأن السلطان أوزبك وأميره على هذه المدينة قطلو دمور من أهل السنة.

وكنت أيام إقامتي بها أصلي الجمعة مع القاضي أبي حفص عمر المذكور بمسجده، فإذا فرغت الصلاة ذهبت معه إلى داره، وهي قريبة من المسجد، فأدخل معه إلى مجلسه، وهو من أبدع المجالس فيه الفرش الحافلة، وحيطانه مكسوة بالملف، فيه طيقان كثيرة، وفي كل طاق منها أواني الفضة المموهة بالذهب، والأواني العراقية. وكذلك عادة أهل تلك البلاد أن يصنعوا في بيوتهم. ثم يأتي بالطعام الكثير، وهو من أهل الرفاهية والمال الكثير والرباع، وهو سلف الأمير قطلودمور متزوج بأخت امرأته، واسمها جيجا آغا، وبهذه المدينة جماعة من الوعاظ والمذكرين أكبرهم مولانا زين الدين المقدسي والخطيب مولانا حسان الدين المشاطي الخطيب المصقع أحد الخطباء الأربعة الذين لم أسمع في الدنيا أحسن منهم.

أمير خوارزم

وهو أمير الكبير قطلودمور، ومعنى اسمه الحديد المبارك لأن قطلو هو المبارك ودمور هو الحديد. وهذا الأمير ابن خالة السلطان المعظم محمد أوزبك، وأكبر أمرائه وهو واليه على خراسان وولده هارون بك متزوج بابنة السلطان المذكور التي أمها الملكة طيطغلي المتقدم ذكرها، وامرأته الخاتون ترابك صاحبة المكارم الشهيرة.

وذكر لي بعض الناس أن تلك السوق يخف زحامها يوم الجمعة لأنهم يسدون سوق القيسارية وغيرها من الأسواق. فركبت يوم الجمعة وتوجهت إلى المسجد الجامع والمدرسة، وهذه المدينة تحت إمرة السلطان أوزبك، وله فيها أمير كبير يسمى قطلودمور، وهو الذي عمر هذه المدرسة وما معها من المواضع المضافة، أما المسجد فعمرته زوجته الخاتون الصالحة ترابك.

وبخوارزم مارستان له طبيب شامي يعرف بالصهيوني نسبة إلى صهيون من بلاد الشام، ولم أر في بلاد الدنيا أحسن أخلاقاً من أهل خوارزم، ولا أكرم نفوساً، ولا أحب في الغرباء.

ولهم عادة جميلة في الصلاة لم أرها لغيرهم، وهي أن المؤذنين بمساجدها يطوف كل واحد منهم على دور جيران مسجده معلماً لهم بحضور الصلاة، فمن لم يحضر الصلاة مع الجماعة ضربه الامام بمحضر الجماعة، وفي كل مسجد درة معلقة برسم ذلك، ويغرم خمسة دنانير تنفق في مصالح المسجد أو طعم للفقراء والمساكين، ويذكرون أن هذه العادة عندهم مستمرة على قديم الزمان.

وبخارج خوارزم نهر جيحون أحد الأنهار الأربعة التي من الجنة وهو يجمد في أوان البرد كما يجمد نهر أتل، ويسلك الناس عليه، وتبقى مدة جموده خمسة أشهر. وربما سلكوا عليه عند أخذه في الذوبان فهلكوا.

ويسافر فيه أيام الصيف بالمراكب إلى ترمذ، ويجلبون منها القمح والشعير، وهي مسيرة عشر للمنحدر. وبخارج خوارزم زاوية مبنية على تربة الشيخ نجم الدين الكبرى، وكان من كبار الصالحين، وفيها الطعام للوارد والصادر، وشيخها المدرس سيف الدين بن عصبة من كبار أهل خوارزم، وبها أيضاً زاوية شيخها الصالح المجاور جلال الدين السمرقندي من كبار الصالحين أضافنا بها، وبخارجها قبر الامام العلامة أبي القاسم محمود بن عمر الزمخشري، وعليه قبة وزمخشر قرية على مسافة أربعة أميال من خوارزم، ولما أتيت هذه المدينة نزلت بخارجها، وتوجه بعض أصحابي إلى القاضي الصدر أبي حفص عمر البكري، فبعث إلى نور الإسلام، فسلم علي ثم عاد إليه ثم أتى القاضي في جماعة من أصحابه فسلم علي، وهو فتي السن، كبير الفعال، وله نائبان أحدهما نور الإسلام

3

رحلة ابن بطوطة إلى آسيا الوسطى

رحلة ابن بطوطة إلى خوارزم وما وراء النهر

فسرنا من السرا عشرة أيام، فوصلنا إلى مدينة سراجوق، ومعنى جوق صغير، فكأنهم قالوا سرا الصغيرة، وهي على شاطئ نهر كبير زخار، يقال له ألوصو ومعناه الماء الكبير، وعليه جسر من قوارب كجسر بغداد، وإلى هذه المدينة انتهى سفرنا بالخيل التي تجر العربات، وبعناها بها بحساب أربعة دنانير دراهم للفرس، وأقل من ذلك لأجل ضعفها ورخصها بهذه المدينة، واكترينا الجمال لجر العربات.

وبهذه المدينة زاوية لرجل صالح معمر من الترك يقال له أطا، ومعناه الوالد، أضافنا بها ودعا لنا، وأضافنا أيضاً قاضيها، ولا أعرف اسمه، ثم سرنا منها ثلاثين يوماً سيراً جاداً لا ننزل إلا ساعتين إحداهما عند الضحى والأخرى عند المغرب، وتكون الإقامة قدر ما يطبخون الدوقي ويشربونه، وهو يطبخ من غلية واحدة، ويكون معهم الخليع من اللحم يجعلونه عليه، ويصبون عليه اللبن، وكل إنسان إنما ينام أو يأكل في عربته حال السير.

وكان لي في عربتي ثلاث من الجواري، ومن عادة المسافرين في هذه البرية الاسراع لقلة أعشابها، والجمال التي تقطعها يهلك معظمها، وما يبقى منها لا ينتفع به، إلا في سنة أخرى بعد أن يسمن. والماء في هذه البرية في مناهل معلومة بعد اليومين والثلاثة، وهو ماء المطر والحسيان.

ثم لما سكنا هذه البرية وقطعناها كما ذكرناه وصلنا إلى خوارزم، وهي أكبر مدن الأتراك وأعظمها وأجملها وأضخمها، لها الأسواق المليحة، والشوارع الفسيحة، والعمارة الكثيرة، والمحاسن الأثيرة، وهي ترتج بسكانها لكثرتهم، وتموج بهم موج البحر، ولقد ركبت بها يوماً ودخلت السوق، فلما توسطته وبلغت منتهى الزحام في موضع يقال له الشور لم أستطع أن أجوز ذلك الموضع لكثرة الازدحام، وأردت الرجوع فما أمكنني لكثرة الناس، فبقيت متحيراً وبعد جهد شديد رجعت.

4

English translation of the section of "The Travels" of Ibn Battuta to Central Asia

After ten days' journey from al-Sarā* [Al-Sarra] we reached the city of Sarāchūq* [Sarajuk] (*chūq* means 'little', so that it is as if they said 'little Sarā'), which lies on the bank of a great and swollen river called Ulūṣū,* meaning 'the great stream'.[1] Over it is a bridge of boats,* like the bridge of Baghdād.[2] At this city we reached the limit of the journey with the horses that draw the waggons. We sold them at the rate of four silver* dinars per head, and even less, on account of their exhaustion and the cheapness of horses in this town, and hired camels to draw the waggons. In this city there is a hospice [zawiya]* belonging to a pious Turk of great age, who is called Aṭā, which means 'father'. He received us hospitably in it and called down a blessing on us. We were hospitably entertained also by the qāḍī of the town, but I do not know his name.

From this place we went on for thirty days by forced marches, halting only for two hours each day, one in the forenoon and the other at sunset. The length of the halt was just as long as the time needed to cook and sup dūqī,[3] and this is cooked with a single boiling. They would have with them [pieces of] dried meat,[4] which they put on top of this and they pour sour milk over the whole. Everybody eats and sleeps in his waggon while it is actually on the move, and I had in my waggon three slavegirls. It is the custom of travellers in this wilderness to use the utmost speed, because of the scarcity of herbage. Of the camels that cross it the majority perish and the remainder are of no use except a year later, after they are fattened up. The water in this desert is at certain known waterpoints, separated by two or three days' march, and is rainwater [in surface pools] and shallow wells under the sand.

1 Saraichiq [Saraychik], about 40 miles from the mouth of the Ural river, called in Turkish *ulu-ṣu*, 'Great River' and by the Arab geographers Yayik.

2 See vol. II, p. 329.

3 See vol. II, p. 474.

4 Arabic *al-khalī'*, apparently a Maghribine term, described by Dozy as salted or marinated beef or mutton, soaked in oil and then sun-dried.

Ibn Baṭṭūṭa's itineraries in Central Asia

After journeying through this desert and traversing it as we have described we arrived at Khwārizm [Khorezm],[5]* which is the largest, greatest, most beautiful and most important city of the Turks. It has fine bazaars and broad streets, a great number of buildings and abundance of commodities;* it shakes under the weight of its population, by reason of their multitude, and is agitated by them [in a manner resembling] the waves of the sea. I rode out one day on horseback and went into the bazaar, but when I got halfway through it and reached the densest pressure of the crowd at a point called al-Shawr,[6]* I could not advance any further because of the multitude of the press, and when I tried to go back I was unable to do that either, because of the crowd of people. So I remained as I was, in perplexity, and only with great exertions did I manage to return. Some person told me that that bazaar is much less crowded on Fridays,* because [on that day] they close the Qaisārīya [Qaysariyya][7]* and other bazaars, so I rode [again] on the Friday and went to the cathedral mosque and the college.*

This city is in the dominions of the sultan Ūzbak,* who is represented in it by a great amīr called Quṭlūdumūr.[8]* It was he who built this college and the dependencies annexed to it. As for the mosque, it was built by his wife, the pious khātūn Turābak [Turabek Khatun].[9]* There is at Khwārizm a hospital, which has a Syrian doctor called al-Ṣahyūnī, after the town of Ṣahyūn in Syria.[10]

Never have I seen in all the lands of the world men more excellent in conduct than the Khwarizmians, more generous in soul, or more friendly to strangers. They have a praiseworthy custom in regard to

5 I.B. does not indicate his pronunciation of this name. The traditional Arabic spelling (adopted here) aims at representing a native pronunciation somewhat like Khōrezm (see Yāqūt's *Geog. Dict.*, s.v.), but by Arabic speakers was commonly read Khuwārizm or Khuwārazm. This was properly the name of the region (Khorezmia), but often applied to its chief city, at this time (Kunya) Urgench, in the delta of the Amu Darya.

6 Apparently a Khwarizmian name.

7 See vol. I, p. 97, n. 115.

8 Qutlugh-tömür (see n. 23 below) had taken the lead in securing the succession of Özbeg Khān to the throne in 1313, and was for a time the administrator of his empire, but was transferred in 1321 to the governorship of Khwārizm.

9 Turābak is buried in the mausoleum at Urgench (see *Āthār al-Islām al-ta' rīkhīya fi 'l-Ittihād al-Sūfiyītī*, p. 27 and plate 18, undated).

10 See vol. I, p. 105.

[the observation of] prayer-services which I have not seen elsewhere, namely that each of the muezzins in their mosques goes round the houses of those persons neighbouring his mosque, giving them notice of the approaching hour of prayer.[11]* Any person who absents himself from the communal prayers is beaten by the imām [who leads the prayers] in the presence of the congregation, and in every mosque there is a whip hung up for this purpose. He is also fined five dinars,* which go towards the expenses of upkeep of the mosque, or of supplying food to the poor and the destitute. They say that this custom has been an uninterrupted tradition amongst them from ancient times.

Outside Khwārizm is the river Jaiḥūn [Jayhun],* one of the four rivers which [flow] from Paradise.[12] It freezes over in the cold season in the same way as the river Itil* freezes over,[13] and people walk upon it. It remains frozen for the space of five months,[14] and often they walk over it when it is beginning to melt and perish in consequence. It is navigable for ships in summer time as far as Tirmidh,[15] from which they import wheat and barley, the journey downstream taking ten days.

Outside [Khwārizm is a hospice built over the tomb of the shaikh Najm al-Dīn al-Kubrā,* who was one of the great saints.[16] Food is supplied in it to all wayfarers,* and its shaikh is the teacher at the college, Saif al-Dīn ibn ‘Aṣaba, one of the principal citizens of Khwārizm. In the town also there is a hospice, whose shaikh is the pious ‘sojourner’[17] Jalāl ad-Dīn al-Samarqandī, one of the most saintly of men. He received us hospitably in it. Outside the city again is the tomb of the most learned imām Abu'l-Qāsim Maḥmūd ibn ‘Omar al-Zamakhsharī [Abu-l-Qasim Mahmud ibn ‘Umar al-Zamakhshari],[18]* with a cupola over it. Zamakhshar* is a village four miles distant from Khwārizm.

11 The other interpretation, ‘warning them to attend the service’, is grammatically possible, but *mu'lim* does not ordinarily convey this meaning.

12 See vol. I, p. 49 and n. 152.

13 See vol. II, p. 497.

14 According to the geographer Yāqūt, it remained frozen over for two months.

15 See p. 570 below.

16 One of the major saints of the Suhrawardī order, killed in the Mongol capture of Gurganj in 1221; see his biography in *Fawa'ih al-Jamal*, ed. F. Meier (Wiesbaden, 1957).

17 A ‘sojourner’ is a scholar devotee who has spent one or more years at Mecca or al-Madīna; see vol. I, pp. 176, 221.

18 Author of a celebrated grammatical commentary on the Qur'ān and other philological works, d. 1143.

When I reached this city I encamped in its outskirts, and one of my companions* went to visit this qāḍī, the *ṣadr* [sadr][19]* Abū Ḥafṣ 'Omar al-Bakrī, whereupon he sent his substitute Nūr al-Islām to me. This man saluted me and then returned to him, and thereafter the qāḍī himself came with a group of his associates and greeted me. He was a man young in years but mature in welldoing. He has two substitutes, one of them Nūr al-Islām, already mentioned, and the other Nūr al-Dīn al-Kirmānī, who is a great jurist, severe in his decisions and vigorous in [defence of] all that pertains to God Most High.

When my meeting with the qāḍī took place he said to me, 'This city is overcrowded, and you will have difficulty in entering it in the daytime. Nūr al-Islām will come to you to conduct you in towards the end of the night.' So we did as he suggested, and lodged in a newly-built college in which no one was living [as yet]. After the dawn prayer, the qāḍī above-mentioned visited us, and together with him a number of the principal men of the city, among them Mawlānā Humām al-Dīn, Mawlānā Zain al-Dīn al-Maqdisī, Mawlānā Raḍīy al-Dīn Yaḥyā, Mawlānā Faḍl Allāh al-Riḍawī, Mawlānā Jalāl al-Dīn al-'Imādī, and Mawlānā [*Mawlana*]* Shams al-Dīn al-Sinjarī, the imām of the governor. They are men of generous nature and virtuous character, and the prevailing school of doctrine among them is the Mu'tazilite,[20]* but they do not make open profession of it because Sultan Ūzbak and Quṭlūdumūr, who is his governor over this city, are adherents of the [orthodox] Sunna.*

During my stay there I used to attend the Friday prayers in company with the above-mentioned qāḍī Abū Ḥafṣ 'Omar in his own mosque, and on the conclusion of the service I went with him to his house, which is close to the mosque. I would then go with him into his reception hall, a most magnificent chamber, furnished with rich carpets, its walls hung with cloth, and a large number of arcaded niches in it, with vessels of silver-gilt and 'Irāqī glass in every niche. Such is the custom followed by the people of this country in [the adornment of] their houses. He would then produce a copious meal, being a man

19 I.B. rarely, if ever, uses the current Egyptian form of abbreviation in which *al-Ṣadr* stands for Ṣadr al-Dīn. In Eastern Persia and Transoxiana it seems that the term *ṣadr* was regularly applied to the chief qāḍī; see Barthold, *Turkestan*, 353–5, and p. 549 below.

20 The rationalizing school of Sunnī theologians; see vol. II, p. 416, n. 18.

amply endowed with great wealth and landed property, and related by marriage to the amīr Quṭlūdumūr, the husband of the sister of his wife, whose name is Jīfā Aghā.[21]

In this city there are a number of admonitory preachers and revivalists,[22] the chief of whom [the notificator]* is Mawlānā Zain al-Dīn al-Maqdisī. The khaṭib at the Friday services is Mawlānā Ḥusām al-Dīn al-Mishāṭī, the eloquent orator, one of the four khaṭibs whom I have never heard surpassed in the whole world.

The Amīr of Khwārizm. He is the great amīr Quṭlūdumūr, and the meaning of his name is 'Blessed Iron', because *Quṭlū* is [in Turkish] 'blessed' and *dumūr* is 'iron'.[23] This amīr is the son of the maternal aunt of the exalted sultan Muḥammad Ūzbak and the greatest of his amīrs. He is the sultan's governor over Khurāsān, and his son Hārūn Bak is married to the daughter of this sultan; her mother is the queen Ṭaiṭughlī, who was mentioned earlier. His wife is the khātūn Turābak, whose name is associated with famous benefactions.

When the qāḍī came to greet me, as I have related, he said to me, 'The amīr has learned of your arrival, but is still suffering from the effects of an illness, which prevent him from coming to visit you,'* so I rode with the qāḍī to visit him. On reaching his residence we entered a large audience-hall, most of the partitions[24] of which were of wood, and went into a small hall; this had a wooden cupola with ornamental embellishments, its walls hung with coloured woollen cloths and its ceiling with gold-embroidered silk. The amīr was [sitting] on a silk [carpet] spread for him, and had a cover over his legs on account of the gout with which they were affected, this being a malady very common among the Turks. I saluted him and he bade me sit beside him. The qāḍī and doctors of the law sat down [likewise]. He questioned me about his sultan, the king Muḥammad Ūzbak, and about the khātūn

21 For the title of *aghā* see vol. II, p. 434, n. 80.

22 *Mudhakkirīn*, literally 'preachers who call men to remembrance', i.e. of the promises of reward and punishment in the Qur'ān.

23 *Qutlugh* = 'fortunate' (Radloff, *Wörterbuch*, II, 996); *tömür* is a dialect form of the normal Turkish *tämür* = 'iron' (P. Pelliot, *Notes sur . . . la Horde d'Or* (Paris 1950), p. 61). *Qutlugh* is commonly rendered by *Quṭlu* or *Quṭluq* in Arabic transcriptions of Turkish names.

24 Literally 'compartments'.

Bayalūn,* and her father and the city of Constantinople. After I had replied to him on all these subjects, tables were brought in with food [of different kinds], roasted fowls, cranes, young pigeons, bread baked with butter, which they call kulījā,[25] biscuits and sweetmeats. After these were brought over tables with fruit, seeded pomegranates in gold and silver vessels with gold spoons, and some in vessels of 'Irāqī glass* with wooden spoons,[26] grapes and wonderful melons.

It is one of the regular practices of this amīr that the qāḍī comes daily to his audience-hall and sits in a place assigned to him, accompanied by the jurists and his clerks. Opposite him sits one of the great amīrs, accompanied by eight of the great amīrs and shaikhs of the Turks, who are called *arghujīs*.[27] The people bring their disputes to them for decision; those that come within the jurisdiction of the religious law[28] are decided by the qāḍī, and all others are decided by those amīrs. Their decisions are well-regulated and just, for they are free from suspicion of partiality and do not accept bribes.

When we returned to the college after our session with the governor, he sent us rice, flour, sheep, butter, spices, and loads of firewood. In all of these countries [the use of] charcoal is unknown, and likewise in India, Khurāsān and Persia.

As for China, there they kindle stones in which the fire blazes up as it does in charcoal; then when they turn to ash, the Chinese knead it with water, dry it in the sun, and it serves them as fuel for cooking again until it is entirely used up.[29]*

Anecdote. A generous act of this qāḍī and of the governor. One Friday, after I had attended the service of prayers, according to my custom, in the mosque of the qāḍī Abū Ḥafṣ, he said to me, 'The amīr commanded that you be given five hundred dirhams, and ordered also that a banquet should be prepared in your honour at a cost of another five hundred dirhams, to be attended by the shaikhs, doctors of the law, and principal

25 A Persian term.
26 See vol. II, p. 442, n. 109.
27 *Arghujī* is for *yarghujī*, the Eastern Turkish word for a person who decides such a lawsuit, from *yarju*, 'a lawsuit', in the language of Khwārizm.
28 Generally those relating to marriage, inheritance and other matters of personal status.
29 SeeYule's *Marco Polo*, I, 442–3.

citizens. When he gave this order I said to him "O amīr, you are preparing a banquet at which those present will eat only a mouthful or two; if you were to give him all of the money it would be more useful[30] to him". He said "I shall do so", and has commanded that you should be given the entire thousand.' A little later the amīr sent this sum, accompanied by this imām Shams al-Dīn al-Sinjarī, in a purse borne by his page. Its value in Moroccan gold was three hundred dinars.[31]* I had bought on the same day a black horse for thirty-five silver dinars and had ridden it on going to the mosque, and it was from that thousand and no other that I paid its price. Thereafter I became possessed of so many horses that they reached a number which I dare not mention lest some sceptic accuse me of lying, and my fortunes never ceased to expand up to the time when I entered the land of India. I had many horses, but I used to prefer this horse, give it special attention, and picket it in front of the others. It remained with me up to the end of three years, and when it died my affairs took a turn for the worse.

The khātūn Jījā Aghā, the wife of the qāḍī, sent me a hundred silver dinars, and her sister Turābak, the governor's wife, gave a banquet in my honour, for which she assembled the doctors of the law and the principal citizens. This was held in the hospice built by her, where food is supplied to all wayfarers [from her benefaction]. She sent a furred robe of sable and an excellent horse. She is one of the most virtuous, pious, and generous of women – God reward her with good.

Anecdote. When I left the banquet which this khātūn had given for me, and went out of the hospice, I found myself face to face with a woman in the gateway. She was wearing soiled garments, had a veil over her head, and was accompanied by several women – I do not know how many. She gave me the word of salutation, and I returned it, but did not stop with her nor give her any attention. Then when I had gone out, a certain person overtook me and said to me, 'The woman that saluted you is the khātūn.' I was covered with confusion on hearing this, and tried to go back to her, but I found that she had departed. So I rent my salutations to her through one of her attendants, together with my apologies for my action, the result of my having no acquaintance with her.

30 The variant reading noted in the edition does not change the sense.

31 A Moroccan dīnār weighed 4.722 grammes (as against the standard weight of 4.233 grammes in the East).

Account of the melons of Khwārizm. The melons of Khwārizm have no equal in any country of the world, East or West, except it may be the melons of Bukhārā, and next to them are the melons of Iṣfahān. Their rind is green, and the flesh is red, of extreme sweetness and firm texture. A remarkable thing is that they are cut into strips, dried in the sun, and packed in reed baskets, as is done in our country with dried figs and Malaga figs.* They are exported from Khwārizm to the remotest parts of India and China, and of all the dried fruits there are none which excel them in sweetness. During my stay at Dihlī in India, whenever a party of travellers arrived, I used to send someone to buy sliced melon for me from them. The king of India, too, when any of it was brought to him, used to send it to me, knowing as he did my fondness for it. It was his way to give pleasure to the foreigners by sending to them the fruit of their own countries, and he used to give special attention to learning their desires and supplying them accordingly.

Anecdote. On my journey from the city of al-Sarā to Khwārizm I had been accompanied by a sharīf, an inhabitant of Karbalā [Karbala']* named 'Alī ibn Manṣūr, who was [by profession] a merchant. I used to commission him to buy robes and other things for me, and he would buy a robe for me for ten dinars, but say 'I bought it for eight', and so charge me with only eight dinars and pay the other two dinars with his own money. I was in total ignorance of what he was doing until I learned of it from remarks made by other persons. Not only that, but he had also lent me a sum of dinars, and when I received the benefaction from the governor of Khwārizm, I repaid him what he had lent me and wished to make a gift to him over and above that in return for his good services, but he refused to accept it and swore that he would never do so. I proposed to make a gift to a slave-boy whom he had, called Kāfūr, but he adjured me not to do so. He was the most generous-hearted of all the 'Irāqīs whom I have met. He made up his mind to travel with me to India, but afterwards a company [of merchants] from his native town arrived at Khwārizm with the intention of proceeding to China, and he took the road with them. I remonstrated with him about this, but he replied 'These men, fellow-citizens of mine, will go back to my family and my kinsmen and will spread the story that I travelled to India to gain a livelihood by begging. This would be a disgrace for me. I shall not do it.' So he set out with them for China. I heard later on during my stay in India, that when he reached the city of

Almaliq[32]* which is the last of the towns in the province of Transoxiana [Mawarannahr]* and the first town in China, he stopped there and sent on a slave-boy of his with what he had of merchandise. The slave-boy was a long time in returning and in the meantime a certain merchant from his native town arrived and put up with him in the same caravanseray.* The sharīf asked him to lend him some money until such time as his slave-boy should arrive. Not only did he refuse to do so but, not content with the vileness of his conduct in failing to succour the sharīf, he tried to bid against him for the lodging that he had in the caravanseray. When the sharīf heard of this he was so upset by it that he went into his room and cut his throat. He was found with a spark of life still in him, but he said to them 'Do not wrong him, it was I who did this by myself,' and expired the same day – God forgive him.[33]

The sharīf had in fact told me [a similar story] about himself. He had once received six thousand dirhams on loan from one of the merchants of Damascus. This merchant met him [one day] in the town of Ḥamāh [Hama],* in Syria, and asked him for the money. He had sold on credit the merchandise that he bought with it, and was so ashamed at [his inability to repay] his creditor that he went into his room, tied his turban to the ceiling of the room, and intended to hang himself. But the appointed hour of his death was not yet come. He remembered a friend of his, a money-broker, went to him and told him his circumstances, and this man lent him some money which he paid to the merchant.

When I prepared to leave Khwārizm I hired camels and bought a double litter, the second side of which was occupied by 'Afīf al-Dīn al-Tūzarī. The servants rode some of the horses and we put horse-cloths on the rest because of the cold. [In this wise] we began our journey through the wilderness which lies between Khwārizm and Bukhārā, eighteen days' march in sands with no permanent settlement in them save one small township.* I took leave of the amīr Quṭlūdumūr, and he presented me with a robe* of honour; the qāḍī too gave me another, and came out with the doctors of the law to bid me farewell.

After travelling for four days we came to the city of al-Kāt [Kat],[34]* the only settled place on this road, small and pretty. We encamped

32 Properly Almaligh, a town in the Ili valley, north-west of modern Kulja.
33 Suicide is regarded as a sin, and is very rare in Islam
34 Kath, the ancient capital of Khorezmia, on the right bank of the Amu Darya, about 35 miles N.E. of Khīva. The old town was undermined by the river, and

outside it, by a lake which was frozen over because of the cold, and the boys were playing on it and sliding over it. The qāḍī of al-Kāt heard of our arrival (he is called Ṣadr al-Sharī'a,[35] and I had already met him at the house of the qāḍī of Khwārizm), and came to greet me, together with the students of religion and the shaikh of the town,* the pious and devout Maḥmūd al-Khīwaqī.[36] The qāḍī suggested that I should go to visit the governor of the town, but the shaikh Maḥmūd said to me, 'It is the one that comes who should be visited, and if this is a matter of concern to us let us go to the governor of the town and bring him.' They did so, and the amīr came after a while, accompanied by his officers and servants, and we saluted him. Our intention was to press on with our journey, but he begged us to stay and gave a banquet for which he assembled the jurists, the chief officers of the troops, and others, [and in the course of which] the poets stood up to declaim his praises.

We continued our journey on the road known as Sībāya [Sibaya].[37]* Through that desert [it is] a journey of six nights without water, at the end of which we reached the town of Wabkana [Wabkanat],* one day's journey from Bukhārā.[38] It is a pretty town, with streams and fruit gardens. Its inhabitants preserve grapes from year to year, and they have there a fruit which they call *'allū*.[39] They dry it, and people carry the dried fruit to India and China. One steeps it in water and drinks the liquid. In its green state the fruit is sweet, but when dried it acquires a slight acidity, and it has a great deal of pulp. I have never seen the like of it in al-Andalus, nor in the Maghrib nor in Syria.

Thereafter we travelled for a whole day through contiguous orchards, with streams, trees and habitations, and arrived at the city of Bukhārā, from which is derived the name of the Imām of the Scholars*

---

the new city described by I.B. was built on a canal some miles to the south-west of the present town.

35 For the title of *ṣadr* see p. 543, n. 19 above.

36 I.e. of Khīva, on the left bank of the Amu Darya and situated on a canal deriving from the river. The exact function of the 'shaikh' of the town is not clear.

37 The term Sībāya does not seem to be found elsewhere. Yāqūt (s.v. Sabīrā) mentions a village Sibārā in the vicinity of Bukhārā. The variant reading Siyāsa is even more unhelpful.

38 Wabkana or Wafkand, a suburb of Bukhārā three farsakhs north-west of the main city.

39 Persian *ālū*, 'plum'. The yellow plums of Bukhārā were especially celebrated.

in Tradition, Abū 'Abdallāh Muḥammad ibn Ismā'īl al-Bukhārī.[40]* This city was formerly the capital of the lands beyond the river Jaiḥūn,[41] but was laid in ruins by the accursed Tankīz,* the Tatar, the ancestor of the kings of al-'Irāq.* So at the present time its mosques, colleges and bazaars are in ruins, all but a few, and its inhabitants are looked down upon and their evidence [in legal cases] is not accepted* in Khwārizm or elsewhere, because of their reputation for factionalism, and making false claims, and denial of the truth. There is not one person in it today who possesses any religious learning or who shows any concern for acquiring it.

Narrative of the Origin of the Tatars and of their devastation of Bukhārā and other cities. Tankīz Khān[42] was a blacksmith in the land of al-Khaṭā [Khata],* and he was a man of generous soul, and strength, and well-developed body. He used to assemble the people and supply them with food.[43] After a while a company [of warriors] gathered around him and appointed him as their commander. He gained the mastery in his own country, grew in strength and power of attack and became a formidable figure. He subdued the king of al-Khaṭā and then the king of China, his armies became immense in size, and he conquered the lands of al-Khutan [Khotan],* Kāshkhar [Kashghar],* and Almaliq.[44]*

40 See vol. I, p. 154, n. 319, and p. 554, n. 57 below.

41 I.e. the Oxus (Amu Darya). 'Transoxiana' reproduces the Arabic name of this province, 'What lies beyond the River.' Bukhārā was the capital of the flourishing Sāmānid kingdom (900–999). Although sacked by Chingiz Khān in 1220, it soon recovered, and its ruinous condition at this time was due to its later destruction by the Mongol Īl-khāns of Persia in 1273 and 1316.

42 Tankīz is an Arabic transcription of Old Turkish *tāniz*, 'ocean' (Radloff, *Wörterbuch*, col. III, 1045), of which Chingiz (*chingiz*) is probably a Mongol dialect form. Tankīz (probably pronounced *tengiz*) frequently appears as the name of Turkish mamlūk amīrs; cf. vol. I, p. 78.

43 One MS. reads 'and stir up their ambitions'. A somewhat similar account of Chingiz Khān's origins is given by William of Rubruck (see M. Komroff, *Contemporaries of Marco Polo*, p. 94), and apparently reflects a popular story based on his original personal name of Temüjin (Turkish for 'blacksmith').

44 Khaṭā or Khiṭāy ('Cathy') was the name given to the northern nd north-western provinces of China, which constituted a separate kingdom under the Khitan or or Liao dynasty (see E. Bretschneider, *Mediaeval Researches from Eastern Asiatic Sources*, London, 1910, I, 208–9). Pekin, the capital of the Chin dynasty in China proper, was captured in 1215. Kāshghar and Khotān (both in Sinkiang) and Almaligh (in Semiryechye; see n. 32 above) were occupied in 1218.

Jalāl al-Dīn Sanjar [Jalal al-din Mankburni], son of Khwārizm Shah,[45]* the king of Khwārizm, Khurāsān, and Transoxiana, [however], possessed great power and military strength, so Tankīz stood in awe of him, kept out of his [territories], and avoided any conflict with him.

It happened that Tankīz sent a party of merchants with the wares of China and al-Khaṭā, such as silk fabrics etc., to the town of Uṭrār [Utrar],* which was the last place in the government of Jalāl al-Dīn. His governor in the town sent a message to him, informing him of this event, and enquiring of him what action he should take in regard to them. Jalāl al-Dīn wrote to him, commanding him to seize their goods, mutilate them, cut off their limbs and send them back to their country – [displaying thereby], because of what God Most High willed to inflict of distress and suffering for their faith upon the peoples of the Eastern lands, weak judgement and a bad and ill-omened management of affairs. So, when he carried out this action, Tankīz made ready to set out in person with an army of uncountable numbers to invade the lands of Islām. When the governor of Uṭrār heard of his advance he sent spies to bring back a report about him, and the story goes that one of them went into the *maḥalla* [mahalla]* of one of the amīrs of of Tankīz, disguised as a beggar. He found nobody to give him food, and took up a position beside one of their men, but he neither saw any provisions with him nor did the man give him anything to eat. In the evening the man brought out some dry intestines that he had with him, moistened them with water, opened a vein of his horse, filled the intestines with its blood, tied them up and cooked them on a fire; this was his food. So the spy returned to Uṭrār, reported on them to the governor, and told him that no one had the power to fight against them. The governor then asked his king, Jalāl al-Dīn, for reinforcements, and the latter sent him a force of sixty thousand men, over and above the troops who were already with him. When the battle was joined, Tankīz defeated them, forced his way into the city of Uṭrār by the sword, killed the men, and

45 This again reflects popular legend, in which Jalāl al-Dīn, the son of Muḥammad Khwārizm-Shāh, has eclipsed the figure of his father, owing to his exploits against the Mongol invaders and later adventurous career in Persia and Azerbaijan; see *Histoire du Sultan Djelāl ed-Dīn* of al-Nasawī, tr. O. Houdas, Paris, 1895. The episode of Uṭār (on the Jaxartes or Sir Darya, 100 miles north of Tashkent), however, is historical; see Barthold, *Turkestan*, 396–9.

enslaved the children. Jalāl al-Dīn [then] came out in person to engage him, and there took place between them battles such as were never known in the history of Islām.[46]

The final result of the matter was that Tankīz gained possession of Transoxiana, laid waster Bukhārā, Samarqand and Tirmidh, crossed the River [i.e. the river of Jaiḥūn] to the city of Balkh* and captured it, then [advanced] to al-Bāmiyān [Bamiyan],[47]* conquered it, and penetrated far into the lands of Khurāsān and 'Irāq al-'Ajam.[48]* The Muslims in Balkh and Transoxiana then revolted against him, so he turned back to deal with them, entered Balkh by the sword and left it 'fallen down upon its roofs'.[49]* He went on to do the same at Tirmidh; it was laid waste and never afterwards repopulated, but a [new] city was built two miles distant from it, which is nowadays called Tirmidh. He slew the population of al-Bāmiyān[50] and destroyed it completely, except for the minaret of its mosque. He pardoned the inhabitants of Bukhārā and Samarqand, and returned thereafter to al-'Irāq. The advance of the Tatars continued to the point that finally they entered Baghdād, the capital of Islām and seat of the Caliphate, by the sword and slaughtered the Caliph al-Musta'ṣim billāh, the 'Abbāsid [Khalifa al-Musta'sim bi-llah al 'Abbasi]* (God's mercy on him).[51]

---

46 Jalāl al-Dīn defeated the Mongol army at Parwān (see p. 589), n. 199 below), but was pursued by Chingiz Khān, hemmed in against the Indus river, and escaped with his life only by swimming across it into Sind: see Barthold, *Turkestan*, 445–6.

47 Transoxiana and Khwārizm were conquered in 1220, Balk and Bāmiyān (at that time the capital of northern Afghanistan) in 1221.

48 The expedition into Khurāsān in 1221 was commanded by Tuluy, the youngest son of Chingiz Khān, and the cities of Merv and Nīshāpūr were totally destroyed; see Barthold, *Turkestan*, 447–9. An expeditionary force under Mongol generals marched in 1220 through Azerbaihan and Transcaucasia into southern Russia.

49 A revolt of the Muslim refugees at Merv and consequent destruction of the cities of eastern Khurāsān is related by Ibn al-Athīr (*Kāmil*, XII, 255–6). Juvainī (I, 130–1), although he places the destruction of Balkh on its first capture, also speaks of a second devastation of the city. The quotation is from Qur'ān, ii, 261.

50 The destruction of Bāmiyān was in revenge for the death of one of his grandsons in the siege of the city: Barthold, *Turkestan*, 443.

51 I.B. here combines two separate campaigns. Chingiz Khān did not 'return to al-'Irāq', but to Mongolia; the capture of Baghdād was the culmination of an expedition under his grandson Hulagu in 1256–9; see vol. II, p. 334.

Ibn Juzayy remarks: Our Shaikh, the Grand Qāḍī Abu'l-Barakāt ibn al-Hājj[52] (God exalt him), related to us that he had heard the *khaṭīb* Abū 'Abdallāh ibn Rashīd say: 'I met in Mecca Nūr al-Dīn b. al-Zajjāj, one of the scholars* of al-'Irāq, who had with him a son of a brother of his. We engaged in conversation, and he said to me, "There perished in the Tatar massacre in al-'Irāq twenty-four thousand men of the class of scholars, and not one of them is left except me and that one", pointing to his brother's son.'

(To return.) We lodged in Bukhārā in its suburb called Fatḥ Abād [Fath'abad],[53]* where there is a tomb of the learned shaikh and pious ascetic Saif al-Dīn al-Bākharzī [Sayf al-Din al-Bakharzi].[54]* He was one of the great saints.* This hospice where we lodged, to which the name of this shaikh has been given, is a large institution with vast endowments from which food is supplied to all corners, and its superior is a descendant of the shaikh's, namely the much-travelled pilgrim Yaḥyā al-Bākharzī [Yahya al-Bakharzi].[55]* This shaikh hospitably entertained me in his residence, and invited all the leading men of the city. The Qur'ān-readers recited with beautiful modulations, the homiletic preacher delivered an address, they then sang melodiously in Turkish and Persian, and [altogether] we passed there an exquisite and most delightful night. I met on this occasion the learned and virtuous jurist Ṣadr al-Sharī'a; he had come from Harāt, and is a pious and excellent man.[56] I visited at Bukhārā also the tomb of the learned Imām Abū 'Abdullāh al-Bukhārī, compiler of *al-Jāmi' al-Ṣaḥīḥ*, the Shaikh of the Muslims (God be pleased with him), and over it is inscribed: 'This is the grave of Muḥammad b.

52 Not mentioned elsewhere.

53 The suburb beyond the Eastern (Qarshī) gate of Bukhārā, still called by the same name.

54 Abu'l Ma'ālī Sa'īd b. al-Muṭahhar, d. 1261, one of the principal disciples of Najm al-Dīn Kubrā (see p. 542, n. 16 above); see *E.I.* s.v. Saif al-Dīn Bākharzī. The hospice or madrasa by his tomb was founded by the mother of the Great Khans Möngke and Qubilai, altogether she herself was a Christian (Juvainī, tr. J. A. Boyle, II, 552). The tomb is still in existence; see G. A. Pugachenkova & L. E. Rempel, *Vydayushchiyesya Pamyatniki Arkhitektury Uzbekistana*, Tashkent, 1958, pp. 72–3 and plates 11, 12.

55 One manuscript repeats here, 'He was one of the great saints.'

56 Presumably Fakhr al-Dīn Khisār (or Khiṭār), entitled Ṣadr al-Dīn, whose appointment and diploma as qāḍī of Herāt in 1314/15 is cited at length in *Ta'rīkh Nāma-i Harāt*, Calcutta, 1944, 609–14.

Ismā'īl al-Bukhārī, who composed such-and-such books.'[57] In the same manner, the tombs of the learned men of Bukhārā are inscribed with their names and the titles of their writings. I had copied a great many of these, but they were lost along with all that I lost when the Indian infidels robbed me at sea.[58]

We resumed our journey from Bukhārā, making for the camp of the pious and exalted sultan 'Alā al-Dīn Ṭarmashīrīn ['Ala' al-din Tarmashirin],* of whom we shall speak presently. We went by way of Nakhshab,* the town from which the shaikh Abū Turāb al-Nakhshabī derives his place-name;[59] it is small and surrounded by gardens and streams. We lodged outside it, in a house that belonged to its governor. I had with me a slavegirl, who was close to the time of her delivery, and I had intended to transport her to Samarqand, so that she might have the child there. It happened that she was inside a litter; the litter was put on a camel and our associates set off during the night, taking her with them, as well as the provisions and other effects of mine. For myself, I remained behind, in order to travel in the daytime, along with some of those who were with me, but the first party went by one road, while I went by another. So we arrived at this sultan's camp late in the evening, very hungry, and one of the merchants lent us a tent in which we spent that night. Our companions set off next morning to look for the camels and the rest of the party, found them in the evening, and returned with them.

The sultan was absent from the maḥalla on a hunting party, so I met his deputy, the amīr Taqbughā, who assigned me a camping ground close to his mosque, and gave me a *kharqa* – this is a kind of tent, a description of which we have given previously.[60] I put the slave-girl into this *kharqa*, and she gave birth to a child that same night. They told me that it was a male child, although it was not so, but after the [ceremony

57 For al-Bukhārī (d. 870), celebrated as the compiler of the *Ṣaḥīḥ*, see vol. I, p. 154, n. 319. According to the early biographers he was buried in the village of Khartang, near Samarqand (*Ta'rīkh Baghdād*, Cairo, 1931, II, 34).

58 In 1346; see *Selections*, p. 265 (vol. IV, 206 Arabic).

59 Nakhshab or Nasaf, about 100 miles S.E. of Bukhārā, and a main station on the old route through the Iron Gate to Tirmidh and Balkh; already coming to be called by its later name, Qarshī (Mongol = 'palace'), from the palace built there by Ṭarmashīrīn's predecessor Kebek Khān. Abū Turāb 'Askar b. Ḥusain (d. 859) was a celebrated early ṣūfī (al-Iṣfahānī, *Ḥilyat al-Awliyā'*, Cairo, 1938, XII, 45–51, and al-Sulamī, *Ṭabaqāt al-Ṣūfiya*, Leiden, 1960, 136–40).

60 See vol. II, p. 440 and n. 103.

of the] *'aqīqa*[61]* one of my companions informed me that the child was a girl. So I summoned the slave-girls and questioned them, and they confirmed the statement. This girl was born under a lucky star, and I experienced everything to give me joy and satisfaction from the time of her birth. She died two months after my arrival in India, as will be related in the sequel.

In this *maḥalla* I met the devout shaikh and doctor of the law Mawlānā Ḥusām al-Dīn al-Yāghī (which in Turkish means 'the rebel'), who is a man of Uṭrār, and the shaikh Ḥasan, who is related to the sultan by marriage.

Account of the Sultan of Transoxiana. He is the exalted sultan 'Alā al-Dīn Ṭarmashīrīn, a man of great distinction, possessed of numerous troops and regiments of cavalry, a vast kingdom and immense power, and just in his government. His territories lie between four of the great kings of the earth, namely the king of China, the king of India, the king of al-'Irāq, and the king Ūzbak, al of whom send him gifts and hold him in high respect and honour. He succeeded to the kingdom after his brother al-Chagaṭay [Al-Jakhatay].* This al-Chagaṭay was an infidel and succeeded his elder brother Kabak [Kebeg],* who was an infidel also, but was just in government, showing equity to the oppressed and favour and respect to the Muslims.[62]]

Anecdote. It is related that this king Kabak, in a conversation on one occasion with Badr al-Dīn al-Maidānī, the jurist and homiletic preacher, said to him: 'You assert that God has mentioned everything in His exalted Book?' 'Yes' said Badr al-Dīn. Then said Kabak 'Where is my name in it?' to which he replied 'It is in His word (most High is He) *In whatsoever form He would He hath composed thee* (*rakkabak*).'* This reply pleased him, he said *Yakhshī* (which means in Turkish 'good') and showed great favour to him and increased respect for the Muslims.*

Anecdote. Among the judgements of Kabak it is related that a woman laid a complaint before him against one of the amīrs. She stated

61 A ceremony on the seventh day after the birth of a child, when it is given a name, and a ram of he-goat (according to the Mālikite rite) is sacrificed. The shorn hair of the child is weighed and an equal weight of gold or silver given in alms; see *E.I.*, s.v.

62 Kebek (1309–26), Iljigadai (1326), and Ṭarmashīrīn (1326–34/5) were all descendants of Chingiz Khān's son Jaghatai in the fifth generation. The fame of Kebek's justice is attested also by the '*Anonym of Iskandar*', pp. 110–11.

that she was a poor woman, with children to support, that she had some milk [for sale] with the price of which she could procure food for them, and that this amīr had taken it from her by force, and drunk it. He said to her, 'I shall cut him in two; if the milk comes out of his belly, he has gone to his fate, but if not I shall cut you in two after him'. The woman said, '[No,] I release him from the obligation, and will make no demand on him.' But Kabak gave the order, the man was cut in two, and the milk came out of his stomach.[63]*

To return to the account of the sultan Ṭarmashīrīn: after I had stayed for some days in the *maḥalla* (which they call the *urdū*),[64] I went one day to the dawn prayer in the mosque, following my usual practice and when I finished the prayer one of those present mentioned to me that the sultan was in the mosque. Accordingly, when he rose up from his prayer carpet, I went forward to salute him. The shaikh Ḥasan and the legist Ḥusām al-Dīn al-Yāghī came up, and told him about me and my arrival some days before. Then he said to me in Turkish *Khush mīsin* [khosh mi-sen],* *yakhshī mīsin, quṭlū ayūsin. Khush mīsin* means 'are you in good health?', *yakhshī mīsin* 'are you well?' and *quṭlū ayūsin* means 'blessed is your arrival'.[65] The sultan was dressed at the time in a cloak* of green Jerusalem stuff, and had a cap like it on his head.

He then returned to his audience hall, and [as he did so] people kept presenting themselves to him with their complaints, and he would stop to [listen to] each petitioner, small or great, male or female. He then sent for me, and when I came I found him in a tent, outside of which there were men ranged to right and left, the amīrs among them [seated] on chairs, with their attendants standing behind and before them. The rest of the troops [too] had sat down in parade order, each man with his weapons in front of him. These were the detachment on duty, who would sit there until the hour of afternoon prayer, when another detachment would come and sit until the end of the night, and there had been rigged up for them there awnings made of cotton fabrics. When I entered the king's presence, inside the tent, I found him seated

63 A similar story has already been related by I.B. concerning a former governor of Tripoli in Syria; see vol. I, p. 89.

64 See vol. II, p. 482, n. 254.

65 Literally 'You are very fortune-bringing', *quṭlū* (*qutlugh*) meaning 'fortunate' (see p. 544, n. 23 above), and *ayū* (*ayugh*) being a strengthening particle.

on a chair, resembling a mosque-pulpit and covered with silk embroidered in gold. The interior of the tent was lined with silken cloth of gold, and a crown set with jewels and precious stones was suspended over the sultan's head at the height of a cubit. The principal amīrs were [ranged] on chairs to right and left of him, and in front of him were the sons of the kings[66] holding fly-whisks in their hands. At the doorway of the tent were the [sultan's] deputy, the vizier, the chamberlain, and the keeper of the sign-manual, whom they call *al ṭamghā* (*al* meaning 'red' and *ṭamghā* meaning 'sign').[67] The four of them rose up to meet me when I entered, and went in with me. After I had saluted him, he questioned me (the keeper of the sign-manual acting as interpreter between us) about Mecca and al-Madīna, Jerusalem (God ennoble her) and [Hebron] the city of al-Khalīl* (upon whom be peace), Damascus and Cairo, al-Malik al-Nāṣir [Al-Nasir],* the two 'Irāqs and their king, and the lands of the non-Arabs.[68] The muezzin then made the call to the midday prayer so we withdrew.

We continued to attend the prayer-services in his company – this was during the period of intense and perishing cold, yet he would never fail to attend the dawn and evening prayers with the congregation.* He used to sit reciting a litany[69] in Turkish after the dawn prayer until sunrise, and all those in the mosque would come up to him and he would take each one by the hand and press with his own hand upon his. They used to do the same thing at the time of the afternoon prayer. When he was brought a present of dried grapes or dates (for dates are rare in their country and are regarded by them as conveying a blessing), he would give some of them with his own hand to everyone who was in the mosque.

Anecdote. [The following is] an instance of the virtues of this king. One day I attended the afternoon prayer [in the mosque]. The sultan had not yet come, but one of his pages came in with a prayer-rug and

66 I.e. the scions of the royal house; see vol. II, p. 484, n. 258.

67 The Red Seal, embodying the ruler's name, was traced or stamped on all official documents to authenticate them; the keeper or the *ṭamgha* was thus a kind of secretary of state; cf. vol. II, p. 307, n. 120. (The Arabic text has 'whom', not 'which'.)

68 Presumably including Anatolia and southern Russia as well as Persia in this context.

69 Literally 'for the *dhikr*'; see vol. I, p. 44, n. 133.

spread it in front of the miḥrāb, where it was his custom to pray, saying to the imām Ḥusām al-Dīn al-Yāghī. 'Our master desires you to hold back the prayer for him a moment while he performs his ablutions.' The imām rose up and said [in Persian] *Namāz* (which means 'the prayer') *birāyi Khudā aw birāyi Ṭarmashīrīn*, that is to say, 'Is prayer for God or for Ṭarmashīrīn?' He then ordered the muezzin to recite the second call for the prayer.[70] The sultan arrived when two bowings had already been completed, and he made the two latter bowings where the ranks ended, that is at the place where peoples' shoes are left near the door of the mosque. He then performed the bowings that he had missed and went up laughing to the imām to shake his hand, and after sitting down opposite to the miḥrāb with the shaikh (that is, the imām) beside him, and I alongside the imām, he said to me 'When you return to your country, tell how a Persian mendicant behaved like this towards the sultan of the Turks.'

This shaikh used to preach to the congregation every Friday, exhorting the sultan to act righteously and forbidding him from evil and tyrannical acts, addressing him in the harshest terms while the sultan listened to him in silence and wept. He would never accept any gift or stipend[71] from the sultan, nor eat of any food of his nor wear any robe from him. This shaikh was indeed one of God's saintly servants. I used often to see him wearing a cotton cloak,* lined and quilted with cotton, which was worn out and in shreds, and on his head a bonnet of felt,* such as would be worth one qīrāṭ [qirat],[72]* and with no turban round it. I said to him one day, 'Master, what is this cloak that you are wearing? It is not fit to be worn', and he replied 'My son, this cloak does not belong to me but to my daughter.' So I begged him to accept one of my robes, but he said to me, 'I made a vow to God fifty years ago never to accept anything from anyone, but if I were to accept [something] from anyone it would be from you.'

70 The call to prayer (*adhān*) is repeated with slight variations inside the mosque when the worshippers have arranged themselves in rows. This is called the *iqāma*, 'summons to rise', i.e. to begin the prayer.

71 The term '*aṭā*' has the double sense.

72 The *qīrāṭ* ('carat') was 1/24th of the gold *mithqāl* or 1/16th of the silver dirham.

When I resolved to proceed on my journey after staying at this sultan's camp for fifty-four days,[73] the sultan gave me seven hundred silver dinars and a sable coat worth a hundred dinars. I had asked him for this on account of the cold weather, and when I mentioned it to him he took hold of my sleeves and kissed his hand after touching them,[74] with his natural humility, generosity and goodness of character. He gave me two horses and two camels also. When I wished to take leave of him, I encountered him in the midst of his way to his hunting-ground. The day was a bitterly cold one, and I swear that I could not utter a single word owing to the severity of the cold, but he understood this, and laughed and gave me his hand, and so I departed.

Two years after my arrival in India, the news reached us that the assembly[75] of his subjects and his amīrs had met in the most remote part of his territories, adjoining China, where the greater part of his troops were [stationed]. They swore allegiance to a paternal cousin of his called Būzun Ughlī [Buzun]* (everyone who is of the sons of the kings is called by them *ughlī*),[76] who was a Muslim, but tainted in faith and evil in conduct. The reason for their [transference of] allegiance to him and deposition of Ṭarmashīrīn was that the latter had contravened the laws of their ancestor, the accursed Tankīz, he who, as related above, devastated the lands of Islām. Now Tankīz had compiled a book on his laws, which is called by them the *Yasāq* [Yasaq],[77]* and they hold that if any [of the princes] contravenes the laws contained in this book his deposition is obligatory. One of its prescriptions is that they shall assemble on one day in each year, which they call the *ṭūy* (meaning the

73 Probably from mid-March to early May, 1333.

74 This, which is the alternative rendering of the French editors (see p. 455 of the edition) for 'kissed them with his hand', corresponds to the traditional phrase and action of 'kissing the ground'.

75 *Al-mala'*, a Qur'ānic term for 'council' (i.e. assembly of shaikhs of clans), seems to be used here for the Mongol term *quriltai*.

76 For Turkish *ughul* + *i*, meaning 'son of'. I.B.'s statement is confirmed by the usage of the Persian chronicler of the Mongols; see Juvainī, *Ta'rīkh-i Jahāngushā*, II (Leyden–London, 1916), Introduction, p. 9 (s.v. *pisar*). Būzun was the son of Duwā Timūr, another brother of Ṭarmashīrīn.

77 For the codification of the 'Great Yasa' of Chingiz Khān see Barthold, *Turkestan*, 41; G. Vernadsky, 'The Scope and Contents of Chingis Khan's Yasa' in *Harvard Journal of Asiatic Studies*, III (1938), 337–60. The form *yasāq* is used also by the author of the '*Anonym of Iskandar*'.

day of the banquet).[78] The descendants of Tankīz and the amīrs come from all quarters, and the khātūns and superior officers of the army also attend. If their sultan should have changed any one of those laws their chiefs will rise up before him and say to him, 'You have changed this and changed that, and you have acted in such-and-such a manner and it is now obligatory to depose you.' They take him by his hand, cause him to rise from the throne of the kingship, and set upon it another of the descendants of Tankīz. If one of the great amīrs should have committed an offence in his territory, they pronounce judgement against him as he deserves.

Now the sultan Ṭarmashīrīn had abrogated the law relating to this day and abolished its practice, and they most violently disapproved of his action; furthermore, they resented his staying for four years in that part of his territories which borders on Khurāsān without ever coming to the region which adjoins China. It was customary for the king to visit that district every year, to investigate its conditions and the state of the troops in it, because it was the cradle of their kingdom, and their seat of kingship is the city of Almāliq.[79]

When the amīrs transferred their allegiance to Būzun, he advanced with a powerful army, and Ṭarmashīrīn, fearing an attempt on his life by his amīrs and not trusting them, rode out with a company of fifteen horsemen, making for the district of Ghazna. This was included in his provinces, and its governor was the chief of his amīrs and his close confidant, Buruntaih.[80] This amīr, a lover of Islām and of the Muslims, had constructed in his province about forty hospices in which food was supplied to travellers, and had under his command many regiments of troops. I have never, among all the human beings that I have seen in all the lands in the world, seen a man of more prodigious stature. When Ṭarmashīrīn had crossed the river Jaiḥūn and taken the road of Balkh, he was seen by a certain Turk in the service of Yanqī, the son of his brother Kabak. Now this sultan Ṭarmashīrīn had killed his brother

78 *Ṭuy* is a variant form of *toi* (Ottoman Turkish *doy*), the common Turkish term for 'feast'; Radloff, *Wörterbuch*, III, coll. 1423, 1141.

79 See p. 548 above. The original *ulus* of Chagatai and his successors was in the vicinity of Almaligh. After the expansion of the Chagatai khanate over Transoxiana, the eastern provinces centred on Almaligh were called Moghulistān or (more popularly) Jatah.

80 Apparently (like Borodai) a modification of the Mongol name Boroldai, 'the grey'; see P. Pelliot, *Notes sur . . . la Horde d'Or*, p. 63.

Kabak,[81] whom we have mentioned above, and the latter's son Yanqī had remained in Balkh. So, when the Turk reported to him that he had seen Ṭarmashīrīn, he said 'He must have taken flight only because of something that has happened to his disadvantage', and he rode out with his officers, seized him and imprisoned him. When Būzun reached Samarqand and Bukhārā and received the allegiance of their inhabitants, Yanqī came to him, bringing Ṭarmashīrīn. It is said that when the latter arrived in Nasaf, which is outside Samarqand, he was killed and buried there,[82] and the shaikh Shams al-Dīn Gardan Burīdā was made guardian of his tomb. But it is said also that he was not killed, as we shall relate [shortly]. *Gardan* means 'neck' [in Persian] and *burīdā* means 'cut', and he was called by this name because of a slash he had on his neck. I saw him, in fact, in the land of India, and the story of [this encounter with] him will be told later.

When Būzun became king, the son of the sultan Ṭarmashīrīn, who was Bashāy Ughlī,[83] fled, together with his sister and her husband Fīrūz, to the king of India. He received them as distinguished guests and lodged them magnificently, on account of the friendship and the exchange of letters and gifts which had existed between himself and Ṭarmashīrīn, whom he used to address [in his letters] as 'brother'.* Some time later, there came a man from the land[84] of Sind,* claiming to be Ṭarmashīrīn himself. Different opinions were expressed about him, and when this came to the ears of 'Imād al-Mulk Sartīz, the slave [ghulam]* of the king of India and governor of the land of Sind[85] (he is called also *Malki 'Ard*, because it is before him that the armies of India are paraded for review and he has general supervision over them,[86] and

81 According to Mu'īn al-Dīn Naṭanzī ('*Anonym of Iskandar*', p. 111), Kebek died a natural death.

82 I.B. seems to be unaware that Nasaf is the same place as Nakhshab, which he had mentioned a few pages earlier (p. 555 above). Mu'īn al-Dīn (*loc. cit.*) also places Ṭarmashīrīn's death at Nakhshab. MS. 2289 reads: 'he [Yanqī] killed him'.

83 So, correctly, here in MS. 2289, against the reading *Ughl* of the other MSS and below.

84 MS. 908 reads 'people'.

85 See p. 593 below.

86 *Malik 'Ard*, 'King of Review', is Indian magniloquence for *'āriḍ*, the officer whose function it was to review the troops from time to time, examine their equipment, numbers and efficiency, and in some instances issue their pay. The French translation, 'il en avait le commandement', although possible, does not agree with the usage.

his residence is in Multān*) he sent some Turks who were acquainted with Ṭarmashīrīn, so he ordered a *sarācha* ["sirraja"]* (that is to say, an *āfrāg* ["afraj"][87]) to be prepared for him, and it was put up outside the city. He also performed the ceremonial duties in the style proper to one of his rank, went out to receive him,* dismounted before him, saluted him, and came to the *sarācha* in attendance on him, while the man entered it on horseback, in the usual manner of kings. No one doubted that it was in fact he. Sartīz sent a despatch about him to the king of India, who sent a group of amīrs to meet him and to welcome him with the [customary] ceremonies of hospitality.

There was in the service of the king of India a physician who had formerly been in the service of Ṭarmashīrīn, and was now chief of the physicians in India. This man said to the king 'I shall go myself to see him and find out the truth of his claim, for I once treated him for a boil under his knee, and since the scar remained I can recognize him by that.' So this doctor went to meet him and welcome him along with the amīrs; he went into his quarters and was constantly beside him, because of his former relations with him. [At an appropriate moment] he took occasion to feel his legs and uncovered the scar, whereupon the man scolded him violently, saying, 'Do you want to see the boil that you healed? Well, here it is,' and showed him the mark of it. The physician was assured that it was he, returned to the king of India, and made his report to him.

Sometime later the vizier Khwāja Jahān Aḥmad b. Aiyās[88] and the Chief of the Amīrs, Quṭlūkhān, who had been the sultan's tutor in his youth, came before the king of India and said to him, 'O Master of the world, here is the sultan Ṭarmashīrīn who has arrived, and it is established that it is really he. There are here of his tribesmen about forty thousand[89] as well as his son and his son-in-law. Have you thought what might happen if they should combine with him?' These words made a powerful impression on the king and he commanded

87 I.e., a royal tent with an enclosure; see vol. II, p. 476.

88 See pp. 617–18, 654–5 below.

89 Ṭarmashīrīn had sent a number of Mongol chiefs, presumably with their followers, to enter the service of Sultan Muḥammad: see Mahdi Husain, *The Rise and Fall of Muḥammad bin Tughluq*, London, 1938, p. 107. Out of this there grew up a legend that Ṭarmashīrīn had invaded India and imposed a humiliating peace on Sultan Muḥammad: ibid. 100–5.

that Ṭarmashīrīn should be fetched at once. When the latter entered his presence, he was ordered to do homage,* like all other visitors, treated without respect, and the sultan said to him *'Yā mādhar kānī* (which is a hideous insult),[90] how dare you lie, claiming to be Ṭarmashīrīn when Ṭarmashīrīn has been killed and here with us is the keeper of his tomb? By God, were it not for incurring disgrace[91] I would kill you. However, give him five thousand[92] dinars, take him to the house of Bashāy Ughul and his sister, the children of Ṭarmashīrīn, and say to them "This liar claims to be your father.'" So he came to their house and saw them, and they recognized him; he spent the night with them under the surveillance of guards, and was taken away the next day. They were afraid that they might be killed because of him, and therefore disowned him. He was exiled from India and Sind, and travelled by way of Kīj and Makrān,[93]* being received by the people of the land [everywhere] with respect, hospitality and gifts. He came [finally] to Shīrāz whose sultan Abū Isḥāq received him honourably and furnished him with an income sufficient for his needs. When on my return journey from India I entered Shīrāz, I was told that he was still living there. I tried to meet him but could not do so, because he was in a house which no one might enter to visit him, except by permission of the sultan Abū Isḥāq. I was afraid of the suspicions that might be aroused by [asking for] this, but afterwards I regretted not having met him.

Our narrative now returns to Būzun, namely that when he became king, he treated the Muslims harshly, oppressed the subjects, and allowed the Christians and Jews to rebuild their churches.* The Muslims were aggrieved by this, and 'waited in readiness for the turns of fortune against him'.[94] The report of this reached Khalīl, son of the sultan al-Yasaur, who had been defeated in [the attempt to seize] Khurāsān.[95] He approached the king of Harāt, the sultan Ḥusain

90 Literally, 'O [son of a] prostitute mother' (*kānī* for Persian *gānī*).
91 By killing a person who had sought his protection.
92 MS. 2289 reads 'three thousand'.
93 See vol. II, p. 342, n. 238 (to p. 341).
94 An allusion to Qur'ān, ix, 99.
95 Yasavur invaded Khurāsān in 1314 and again in 1319; after his second failure he was pursued by a force of Chagatai troops under Iljigadai (see p. 556, n. 62 above) and killed in 1320.

[Husayn], son of the sultan Ghiyāth al-Dīn al-Ghūrī,[96]* told him what was in his mind, and asked him for assistance in troops and money on the condition that he, Khalīl, would give half of his kingdom to him when it was firmly under his control. The king Ḥusain thereupon sent a large force of troops with him, the distance between Harāt and al-Tirmidh being nine days' [journey]. When the Muslim amīrs[97] heard of Khalīl's arrival they received him with tokens of submission and of desire to engage in *jihād* against the enemy.[98] The first man to join him was 'Alā al-Mulk Khudhāwand-zāda, the lord of Tirmidh; he was a great amīr, a sharīf by descent from Ḥusain [Husayn],* and he came to Khalīl with four thousand Muslim [troops]. Khalīl was filled with joy at his adhesion, appointed him as his vizier and confided to him the management of his affairs. He was a man of great courage. [Other] amīrs too arrived from every quarter and assembled around Khalīl. When he engaged Būzun in battle, the troops passed over to Khalīl, brought along Būzun as a prisoner, and delivered him up, whereupon Khalîl executed him by strangulation with bow-strings, it being a custom among them never to put any of the sons of the kings to death except by strangulation.

Khalīl was now firmly established in his kingship,[99] and held a review of his troops at Samarqand. They amounted to eighty thousand men, clad, both they and their horses, in armour.[100] He discharged the troops that he had brought with him from Harāt, and marched toward the land of Almāliq. The Tatars appointed one of their own number as their commander, and met him at a distance of three nights' journey from Almāliq, in the vicinity of Ṭarāz [Taraz].[101]* The battle grew fierce

96 See vol. II, p. 341, n. 237.

97 The phrase used is 'the amīrs of al-Islām', apparently referring to those of the Mongol leaders who had become Muslims; cf. 'the troops of al-Islām' on p. 567 for the Muslim troops.

98 I.e. the pagan khān and his followers.

99 This account of Khalīl and his reign may be fantastic history, but it seems that a Turkish *faqīr* named Khalīl did succeed in establishing his rule in Bukhārā about 1340; see W. Barthold, *Histoire des Tures d'Asie centrale*, Paris, 1945, pp. 159–60.

100 Literally 'in breastplates', but the term seems to be used here in a general sense. On the armour for men and horses in the Mongol army see Plano Carpini, cap. xv, in M. Komroff, *Contemporaries of Marco Polo*, p. 25, and B. Spuler, *Die Mongolen in Iran*², Berlin, 1955, 410 ff.

101 The text has Aṭrāz, possibly by confusion with Uṭrār. Taraz, on the river Talas, in the vicinity of the modern Aulié-Ata, was about 150 m. east of Uṭrār and some 300 miles west of Almaligh.

and both parties stood firm, when the amīr Khudhāwand-zāda, Khalīl's vizier, with twenty thousand Muslim troops led a charge before which the Tatars could not stand their ground, but were driven in flight and slaughtered in great numbers. Khalīl stayed in Almāliq for three nights, then went out to extirpate all that remained of the Tatars. They submitted to him, and he crossed to the frontiers of al-Khaṭā and China and captured the city of Qarāqurum [Qara-Qorum]* and the city of Bishbāligh [Besh-Baligh].[102]* The sultan of al-Khaṭā sent troops against him, but eventually peace was made between them. Khalīl became so powerful that the kings stood in awe of him; he showed himself a just ruler, established a body of troops in Almāliq, leaving there [as his deputy] his vizier Khudhāwand-zāda, and returned to Samarqand and Bukhārā.

Somewhat later, the Turks, seeking to stir up disorder, calumniated this vizier to Khalīl, asserting that he was planning to revolt and that he claimed that he had a better title to the royal power, by reason of his relationship to the Prophet (God bless him and give him peace), his generosity, and his bravery. Khalīl then sent a governor to Almāliq to replace him, and ordered him to come and present himself at the court with a small body of his associates. Then when he presented himself, Khalīl executed him as soon as he arrived, without further investigation. But this became the cause of the ruin of his kingdom. When Khalīl became so powerful, he had acted in an insolent manner towards the lord of Harāt, who had caused him to inherit the kingship and furnished him with troops and money; he wrote to him demanding that the *khuṭba* should be recited in his territories in Khalīl's name,[103] and that his name* should be struck on the dīnārs and dirhams. The king Ḥusain was enraged at this and indignantly replied to him in the rudest of terms, whereupon Khalīl made preparations for war with him. But the Muslim troops refused to support him, and regarded him as an aggressor against the king of Harāt. When the report of this reached the king Ḥusain, he despatched troops under the command of his paternal cousin Malik Warnā. The two armies met, and Khalīl was routed and brought as a captive before the king Ḥusain. He spared Khalīl's life,

---

102 I.e. the original centres of Mongol rule, on the Orkhon river and in the vicinity of Turfan. There was no sultanate of Cathay at this time, these territories being incorporated in the Mongol empire of China.

103 The traditional form of public recognition of suzerainty; see vol. I, pp. 232–3.

assigned him a residence, gave him a slave-girl and made him a regular allowance for his upkeep. It was in this condition that I left Khalīl [still residing] with him, at the end of the year 47,* when I returned from India.[104]

Let us now return to where we were. When I took leave of the sultan Ṭarmashīrīn I journeyed to the city of Samarqand, which is one of the greatest and finest cities, and most perfect of them in beauty. It is built on the bank of the river called Wādi'l-Qaṣṣārīn,[105]* along which there are norias [nawa'ir]* to supply water to the orchards. The population of the town gather there after the 'aṣr prayer to divert themselves and to promenade. Benches and seats are provided for them to sit on alongside the river, and there are booths in which fruit and other edibles are sold. There were formerly great palaces on its bank, and constructions which bear witness to the lofty aspirations of the townsfolk, but most of this is obliterated, and most of the city itself has also fallen into ruin. It has no city wall, and no gates, and there are gardens inside it. The inhabitants of Samarqand possess generous qualities; they are affectionate towards the stranger and are better than the people of Bukhārā.

In the outskirts of Samarqand is the tomb of Qutham, son of Al-'Abbās b. 'Abd al-Muṭṭalib* (God be pleased with both al-'Abbās and his son), who met a martyr's death at the time of its conquest.[106] The people of Samarqand go out to visit it on the eve of every Tuesday and Friday,[107] and the Tatars too come to visit it, and make large votive offerings to it, bringing to it cattle, sheep, dirhams and dinars, [all of] which is devoted to expenditure for the maintenance of travellers and the servitors of the hospice and the blessed tomb. The latter is surmounted

104 Since I.B. did not visit Herāt in 747/1347, this sentence must be taken to mean 'When I left India in 747, Khalīl was still in captivity in Herāt.' Ḥusain died in 1370–1.

105 Samarqand was situated on a mound on the west (left) bank of the Zarafshān river. I.B. has confused its name with that of the river which flows by Nakhshab and Kish, literally 'The Fullers' stream'.

106 The report of Qutham's death in 676, when the Arab general Sa'īd b. 'Othmān is said to have besieged and forced the surrender of Samarqand, is attested at a fairly early date (Ibn Sa'd, *Ṭabaqāt*, VII/I, p. 101). But it is very doubtful whether Sa'īd did besiege Samarqand, and evident on the other hand that the cult of Qutham was promoted by the 'Abbāsid caliphs after 750: cf. Barthold, Turkestan, 91.

107 I.e., every Monday and Thursday night. It is strictly the saint himself, not his tomb, which is the object of visitation.

by a dome resting on four pilasters, each of which is combined with two marble columns, green, black, white and red. The walls of the [cell beneath the] cupola are of marble inlaid with different colours[108] and decorated with gold, and its roof is made of lead. The tomb itself is covered with planks of ebony inlaid [with gold and jewels][109] and with silver corner-pieces; above it are three silver lamps. The hangings of the dome[110] are of wool and cotton. Outside it is a large canal, which traverses the hospice at that place, and has on both its banks trees, grape-vines, and jasmine. In the hospice there are chambers for the lodging of travellers. The Tatars, in the time of their infidelity, did not injure in any way the condition of this blessed site; on the contrary, they used to visit it to gain blessing as the result of the miraculous signs which they witnessed on its behalf.

The superintendent of everything to do with111 this blessed sepulchre and the adjoining buildings at the time of our lodging there was the amīr Ghiyāth al-Dīn Muḥammad b. 'Abd al-Qādir b. 'Abd al-'Azīz b. Yūsuf, son of the 'Abbāsid Caliph al-Mustanṣir billāh. He was appointed to this office by the sultan Ṭarmashīrīn, when he came to his court from al-'Irāq, but is now in the service of the king of India, and we shall speak of him later.[112] I met at Samarqand its qāḍī, who was known among them by the title of Ṣadr al-Jahān,[113]* and was a worthy and generous man. He made the journey to India after I went there, but was overtaken by death in the city of Multān, the capital of the land of Sind.

108 *mujazza'*, see vol. I, p. 195, n. 30.

109 *muraṣṣa'*, see vol. II, p. 477, n. 237.

110 The term *farsh* seems here to apply to the fabrics suspended over and around the tomb rather than to the floor coverings. This monument, known also as Mazārshāh, and now called Shāh Zindeh, is still one of the principal antiquities of Samarqand; see Pugachenkova-Rempel, *Pamyatniki Uzbekis*-antiquities of Samarqand; see Pugachenkova and Rempel, *Pamyatniki Uzbekistana*, 108 ff. and plates 63–74, and *Athār al-Islām al ta'rīkhīya fi 'l-Ittihād al-Sufīyītī*, plate 21.

111 MS. 2289 vocalizes *ḥāli*. The superintendent (*nāẓir*) is the controller of the revenues from the endowments affected to a mosque or other institution.

112 See pp. 679–85 below.

113 For the title of *ṣadr* applied to chief qāḍīs in this region see p. 543, n. 19 above. *Ṣadr al-Jahān* thus means 'Chief Judge of the World', and was apparently the traditional title of the Grand Qāḍī of Samarqand.

Anecdote. When this qāḍī died at Multān, the intelligence officer [Sahib al-khabar]* sent a report about him to the king of India, stating that he had come with the object of presenting himself at the court[114] but had been cut off before doing so. When this report reached the king, he commanded that there be sent to his sons a sum which I cannot now recall of some thousands of dinars, and that there be given to his associates what he would have given them if they had arrived in his company during his lifetime. The king of India maintains in every one of his towns an intelligence officer, who writes to him to report everything that happens in that town, and about every traveller that arrives in it. When a traveller comes, they record from what land he has come, his name, description, clothes, companions, horses, servants, his manner of sitting and of eating, and all of his affairs and activities, and what may be remarked about him in the way of good qualities or the opposite. In this way no new arrival comes to the king without his being advised of everything about him, so that his generosity may be proportioned to the newcomer's merits.

We set out from Samarqand and came in passing to the township of Nasaf, from which comes the ethnic of Abū Ḥafṣ 'Omar al-Nasafī [Abu Hafs 'Umar al-Nasafi],* the author of the book of rhyming verses on the points of difference between the four jurists [who were the founders of the four Sunni schools of law] (God be pleased with them).[115]

We then came to the city of Tirmidh, from which comes the ethnic of the Imām Abū 'Īsā Muḥammad b. 'Īsā b. Sūra al-Tirmidhī, composer of the 'Great Collection' on the Tradition of the Prophet.[116] It is a large city with fine buildings and bazaars, traversed by camels, and with many gardens. It abounds in grapes and quinces of exquisite flavour, as well as in flesh-meats and milk of all kinds. Its inhabitants

114 *Birasmi bābihi.*

115 Rhyming couplets (*rajaz*) were a favourite medium for the composition of college textbooks on subjects of all sorts, in order to facilitate their memorization. This poem of al-Nasafī (d. 1142) contained 2700 verses. The road from Samarqand to Tirmidh, however, does not pass through Nasaf, but through Kish (later called Shahr-i Sabz), over 100 miles east of Nasaf and on the higher reaches of the same river. I suspect that Ibn Baṭṭūṭa has confused the two cities; hence his distinction between Nasaf and Nakhshab, see p. 562, n. 82 above.

116 One of the six 'canonical' collections of Prophetic Tradition, second in repute only to the *Ṣaḥīḥ* of al-Bukhārī. Al-Tirmidhī d. 892.

wash their heads in the bath-house with milk instead of fuller's earth [tafl];* the proprietor of every bath-house has large jars filled with milk, and each man as he enters the establishment takes some of it in a small jug, and then washes his head. It makes the hair fresh and glossy. The Indians put oil of sesame (which they call *sīrāj*)[117] on their heads and afterwards wash their hair with fuller's earth. This gives a smoothness to the body and makes the hair glossy and long, and that is the reason why the Indians and those who live among them have long beards.

The old city of Tirmidh was built on the bank of the Jaiḥūn, and when it was laid in ruins by Tankīz[118] this new city was built two miles from the river. Our lodging there was in the hospice of the pious shaikh 'Azīzān, one of the great and most generous shaikhs, who possesses great wealth and house property and orchards and spends of his wealth to [supply the needs of] travellers. Before arriving in this city, I had met its ruler, 'Alā al-Mulk Khudhāwand-Zāda,[119] who sent in writing an order to the city for my entertainment as a guest, and every day during our stay in it provisions were brought to us. I met also its qāḍī, Qiwām al-Dīn, who was on his way to see the sultan Ṭarmashīrīn and to ask for his permission to him to travel to India. The story of my meeting with him thereafter, and with his brothers Ḍiyā al-Dīn and Burhān al-Dīn, at Multān and of our journey together to India will follow later.[120] [We shall relate also] the story of his two brothers 'Imād al-Dīn and Saif al-Dīn, and my meeting with them at the court of the king of India, as well as of his two sons, their coming to the king of India after the killing of their father, and their marriage to the two daughters of the vizier Khwāja Jahān and all that happened in that connection, if God Most High will.[121]

Next we crossed the river Jaiḥūn into the land of Khurāsān, and marched for a day and a half after leaving Tirmidh and crossing the river through uninhabited desert and sands to the city of Balkh. It is completely dilapidated and uninhabited, but anyone seeing it would think it to be inhabited because of the solidity of its construction (for it

117 Arabic *sīraj* or *shairaj*, 'sesame-oil'.
118 See p. 553 above.
119 See p. 565 above.
120 See pp. 606–7 below.
121 See pp. 692, 735 below.

was a vast and important city), and its mosques and colleges preserve their outward appearance even now, with the inscriptions on their buildings incised[122] with lapis-blue paints. People generally attribute the lapis-stone[123] to Khurāsān, but in reality it is imported from the mountains of [the province of] Badakhshān, which has given its name also to the ruby called *badakhshī* pronounced by the vulgar *balakhshī*),[124] and which will be mentioned later, if God will.

The accursed Tankīz devastated this city[125] and pulled down about a third of its mosque because of a treasure which he was told lay under one of its columns.[126] It is one of the finest and most spacious mosques in the world; the mosque of Ribāṭ al-Fatḥ in the Maghrib resembles it in the size of its columns,[127] but the mosque of Balkh is more beautiful than it in all other respects.

Anecdote. I was told by a certain historian that the mosque at Balkh was built by a woman whose husband was governor of Balkh for the 'Abbāsid [Caliphs], and was called Dā'ūd b. 'Alī.[128] It happened that the Caliph on one occasion, in a fit of anger against the people of Balkh for some rebellious act on their part, sent an agent to them to exact a crushing indemnity from them. On his arrival at Balkh, the women and the children of the city came to this woman who had built the mosque i.e. the wife of their governor, and complained of their situation and [the suffering which] they had to endure because of this indemnity. Thereupon she sent to the amīr who had come to levy this tax on them a garment of her own, embroidered with jewels and of a

122 Arabic *mudkhala*, which seems to imply something put into another thing, but I have found no example of its use as a technical term.

123 Lapis-lazuli, Arabic *lāzward*. The mines are in the upper valley of the Kokcha river; see Yule's *Marco Polo*, I, 162.

124 Cf. Marco Polo on the *balas* rubies and azure-stone: Yule, I, 161. I.B. has apparently forgotten his own 'vulgar' pronunciation in an earlier passage.

125 See p. 553 above.

126 Ibn al-Athīr (*Kāmil*, XII, 256) accuses the Tatars of digging up graves in search of treasure.

127 The great mosque of Rabat in Morocco called the Mosque of Ḥassān, begun by the Almohad caliph Abū Yūsuf Ya'qūb (1189–99) but apparently never completed; see J. Caillé, *La Mosquée de Hassan à Rabāt*, Paris, 1954, 2 vols.

128 This story, which I have not traced in any other source, apparently refers to Dā'ūd b. al-'Abbās, a descendant of one of the local princely families, d.c. 871; see J. Marquart, *Erānsahr*, Berlin, 1901, p. 301.

value greater than the indemnity that he had been ordered to collect, [with a message] to him, saying 'Take this robe to the Caliph, for I give it to him as alms on behalf of the people of Balkh, in view of their poverty.' So he went off with it to the Caliph, laid the robe before him, and related the story to him. The Caliph was covered with shame and exclaiming 'Shall the woman be more generous than we?' commanded him to annul the indemnity extracted from the inhabitants of Balkh, and to return there to restore the woman's robe to her. He also remitted one year's taxes to the people of Balkh. When the amīr returned to Balkh, he went to the woman's dwelling, related to her what the Caliph had said, and gave the robe back to her. Then she said to him, 'Did the Caliph's eye light upon this robe?' He said 'Yes'. She said, 'I shall not wear a robe upon which there has lighted the eye of any man other than those within the forbidden degrees of relationship to me.'[129] She ordered the robe to be sold and built with its price the mosque, the hospice, and a convent [for ṣūfī devotees] opposite it, the latter built of tufa[130]* and still in habitable condition today. [After the buildings were completed] there remained of the [price of the] robe as much as one-third, and the story goes that she ordered it to be buried under one of the columns of the mosque, that it might be available and come to light[131] if it should be needed. This tradition was related to Tankīz, who gave orders in consequence to pull down the columns in the mosque. After about a third had been pulled down without finding anything, he left the rest as they were.

Outside [the city of] Balkh is a tomb said to be that of 'Okkāsha ibn Miḥṣan of the tribe of Asad ['Akkasha ibn Mihsan al-Asadi],* the Companion of the Apostle of God (God bless him and give him peace) who will enter Paradise without a reckoning [on the Day of Judgement].[132] Over it is a splendid hospice in which we had our lodging. Outside of this is a wonderful pool of water, beside which there is an immense walnut tree, under whose shade travellers alight during the

129 I.e., those male relatives with whom marriage is forbidden (father, brother, son, and other ascendants and descendants).

130 *Kadhdhān*, see R. Dozy, *Supplément aux dictionnaires arabes*, s.v.

131 *Kharaja* is so vocalized in MS. 2289.

132 The tradition is an early one (see Ibn Qutaiba, *Kitāb al-Ma'ārif*, Göttingen, 1850, p. 139), although not mentioned by Ibn Sa'd. 'Okkāsha was killed in the tribal war in Arabia in 632.

summer. The shaikh of this hospice is known as al-Ḥajj Khurd[133] (which means [in Persian] 'the little'), a worthy man, who rode with us and showed us the places* in this city. Among them is the tomb of the prophet Ḥizkīl [Hizqil][134]* (upon whom be peace), over which there is a fine dome. We visited there also many tombs of saintly men, which I cannot recall now. We stopped by the house of Ibrāhīm b. Adham [Ibrahim ibn Adham][135]* (God be pleased with him), which is a vast edifice constructed of white stone which resembles tufa. It was used as a storehouse for the grain belonging to the hospice [from its endowed lands] and was barricaded [to prevent access] to it, so we did not go into it. It is in the vicinity of the cathedral mosque.

We resumed our journey from the city of Balkh, and travelled for seven days through the mountains of Qūh Istān.[136] These [contain] many inhabited villages, in which there are running streams and leafy trees, most of them fig-trees, and many hospices inhabited by pious devotees consecrated to the service of God Most High. Thereafter we arrived at the city of Harāt [Herat],* the largest of the inhabited cities in Khurāsān. The great cities of Khurāsān are four; two of them are inhabited, namely Harāt and Naisābūr [Naysabur],* and two are in ruins, namely Balkh and Marw.[137]* The city of Harāt is very extensive and has a large population. Its inhabitants are men of rectitude, abstention from unlawful pleasures, and sincerity in religion; they follow the school of the Imām Abū Ḥanīfa (God be pleased with him), and their city is [kept] pure of all vice.

Account of the Sultan of Harāt. He is the exalted sultan Ḥusain, son of the sultan Ghiyāth al-Dīn al-Ghūrī,[138] a man of notorious bravery

133 Ms. 2289 reads *Fard*, obviously in error.

134 I.e. Ezekiel. The more celebrated tomb is in the vicinity of al-Ḥilla (see vol. II, p. 324, n. 173), but it not mentioned by I.B. in that context.

135 See vol. I, p. 110, n. 160. According to the legend his father was a king in or near Balkh.

136 As a geographical term Quhistan ('mountain land') was the province lying to the *west* of Balkh. The main road from Balkh to Herāt did not touch this province, but ran via Merv ar-Rūd (now Bala Murghab), the total length being 109 or 117 farsakhs (320 or 350 miles, by alternative roads): Mustawfī, tr. Le Strange, 169, 171–2.

137 For Naisābūr (Nīshāpūr) see pp. 583–4 below. Merv was totally destroyed by the Mongols under Chingiz Khān: Barthold, *Turkestan*, 446–9.

138 See vol. II, p. 339, n. 223. Mu'izz al-Dīn Ḥusain (1332–70) was the third son of Ghiyāth al-Dīn to succeed to the throne of Herāt. *Ghūrī* is the usual vocalization, derived from their habitat in the Ghōr (Ghūr) mountains in south-western Afghanistan, but I.B. evidently pronounced it Ghawrī (see p. 576 below).

and favoured by divine aid and felicity. That which was manifested to him of aid and succour by God Most High on two fields of battle[139] is of a nature to excite astonishment. The first of these was when his army engaged the sultan Khalīl, who had behaved insolently towards him and who ended by becoming a captive in the hands of the sultan Ḥusain.[140] The second occasion was when he engaged in person Mas'ūd, the sultan of the Rāfiḍīs; this ended for the latter with the dispersal of his troops, his own flight, and the loss of his kingdom. The sultan Ḥusain [Husayn] succeeded to the kingship after his brother called al-Ḥāfiẓ [Hafiz], this brother having succeeded his father Ghiyāth al-Dīn.*

Account of the Rāfiḍīs [Rafidits].* There were in Khurāsān two men, one of them called Mas'ūd and the other called Muḥammad. These two had five associates [desperadoes who go by the name] of *futtāk*, known in al-'Irāq as *shuṭṭār* [shuttar],* in Khurāsām as *sarbadālān*, and in the Maghrib as *ṣuqūra*.[141] The seven of them made a compact to engage in disorder, highway robbery, and pillaging of goods and properties, and their exploits became known far and wide. They took up their abode in an impregnable mountain near the city of Baihaq (which is called also Sabzār);[142] they would remain in hiding by day, and at nightfall or later they would come out and make sudden raids upon the villages, engage in highway robbery, and seize people's goods. There poured in to join them a horde of men like themselves, doers of evil and creators of disorder; thus their numbers increased, their power of attack was strengthened, and they became a terror to men. After capturing the city of Baihaq by a sudden assault, they went on to seize other cities, and acquired revenues [with which] they enrolled troops and mounted a corps of cavalry. Mas'ūd [now] took the title of Sultan. Slaves used to

139 Arabic *mawṭinain*; perhaps a better rendering would be 'notable occasions'.

140 See pp. 565–7 above.

141 All of these are terms for the leaders and participants in popular movements against local authorities; *futtāk* = 'assassins', *shuṭṭār* = 'vagabonds', *ṣuqūra* = 'hawks'. I.B.'s account of the Serbedārs (= 'desperadoes', literally 'head-on-the-gallows') is extremely confused in parts; their first leader was a certain 'Abd al-Razzāq; he was murdered by his brother Mas'ūd, under whose leadership (1338–44) the movement reached its peak; see *E.I.*, s.v. Serbedārs. The form Sarbadāl is, however, used also by the local chronicler Naṭanzī (*'Anonym of Iskandar'*, 158–9, 231–2).

142 Sābzawār (colloquially pronounce Sabzūr, according to Yāqūt, s.v. Baihaq), 64 miles west of Nīshāpūr, was the chief city of the district of Baihaq. It was captured by the Serbedārs in 1337/8.

escape from their master to join him; to each of these fugitive slaves he would give a horse and money, and if the man showed himself courageous he made him commander of a section. So his army grew mightily, and he became a serious menace. The entire body of them made a profession of Shīʻism, and aspired to root out the followers of the Sunna in Khurāsān and convert it wholly to the Rāfiḍī cause.

There was in Mashhad Ṭūs[143] a Rāfiḍī shaikh called Ḥasan, who was held by them to be a saint. He supported them in this enterprise and they gave him the title of Caliph. He bade them observe the principles of justice, and they did indeed exhibit it to such a degree that dirhams and dinars would fall to the ground in their camp and not one person would pick them up until their owner came and took them. They captured Naisābūr, and when the sultan Ṭughaitumūr[144] sent troops against them, they routed them. He then sent against them his deputy, Arghūn Shāh, and they routed him too and captured him, but spared his life. After this Ṭughaitumūr mounted an expedition against them in person, at the head of fifty thousand Tatars, but they routed him, took possession of the province, and captured Sarakhs, al-Zāwa, and Ṭūs, which are among the principal towns of Khurāsān. They established their caliph in Mashhad ʻAlī al-Riḍā, son of Mūsā,[145] captured the city of al-Jām, and encamped outside it [with the intention of] advancing to the city of Harāt, at a distance of six nights' journey from there.

When the report of this reached the king Ḥusain, he assembled the amīrs, the troops and the citizens, and asked their advice whether they should await the arrival of these folk or march out towards them and engage them in battle, and the general agreement was for going out to meet them. [The men of Harāt] all belong to a single tribe called the Ghawrīya, and are said to derive both their name and their origin from the Ghawr of Syria.[146] So they prepared for the expedition en masse, and assembled from all parts of the region, for they are settled

143 The modern Meshed, see p. 582 below. The shaikh referred to by I.B. was Shaikh Ḥasan Jūrī, a noted Shīʻite leader.

144 See vol. II, p. 341, n. 236.

145 I.e. Mashhad Ṭūs (see p. 582, n. 166). For al-Jām see p. 580 below.

146 For the Ghawr of Syria see vol. I, p. 82. I.B.'s confusion of the Ghōr (see n. 138 above) with the Ghawr is due to the similarity of the Arabic spelling. The supposed origin of the Ghūrids from Syria is, of course, fictitious.

in the villages and in the open country of Badghīs,[147] which extends over a journey of four nights. Its herbage always remains green and serves as pasture for their cattle and horses; most of its trees are pistachios, which are exported from it to the land of al-'Irāq. The troops of Harāt were reinforced by the men of Simnān,[148] and they set out in a body to meet the Rāfiḍīs, twenty-four thousand of them, counting both foot-soldiers and horse men, under the command of the king Ḥusain. The Rāfiḍīs assembled in a force of a hundred and fifty thousand horse men and the encounter took place in the plain of Būshanj.[149] Both parties alike held their ground, but finally the battle turned against the Rāfiḍīs, and their sultan, Mas'ūd, fled. Their caliph, Ḥasan, stood firm with twenty thousand men until he was killed along with most of them, and about four thousand of them were taken prisoner. One of those who was present at this battle told me that the fighting began shortly after sunrise and the flight [of the Sarbadārs] was just after midday. The king Ḥusain dismounted after [the hour of] midday prayer, and when he had performed the prayer food was brought. He and his principal associates then continued to eat while the remainder of the troops were beheading the prisoners. He returned to his capital after this signal victory, when God had supported with His aid the [adherents of the] Sunna at his hands and quenched the fire of discord. This battle took place after my departure from India in the year [seven hundred and] forty-eight.[150*]

There grew up in Harāt a certain pious man, of eminent virtue and ascetic life, whose name was Niẓām al-Dīn Mawlānā [Nizam al-Din].[151*] The citizens of Harāt held him in high esteem and used to follow his instructions, while he would admonish them and discourse to them [on the punishment of the wicked in Hell]. They made a compact with him

147 The region between the Harī Rūd and the upper Murghāb, to the north of Herāt. In all MSS the name is spelled Marghīs.

148 Simnān, 100 miles east of Tehrān (see P. Schwarz, *Iran im Mittelalter*, pt. VI, Leipzig, 1929, 819–20), was occupied after the break-up of the Ilkhanate by the hereditary prince of Māzenderān, Jalāl al-Dawla Iskandar b. Ziyār (1334–60). The Serbedār Mas'ūd was killed in battle with him in 1344.

149 The battle was fought at Zāwa (see p. 583 below) in July 1342.

150 A singular example of I.B.'s haphazard dating; see the two preceding notes.

151 So in the printed text, but MS. 2289 omits 'Mawlānā'. For the following narrative see the note of the French translators (pp. 456–7) from the historian Khwāndemīr, who confirms I.B.'s account in its general lines, but with considerable variation in details.

to 'redress the evil',[152] and were joined in this undertaking by the khaṭīb of the city [Khatib al-madina],* known as Malik Warnā, who was the paternal cousin of the king Ḥusain and married to his father's widow. (He was one of the most handsome of men in form and conduct, and the king was afraid of him for his own sake and [got rid of him as] we shall relate). Whenever they learned of some action contrary to the law, even were it on the part of the king himself, they redressed it.

Anecdote. It was told me that they were apprised one day that there was committed an unlawful act in the palace of the king Ḥusain, whereupon they assembled for the purpose of redressing it. The king barricaded himself against them inside his palace, but they gathered at the gate to the number of six thousand men, and in fear of them he allowed the jurist [Niẓām al-Dīn] and the principal citizens to be admitted. He had in fact been drinking wine, so they executed upon him the legal penalty[153] inside his palace, and withdrew.

Narrative on[154] *the cause of the killing of the aforementioned jurist Niẓām al-Dīn*. The Turks who inhabit the environs of the city of Harāt and who live in the open country, along with their king Ṭughaitumūr (whom we have already mentioned),[155] to the number of about 50,000, used to be a cause of terror to the king Ḥusain, and he would send gifts to them every year and endeavour to gain their good will. This was before his defeat of the Rāfiḍīs; after routing the latter, he imposed his control on the Turks [also]. It was a custom of these Turks to visit the city of Harāt from time to time, and they often drank wine in it, or a man of them would come to it in a state of intoxication; then Niẓām al-Dīn would inflict the legal penalty upon those of them that he found drunk. Now these Turks are pugnacious and violent, and they continually make descents on the towns of India, and carry off [their inhabitants] as captives or kill [them]. Sometimes they would take captive some of the Muslim women who live in the land of India among the infidels, and when they brought them back to Khurāsān Niẓām al-Dīn would release the Muslim women from the hands of the Turks. The mark of Muslim

152 A traditional Qur'ānic phrase for the punishment or suppression of acts contrary to the Sacred Law.

153 The *ḥadd* or canonical penalty for wine-drinking is, under the Ḥanafī code, eighty lashes in the case of a free man.

154 MS. 2289 reads *wahiya*.

155 See p. 576 above.

women in India is that they do not pierce their ears, whereas the infidel women have their ears pierced. It happened once that one of the amīrs of the Turks called Ṭumūraltī captured a woman and conceived a violent passion for her.[156] She stated that she was a Muslim, whereupon the jurist forced him to release her. This action enraged the Turk; he rode out with some thousands of his men, raided the horses of Harāt in their pasturage in the plain of Badghīs, carried them off and left nothing for the men of Harāt to ride on or to milk. They took them up into a mountain in those parts where no one could prevail against them, and neither the sultan nor his soldiers could find horses with which to pursue them. The sultan then sent an envoy to them, and neither the sultan nor his soldiers could find horses with which to pursue them. The sultan then sent an envoy to them, to request them to restore the cattle and horses that they had seized and to remind them of the pact between them and himself. They replied that they would not restore their booty until he should allow them to lay hands on the jurist Niẓām al-Dīn, but the sultan refused to consent to this. The shaikh Abū Aḥmad al-Jishtī, the grandson of the shaikh Mawdūd al-Jiṣhtī,[157] enjoyed a great reputation in Khurāsān and his word was held in high esteem by its people. This man rode [to the sultan] with a mounted company of his disciples and mamlūks* and said 'I shall personally conduct the faqīh Niẓām al-Dīn to the Turks, so that they may be placated by this, and then I shall bring him back again.' Since those present were in favour of his proposal, the faqīh Niẓām al-Dīn, seeing their unanimous agreement upon it, rode out with the shaikh Abū Aḥmad and arrived at [the camp of] the Turks. The amīr Tumūraltī rose up at his approach, and, saying to him 'It was you who took my woman from me,' struck him with his mace and smashed his brain, so that he fell dead. The shaikh Abū Aḥmad, vexed and disconcerted, returned from the place to his town, and the Turks restored the horses and cattle that they had seized.

Some time later this same Turk who had killed the faqīh came to the city of Harāt. He was met by a body of the faqīh's associates who

156 MS. 2289 vocalizes *kalifa*.

157 I.e. al-Chishtī (from the village of Chisht in Sijistān), one of the founders of the famous Eastern order of the Chishtīya (see *E.I.*, s.v.), d. 1132/3. In the contemporary *Ta'rīkh Nāma-i Harāt* (Calcutta, 1944, p. 647) Abū Aḥmad is mentioned (with the title *Shaikh al-Islām*) in company with Niẓām al-Dīn.

came up to him as though to salute him, but with swords under their robes, and they killed him, while his companions fled for their lives. After this event the king Ḥusain sent his uncle's son Malik Warnā, who had been the partner of the faqīh Niẓām al-Dīn in [the campaign for] the reform of unlawful conduct, as envoy to the king of Sijistān.[158] On his arrival there, the king Ḥusain sent an order to him to remain in Sijistān and not to return to him. He set out to go to India, in consequence, and I met him, as I was leaving the country, at the city of Sīwasitān [Suyustan]* in Sind.[159] He was an excellent man, who had a natural liking for positions of authority, and for hunting, falcons, horses, slaves, attendants, and royal garments made of rich stuffs. Now a man of this order will find himself in no happy situation in the land of India. In his case, the king of India made him governor of a small town, and he was assassinated there on account of a slave-girl by one of the men of Harāt who were living in India. It was said that the king of India had secretly employed the man to assassinate him at the instigation of the king Ḥusain, and it was for this reason that the king Ḥusain acknowledged the king of India as his suzerain after the death of the aforementioned Malik Warnā. The king of India exchanged gifts with him and gave him the city of Bakār in Sind, whose tax-yield is fifty thousand silvar dinars a year.[160]

Let us return now to our narrative: From Harāt we travelled to the city of al-Jām, a place of middling size, pretty, with orchards and trees, abundance of springs, and flowing streams. Most of its trees are mulberries, and silk is to be had there in quantities.[161] The town takes

158 Sijistān (Sīstān) was ruled under the Mongols and their successors by a line of descendants from the Ṣaffārid house, which had survived through all the vicissitudes of the preceding centuries. The ruling princes at this time were Quṭb al-Dīn Muḥammad (1331–45; succeeded by his son Tāj al-Dīn, d. 1350) and his brother 'Izz al-Dīn (1333–82).

159 A statement referring to his visit to the Sultan Muḥammad ibn Tughluq during the latter's stay in Sīwasitān, when I.B. asked to be allowed to go to the Ḥijāz (see p. 766 below).

160 Presumably Bhakkār, on the left bank of the Indus, about 120 miles north of Multān. These negotiations with the king of Herāt are apparently passed over in silence by the Indian historians.

161 In modern times called Turbat-i Shaikh Jām, formerly Būzjān or Pūchkān, in Quhistan on the borders of Bādghīs, and on the direct road from Herāt to Nīshāpūr and Ṭūs. Mustawfī (p. 171) gives the distances as 30 farsakhs from Herāt

its name from the self-denying and ascetic saint Shihāb al-Dīn Aḥmad al-Jām, whose history we shall relate shortly. His grandson was the shaikh Aḥmad, known as Zāda, who was executed by the king of India, and the city is now in the hands of his sons. It is exempted from paying taxes to the sultan, and [the members of the shaikh's house] live there in well-being and opulence. It was told me by a person in whom I have confidence that the sultan Abū Sa'īd, the king of al-'Irāq, came to Khurāsān on one occasion and encamped in this city, in which is the hospice of the shaikh. Whereupon the shaikh [Aḥmad] entertained him with an immense [display of] hospitality; he gave one sheep to every tent in the sultan's *maḥalla*, one sheep to every four men, and to every riding-beast in the *maḥalla*, whether horse, mule, or ass, one night's forage, so that not a single animal was left in the *maḥalla* without receiving [its share of] his hospitality.

History of the Shaikh Shihāb al-Dīn, after whom the city of al-Jām is named:* It is related that [in his youth] he was given to pleasure and addicted to drinking. He had about sixty drinking-companions, and it was their custom to meet for one day in the house of each one of them, so that each man's turn came round every two months. They continued in this fashion for a time. At length one day when the turn of the shaikh Shihāb al-Dīn arrived, on the eve of his turn he made a resolution to repent and determined to set himself aright [to settle affairs] with his Lord.* He said to himself, 'If I say to my associates that I repented before their meeting in my house, they will impute my statement to inability to entertain them,' so he made the same preparations as had formerly been made by any one of his fellows in the way of food and drink, and put the wine into wineskins. His companions arrived, and on preparing to drink opened a skin, but when one of them tasted it he found it to be sweet.[162] They then opened another, found it the same, then a third, and found it likewise, and proceeded to expostulate with the shaikh on this score. Thereupon he confessed to them the true state of his affair, made a clean breast of the circumstances,[163] and

---

to Pūchkān, and 38 from Pūchkān to Nīshāpūr. Shaikh Aḥmad of Jām lived 1049–1142.

162 Arabic *ḥulwan*, apparently in the sense of 'non-intoxicating'.

163 I use this idiomatic phrase to reproduce the Arabic idiom, 'He told them truthfully the age of his young camel.' For the variant, but certainly incorrect, readings see the French editors' note on p. 457.

informed them of his repentance, adding 'By God, this wine is no different from what you have been in the habit of drinking in the past.' Whereupon they all repented, turning to God Most High, built that hospice, and devoted themselves to the service of God Most High. Many miraculous graces and divinations[164] have been made manifest at the hand of this shaikh.

We travelled on from al-Jām to the city of Ṭūs, which is one of the largest and most illustrious cities of Khurāsān, the home-town of the celebrated Imām Abū Ḥāmid al-Ghazālī* (God be pleased with him), and the place of his tomb.[165] Thence we went on to the city of Mashhad al-Riḍā, al-Riḍā being 'Alī b. Mūsā al-Kāẓim b. Ja'far al-Ṣādiq b. Muḥammad al-Bāqir b. 'Alī Zain al-'Ābidīn b. Ḥusain al-Shāhid, son of 'Alī b. Abī Ṭālib (God be pleased with them).[166] This too is a large and important city, with abundance of fruits, streams, and grinding-mills. Living there was al-Ṭahir Muḥammad Shāh (*al-Ṭāhir* has among them the same significance as *al-Naqīb* [Naqib]* among the people of Egypt, Syria, and al-'Irāq).[167] The people of India and Sind and Turkistān say 'Al-Sayyid al-Ajall'.[168] Also at this sanctuary was the qāḍī, the sharīf Jalāl al-Dīn (I met him in India), and sharīf 'Alī[169] and his two sons, Amīr Hindū and Dawlat Shāh – these accompanied me from Tirmidh to India.[170] They were [all] men of eminent virtue.

164 For this sense of *mukāshafāt* cf. vol. II, p. 471, 2 lines from foot.

165 Ṭūs, a few miles to the north of Meshed, was destroyed by the Mongols in 1220, but apparently recovered, since it had a Mongol governor and a Nestorian bishop (see *E.I.*, s.v.). Al-Ghazālī (d. 1111) was one of the greatest of the mediaeval doctors in Islam, and is the subject of a vast literature. The site of his tomb is not now known.

166 The eighth Imām of the 'Twelver' Shī'ites (see vol. II, p. 325, n. 175), who died (or, according to the Shī'ites, was poisoned) at the village of Sanābādh, outside Ṭūs, in 818, after being proclaimed heir-presumptive by the 'Abbāsid caliph al-Ma'mūn, son of al-Rashīd. His shrine became 'one of the most venerated of holy places', in the words of I.B.'s contemporary Mustawfi, who adds that 'at the present day it has become a little town' (tr. 149). See also *E.I.*, s.v. Meshhed.

167 I.e. Marshal of the Sharīfs; see vol. I, p. 258, n. 50. *Ṭāhir* means literally 'pure, free from vice'.

168 'The Most Eminent Sayyid', i.e. the most excellent among the Sayyids.

169 Apparently the same as the sharīf Amīr 'Alī, mentioned later in this volume. But he does not mention the sharīf Jalāl al-Dīn elsewhere. MS. 2289 vocalizes the last name as Dūlat Shah, and reads 'He (i.e. Sharīf 'Alī) was a man of eminent virtue'.

170 The Sharīf 'Alī and his two sons joined I.B. at Tirmidh and accompanied him to India.

The noble sanctuary is surmounted by a great dome inside a hospice, with a college and a mosque adjoining it. All these buildings are of elegant construction, their walls being colourfully decorated[171] with Qāshānī [tiles]. Over the tomb is a wooden staging coated with plaques of silver, with a silver candelabra suspended above it. The threshold of the door of the dome-chamber is of silver, and over the door itself is a curtain of gold-embroidered silk. The chamber is carpeted with different sorts of rugs. Facing this tomb is the tomb of Hārūn al-Rashīd, the Commander of the Faithful (God be pleased with him), and over it is a staging on which they place candlesticks (which the people of the Maghrib call by the name of *ḥasaka* and *manāra*).[172] When a Rāfiḍī enters to visit [the tomb of al-Riḍā], he kicks the tomb of al-Rashīd with his foot and pronounces a blessing on al-Riḍā.[173]

We went on next to the city of Sarakhs, after which is named the pious shaikh Luqmān al-Sarakhsī (God be pleased with him).[174] Thence we travelled to the city of Zāwa, which is the city of the pious shaikh Quṭb al-Din Ḥaidar, who has given his name to the Ḥaidarī group of poor brethren.[175] These are [the faqīrs] who put iron rings in their hands, necks, and ears, and they go so far as to put them also on their penes so that they cannot perform the act of copulation.

We continued our journey from there and came to the city of Naisābūr, which is one of the four metropolitan cities of Khurāsān.[176] It is [sometimes] called 'Little Damascus', because of its quantities of

171 I read *maṣbūgh* with MS. 2289. For *qāshānī* see vol. I, p. 256, n. 42.

172 The text has *shama'dānāt*, a term presumably unknown in Morocco, hence I.B.'s explanation by a word of local use (*ḥasaka* in literary Arabic meaning 'thistle') and a common Arabic term for any kind of stand for a light.

173 Hārūn al-Rashīd died at Ṭūs while leading an expedition to Khurāsān in 809. According to the geographer al-Qazwīnī (cited by Le Strange, *Lands*, 390), the caliph al-Ma'mūn (see n. 166 above) made both graves exactly alike so that they could not be distinguished.

174 Luqmān is mentioned (without dates) by Jāmī, *Nafaḥat al-Uns*, 296–7.

175 A devotee in the thirteenth century, associated with the Qalandarī darwīshes (see vol. I, p. 37, n. 108). According to al-Maqrīzī, 'Treatise on Hemp' (trans. S. de Sacy, *Chrestomathie arabe*, Paris 1806, II, 120–34), he is credited (obviously without foundation) with having introduced the use of *ḥashīsh* into Persia.

176 The old city of Nīshāpūr, which survived the Mongol invasion, was destroyed by an earthquake in 1280 and a new city built in its vicinity (Mustawfī, 147; the translation has 629 (A.H.) for 679).

fruits, orchards and streams, and by reason of its beauty. It is traversed by four canals, and its bazaars are excellent and extensive. Its mosque is exquisite; it is situated in the centre of the bazaar and close by it four colleges, with an abundant supply of running water. They are inhabited by a great host of students studying the Qur'ān and jurisprudence, and are among the good colleges of that land. [But] the colleges of Khurāsān, the two 'Irāqs, Damascus, Baghdād and Cairo, although they attain the highest architectural skill and beauty, yet all of them fall short of the college established by our Master, the Commander of the Faithful, al-Mutawakkil 'ala'llāh, the warrior in the cause of God, the man of learning among kings, and the centrepiece of the necklace of justice-loving Caliphs, Abū 'Inān* (God extend his felicity and give victory to his army),[177] namely the college near the *qaṣba*[178] of the capital city of Fez (God Most High protect her). For this college has no rival in size, elevation, or the decorative plasterwork in it – [indeed] the people of the East have no ability to produce such [plasterwork].[179] There are manufactured at Naisābūr silk fabrics of *nakh*, *kamkhā*[180] and other kinds, and these are exported from it to India. In this city is the hospice of the shaikh and learned imām, the devout Pole* Quṭb al-Dīn al-Naisābūrī [Qutb al-Din al-Naysaburi], one of the saintly homiletic preachers and scholars, with whom I lodged. He gave me excellent and most generous hospitality, and I was witness to some astonishing proofs[181] and graces accorded to him.

A miraculous grace of his. I had purchased in Naisābūr a Turkish slave-boy, and this shaikh, seeing him with me, said to me 'This boy is no good to you; sell him.' I said to him 'Very well', and sold the boy on the very next day, when he was brought by a certain merchant. I took leave of the shaikh and went on my way; afterwards when I stopped in

177 For Sultan Abū 'Inān see vol. I, p. 3, n. 8, and for the Bū 'Inānīya college ibid., p. 53, n. 166.

178 Arabic *al-qaṣaba*, originally and commonly meaning 'fortress', but frequently applied in North Africa to the fortified quarter of a city which contained the palace and its dependencies; see G. Marçais, *L'Architecture musulmane d'Occident*, Paris 1954, 407–8.

179 On the special techniques applied to stucco work in Granada and the Maghrib see G. Marçais, op. cit., 228–31, 331–2.

180 For these fabrics see vol. II, p. 445, n. 117, and 446, n. 122.

181 'Proofs' (*barāhīn*) in the sense of evidentiary miracles testifying to his quality as a saint.

the city of Bisṭām, one of my friends wrote to me from Naisābūr to relate that this slave-boy had killed a Turkish boy and been put to death in retaliation for him. This is an evident miraculous grace accorded to this shaikh (God be pleased with him).

From Naisābūr I went on to the city of Bisṭām, which has given its name to the celebrated shaikh and knower [of the mysteries] Abū Yazīd al-Bisṭāmī [Abu Yazid (Bayazid) Tayfur ibn 'Isa].[182]* In this city is his tomb, beside which, under the same cupola, is [the tomb of] one of the sons of Ja'far al-Ṣādiq (God be pleased with him).[183] In Bisṭām also is the tomb of the pious shaikh and saint Abu'l-Ḥasan al-Kharaqānī.[184] My lodging in this city was in the hospice of the shaikh Abū Yazīd al-Bisṭāmī (God be pleased with him).

I continued my journey from this city by way of Hindukhīr[185] to Qundūs and Baghlān, which are [regions of] villages where there are to be found shaikhs and pious men, and with fruit-gardens and streams.[186] We encamped at Qundūs by a flowing river,[187] where there was a hospice belonging to one of the shaikhs of the poor brethren, an Egyptian who was called *Shīr Siyāh*, and that means 'The Black Lion'.[188] We were entertained there by the governor of that land, who was a man from al-Mawṣil, living in a large garden thereabouts. We remained on the outskirts of this village for about forty days, in order to pasture the camels

---

182 Commonly called Bāyezīd, one of the most famous of the ecstatic mystics of Islam, d. 874; see *E.I.*², s.v. Abū Yazīd, and L. Massignon, *Lexique technique de la Mystique musulmane*, Paris 1922, 243–56. There is a photograph of the tomb in E. Diez, *Kunst der islamischen Völker*, Berlin, 1917, p. 69.

183 Not mentioned elsewhere, and perhaps a confusion with the reputed tomb of Muḥammad b. Ja'far al-Ṣādiq in Jurjān (Mustawfī, tr., 156).

184 Abu'l-Ḥasan 'Alī b. Aḥmad, d. 1035, a later disciple of Bāyezīd; see al-Sam'ānī, *Ansāb*, s.v. al-Kharaqānī.

185 This is the reading adopted by the French editors from MS. 2289, but the preferable reading is that of two other MSS, Hindukhā, for Hindakhū. Their suggestion that this stands for Andakhūdh (now Andkhoy), 100 miles west of Balkh, is apparently confirmed by the marginal reading *Indkhū* in *Ḥudūd al-'Ālam* (tr. V. Minorsky, London, 1937, p. 107, n. 2).

186 Qundūz still exists with the same name, on the lower course of the river called after it, before its junction with the Amu Darya. Baghlān (now an industrial centre) was the name of the region on its middle reaches (here called Surkhāb) between Qundūz and Bāmiyān. See J. Humlum, *La Géographie de l'Afghanistan*, Copenhagen 1959, p. 155.

187 Literally 'by a stream of water'.

188 Not known.

and horses. At that place there are excellent pastures and quantities of herbage, and security there is universally established by reason of the severity of the judgements given by the amīr Buruntaih.[189] We have already said that by the laws of the Turks anyone who steals a horse must [restore it and] give along with it nine like it; if he cannot find this [number] his sons are taken in their place, and if he has no sons he is slaughtered like a sheep. The people [there] leave their animals to graze at will, without any herdsman, after each one has branded his animals on their thighs, and so also did we do in this country. It happened that we made a check of our horses after we had camped there for ten nights, and found three of them missing, but after half a month the Tatars brought them to us at our camp, for fear of what might befall them from the [application of the] laws. We used to picket two horses opposite out tents every night to deal with anything that might happen at night-time. We did lose two horses one night [just before] we set out from there, and twenty-two days later they brought them both back to us while we were on the road.

Another reason for out halt was fear of the snow. For upon this road there is a mountain called Hindūkūsh, which means 'the slayer of the Indians',[190] because the slave-boys and girls who are brought from the land of India die there in large numbers as a result of the extreme cold and the great quantity of snow. [The passage of] it extends for a whole day's march. We stayed until the warm weather had definitely set in and crossed this mountain, [setting out] about the end of the night and travelling on it all day long until sunset. We kept spreading felt cloths in front of the camels for them to tread on, so that they should not sink in the snow.

[On setting out from Baghlān][191] we journeyed to a place called Andar.[192] There existed there in former times a city, whose traces have been obliterated ["the traces of whom were wiped out . . ."]*, and we

189 See p. 561 above, and for the laws on horse-stealing vol. II, p. 474.

190 This seems to be the earliest, or one of the earliest, occurrences of this name.

191 See n. 186 above.

192 Andarāb, on the headwaters of the Doshi (Surkhāb) river. It was the place at which the silver from the mines of Panjhīr was formerly minted as dirhams; see V. Minorsky, *Ḥudūd al-ʿĀlam*, p. 341. The valley of Andarāb leads to the Khāwak Pass (13,000 feet); the hot springs in the upper valley have temperatures of 108° and 124° Fahr. (H. Yule, *Cathay and the Way Thither*, IV, 258, n. 2).

alighted in a large village in which there was a hospice belonging to an excellent man named Muḥammad al-Mahrawī. We lodged with him and he treated us with consideration. When we washed our hands after eating, he would drink the water in which we had washed because of his strong belief [in our merits] and his benevolence. He travelled with us until we scaled the mountain of Hindūkūsh mentioned above. We found on this mountain a spring of warm water, but when we washed our faces with it the skin peeled off and we suffered sorely in consequence.

[After crossing the mountain] we halted at a place called Banj Hīr (*banj* means 'five' and *hīr* means 'mountain', so that the name means 'five mountains'.[193] There was there [in former times] a fine and populous city on a great river of blue water, resembling a sea,[194] which comes down from the mountains of Badakhshān (it is in these mountains that there are found the rubies that are called by people *balakhsh*).[195] This land was devastated by Tankīz, the king of the Tatars, and has not recovered its prosperity since. In this city is the mausoleum of the shaikh Sa'īd al-Makkī, who is greatly venerated among them.[196]

We came to the mountains of Pashāy, where there is the hospice of the saintly shaikh Aṭā Awliyā'.[197] *Aṭā* means, in Turkish, 'father', and *awliyā'* is Arabic [meaning 'friends [of God]', i.e. saints], so his name means 'Father of the Saints'. He is called also by the name of *Sīṣad Sālah*, *sīṣad* in Persian meaning 'three hundred', and *sālah* meaning 'year', since they state that his age is three hundred and fifty years. They have a strong belief in his merits [as a saint], and come to visit him from the towns and villages, and the sultans and the princesses visit him too. He showed us honour and entertained us as his guests. We encamped by a river near his hospice and went to visit him, and when I saluted him he embraced me. His skin is fresh and smoother than

193 Panjhīr was formerly of great importance for its silver mines, and noted for its unruly population. In modern times the ancient term *hīr* (= mountain) was replaced by *shīr* (= lion).

194 Not 'blue like the sea', but in volume 'comparable to a sea'. The Panjhīr river is the principal tributary of the Kābul river.

195 See p. 571 and n. 124 above.

196 Not known.

197 Literally 'Father of the Saints', but not identified. Pashai is the name of a tribe (formerly *kāfir*, i.e. pagan) in the Panjhīr valley and the region to the south of it, still called Kāfiristān (see *E.I.*, s.v.); cf. Marco Polo, cap. xxx (Yule, I, 164–5).

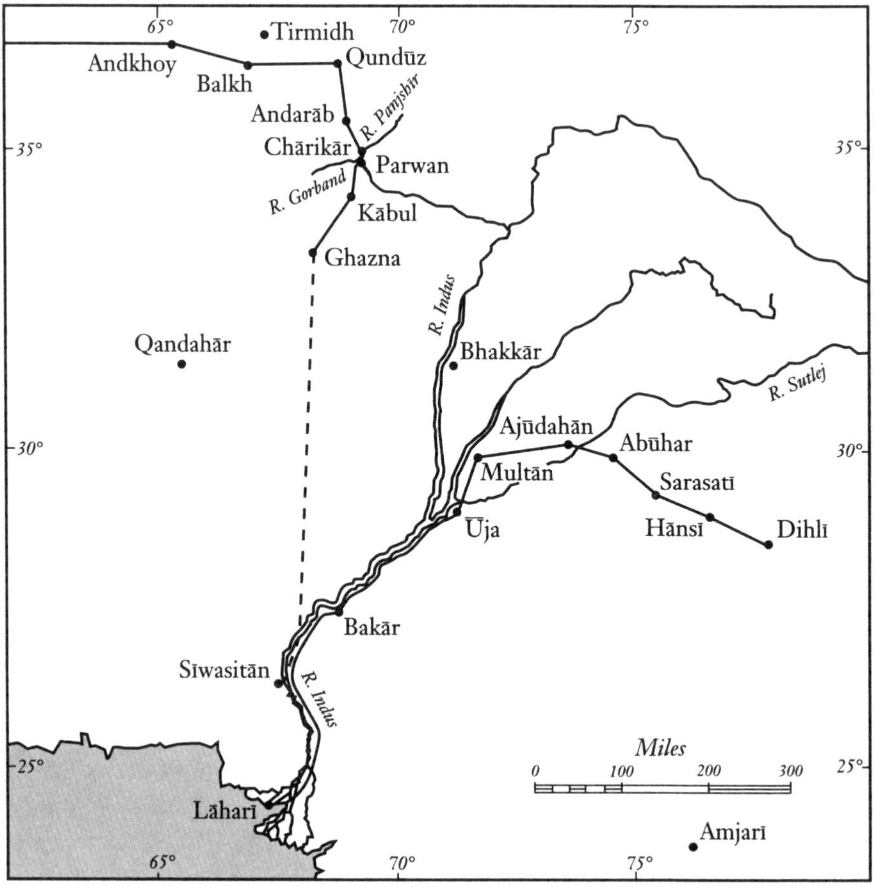

Ibn Baṭṭūṭa's itineraries in Afghanistan, Sind and the Punjab

any that I have seen; anyone seeing him would take him to be fifty years old. He informed me that every hundred years there grew on him [new] hair and teeth, and that he had seen Abū Ruhm, whose tomb is at Multān in Sind. I asked him whether he had any Traditions [of the Prophet] to transmit,[198] and he told me a lot of tales. I had some doubts about him, and God knows how much truth there was in what he claimed.

We went on next to Parwan,[199] where I met the amīr Buruntaih. He made gifts to me, showed me consideration and wrote to his deputies in the city of Ghazna that they should treat me honourably. I have already spoken of him, and have mentioned the immensity of stature with which he was endowed.[200] H had in his company a group of shaikhs and poor brethren, hospice folk. We travelled next to the village of al-Chark, a large place with many fruit-gardens and excellent fruit.[201] We arrived there in the height of summer, and found in it a company of poor brethren and students of religion. We prayed the Friday prayers in it, and its governor, Muḥammad al-Charkhī, offered us hospitality. I met him [again] later in India.

We then journeyed to the city of Ghazna, the town [associated with] the sultan and warrior for the Faith Maḥmūd b. Subuktakīn [Mahmud Ghaznaw],* of famous name.[202] He was one of the greatest of rulers, was given the title of Yamīn al-Dawla,[203] and made frequent incursions into the land of India, where he captured cities and fortresses. His tomb is in this city, with a hospice around it. The greater part of the town is in ruins, with nothing but a fraction of it still standing,

198 The hearing of Traditions from aged persons was eagerly sought, since they shortened the chain of transmittors from the original source; cf. vol. I, p. 155.

199 At the junction of the Panjhīr and Ghōrband rivers, 45 miles north of Kābul.

200 See p. 561 and n. 80 above.

201 Chārikār, ten miles south of Parwan.

202 In Persian pronunciation Ghaznī, 75 miles south by west of Kābul; see *E.I.*, s.v. It was the capital of the dynasty of Turkish princes called after it Ghaznevids (962–1186), and suffered severely from the Ghūrids and later invaders.

203 Maḥmūd (reigned 999–1030) acquired an immense reputation by his raids into India, by which the foundations were laid for the future Islamic sultanate of Dihlī. The title of 'Right Hand of the State' was conferred on him by the 'Abbāsid caliph al-Qādir; see *E.I.*, s.v., and M. Nazim, *The Life and Times of Sultan Mahmud of Ghazna*, Cambridge 1931. The later history of his tomb is related ibid., p. 124, n. 3.

although it was [formerly] a great city. It has an exceedingly cold climate, and the inhabitants move out of it in the cold season to the city of al-Qandahār.[204] This is a large and fertile place, but I did not visit it; it is three nights' journey from Ghazan. We encamped outside Ghazna, in a village there on a stream [that flows] below it citadel. We were honourably received by its governor, Mardak Aghā (*mardak* meaning [in Persian] 'little [man]' and *aghā* meaning 'of great family').[205]

We travelled next to Kābul. This was in former times a great city,[206] and on its site there is now a village inhabited by a tribe of Persians called al-Afghān.[207] They hold mountains and defiles and have powerful forces at their disposal, and the majority of them are brigands. Their principal mountain is called Kūh Sulaimān.[208] It is related that the Prophet of God Sulaimān (peace be upon him) climbed this mountain and looked out over the land of India, which was [then] covered with darkness, but returned without entering it, so the mountain was named after him. It is in this mountain that the king of Afghān resides. At Kābul is the hospice of the shaikh Ismā'īl al-Afghānī, the disciple of the shaikh 'Abbās, who was one of the great saints.[209]

From there we rode to Karmāsh, which is a fortress[210] between two mountains, where the Afghān intercept travellers. During our passage

204 Ghazna, at an altitude of 2,200 metres, has a mean January temperature of -6.7° Cent., Kandahār, 200 miles to the south-west, at an altitude of 1,040 metres, has +5.6° (Humlum, p. 56).

205 See vol. II, p. 434, n. 80.

206 This is probably a reminiscence of the expeditions to Kābul in the early centuries of Islam, but al-Idrīsī also speaks of Kābul as a great Hindu city; see *E.I.*, s.v. It is difficult to see how I.B. could have visited Ghazna from Parwan without first passing through Kābul; most probably the paragraph on Kābul precedes that on Ghazna.

207 At this time the term seems to have been applied only to the tribes in the south-eastern region of modern Afghanistan; see *E.I.*, s.v.

208 The Sulaimān range, to the east of Quetta, overlooking the plain of the Indus, the highest point of which (11,295 ft.) is called Takht-i Sulaimān ('Solomon's Throne').

209 Probably the mausoleum of Jābir al-Anṣārī (5th/11th cent.), son of the Herāt philosopher and poet 'Abdallāh al-Anṣārī: see Wolfe, *An Historical Guide to Kabul*, Kabul, 1965, p. 95.

210 MS. 2289 reads 'a narrow defile', as against the other MSS. From the context it would seem that the original reading was 'a fort in a narrow defile'. Karmāsh is a mountainous tract to the south-east of Gardīz, which is 35 miles east of Ghazna (H. G. Raverty, *Afghanistan and Part of Baluchistan*, London, 1880, p. 91).

of the defile we had an engagement with them. They were on the slope of the mountain, but we shot arrows at them and they fled. Our party was travelling light [without baggage-train] and had with them about four thousand horses. I had some camels,[211] as a result of which I got separated from the caravan, along with a company, some of them being Afghān. We jettisoned some of our provisions, and abandoned the loads of those camels that were jaded on the way, but next day our horsemen returned to the place and picked them up. We rejoined the caravan after the last evening prayer, and spent the night at the station of Shāshnagār, which is the last inhabited place on the confines of the land of the Turks.[212] From there we entered the great desert, which extends for a space of fifteen nights' march;[213] it cannot be entered except in one season of the year, namely after the rains have fallen in the land of Sind and India, which is in the first days of the month of July [Yuliyu].* There blows in this desert the deadly *samūm* wind, which causes bodies to crumble through putrefaction, so that when a man dies his limbs fall apart. We have already mentioned that this wind blows also in the desert between Hurmuz and Shīrāz.[214] A large party, which included Khudhāwand-Zāda, the qāḍī of Tirmidh,[215] had preceded us, and they lost by death many camels and horses. Our company arrived safely (praise be to God Most High) at Banj Āb, which is the water of Sind. *Banj* means 'five' and *āb* means 'water', so the [whole]

211 MS. 2289 reads 'a fever' (*ḥummā*).

212 Shāshnagār is commonly identified with the district of Hashtnagar, 16 miles north-east of Peshāwar, but this cannot be reconciled with the probable identification of Karmash (n. 209 above), nor with the following narrative.

213 The Indus river at Attock is only 40 miles from Hashtnagar, so that the journey from there should require less than two days. The statement in the text requires a journey of well over 300 miles. In conjunction with I.B.'s later statement that he crossed the Indus at some point three or four days' journey from Siwāsitān (Sehwan; see pp. 596–7 below), the only plausible identification of his route is one that went southwards from Ghazna through the desert west of the Sulaimān range (note his reference to it, p. 590 above), thence into the plain of Sind, and reached the Indus as some point in the district of Lārkāna, a total distance of about 350 miles from the point indicated here.

214 See vol. II, p. 404 and n. 130.

215 On p. 565 above Khudhāwand Zāda is called the ruler of Tirmidh, and clearly distinguished from the qāḍī, but in the later narrative (p. 606 below) he is again called the qāḍī.

name means 'The five rivers'.[216] These flow into the main river and irrigate those districts, as we shall mention later, if God will. Our arrival at this river was on the last day of Dhu'l-Ḥijja, and there rose upon us that night the new moon of al-Muḥarram of the year 734.[217] From this point the intelligence officers wrote a report about us to the land of India, and gave its king a detailed account of our circumstances.

Here ends what we have to say concerning the first journey. Praise be to God, Lord of the Worlds.

216 *Banj* for Persian *panj*. As already seen (vol. I, p. 50), I.B. does not clearly distinguish for the Indus proper from the five-river complex of the Panjāb. His term 'water of Sind' in the preceding sentence probably reflects the Persian usage.

217 12 September 1333.

5

Commentary on Chapter 4

Page 93

* Al-Sarra – the city of Saray; this is what Ibn Battuta calls the capital of the Golden Horde. There were two cities with the same name: Saray Batu, the old capital of the Golden Horde, named after Batu Khan (1227–1255); and Saray Berke, founded by Berke Khan (1257–1267) – the brother of Batu – where the capital was moved during the reign of Uzbek Khan (1312–1341), probably before Ibn Battuta arrived there. In historic literature these cities are known as Old and New Saray. The ruins of Saray Berke were discovered in the vicinity of Leninsk town, the contemporary Volgograd district. This city was destroyed by Timur in 1395 [135; 137; 130].

* Sarajuk or Sarajik ("Saraychik") – Maliy (a small) Saray. The ruins of this medieval city are located 1.5 km away from the contemporary town of Saraychik (58 km away from the city of Atirau in the Republic of Kazakhstan). In the fifteenth and sixteenth centuries it was an important trade centre where the foreign merchants used to come to trade with the peoples of Central Asia [130, 88].

* Ulūsū – the river Ural.

* It looks like a pontoon bridge, but for stylistic considerations this word is not used. In Baghdad there were two pontoon bridges: "Upper" and "Lower" [165, 77]. One of the best and most detailed descriptions was made by al-Ja'qubi [54, 333–354].

* Arba'atu dananir darahim. V. Tizengauzen translates this expression as "four silver dinars" [74, 308]). However, there are other considerations: it is not really possible, even in the colloquial speech, to use the word "darahim" with the attributive connotation of "silver"; additionally, dirham is not an Arabic word but was borrowed from the Greek (*drahm*). But used in the plural, darahim acquired the popular and generalized

meaning of "money". It was utilized in colloquial Arabic, first of all in the Moroccan dialect, as a part of proverbs and sayings (al-darahim, marahim – "the money is the remedy against all disease"). Here and in a few other cases it means "four dinars of money" or "four dinars by money". This statement is supported by the fact that on more than one occasion we come across the expression "mi'at dinar darahim" ("one hundred dinars of money"), where the word "dinar" is in the singular and "dirham" is in the plural. It is impossible to suppose the omittance of consequence in such a case; moreover the word "dinar" is in the masculine gender.

* Zawiyas were numerous all over Central Asia in the fourteenth century. According to the written sources the "zawiya" looked like a vagabond abode and a religious house where strangers were fed, especially those returning from pilgrimage. Most of the zawiyas were located together with *mazars* (that is, places of worship) – the graves of the local "saints".

Page 95

* Here it is referred to as Khorezm – the region in the lower flow of the Amudarya (part of the Golden Horde at the time of Ibn Battuta), but the city of Urgench – the capital of Khorezm – also had the name of Khorezm. The ruins of Urgench are described in detail by A.Y. Yakubovskiy [136, 68]. Using the data provided by Ibn Battuta, A.Y. Yakubovskiy came to recognize their identity with the preserved monuments of Urgench and its environs – the mausoleum of Najm al-Din al-Kubra, the mausoleum of Turabek Khatun, the Urgench mosque minaret and so on (the monuments preserved from the time of Ibn Battuta). He proves the fact that the minaret was erected at the time of Qutlugh Timur. The title of Qutlugh Timur (the name is given according to A.Y. Yakubovskiy) signifies the importance of Khorezm in the Golden Horde. This is confirmed by Ibn Battuta's description [ref. 136]. Regarding the architectural monuments of Urgench, refer to the book by V.I. Piliavskiy [121] where he uses a great deal of data provided by Ibn Battuta.

* This short extract was written in rhymed prose and undoubtedly belonged to Ibn Juzayy – Ibn Battuta's "editor" – though the rhyme is very simple and far from literary excellence.

* The French editors of Ibn Battuta think here of the Persian word "shur" ("riot", "dispute" and "stables") [79, III, 57, note 40].

* This is the case on a Friday – the holiday for Muslims, when they close their shops or the whole of the market. This is why V. Tizengauzen's translation of the following sentence was not correct and why it was followed by V.V. Bartol'd: "Because they (Khorezmians) 'damn' the Qaysari bazaar (this day) and other markets" [29, 308].

* Qaysariyya – a kind of guest house, where merchants used to keep their goods guarded and guaranteed by the state [153, II, 433].

* The word *madrasa* was translated by V. Tizengauzen as "a vocational school" [29, 308]. However, since this word has a specific meaning it is better to leave it as it is (Muslim educational establishment).

* This is Sultan Uzbek – the ninth khan of the Golden Horde – who ruled from 1312 until 1341. In Russian folk literature he is known as "Tzar Azvyak".

* A.Y. Yakubovskiy gives it as "Qutlugh Timur". According to Ibn Duqmaq he was appointed as a viceroy in Khorezm and lived there on a permanent basis [74, 1, 328]. Ibn Khaldun notes that Qutlugh Timur was the viceroy in Khorezm with certain intervals, because in 721/1321 he was dismissed from the vicegerency in Crimea and in 724/1323 was appointed there again [74, 388, 143, 18]. According to Mirkhwand, he died in 763/1361. But A.Y. Yakubovskiy remarked that "these words are not right, because the inscription on a stone plate, preserved in Oghuz [Crimea] reads 'This blessing well . . . was built by the order of the Great Amir Qutlugh – Timur-bek . . . 767 by Hijra (1368 A.D.)'"; he refers to 'Uthman Okgak-Rakli as: "Old Crimean and Oghuz inscriptions", p. 7 [136, 18]. Qutlugh Timur, as a close relative of Uzbek Khan, helped the latter to ascend the throne [29, 384] and played a very important role at court. "According to Ibn Battuta and especially if you look at the preserved monuments of Urgench, one can say that the long reign of Qutlugh Timur was marked by the considerable raise of the city and excellent constructions which added to its beauty" [136, 19]. As is clear from the archeological excavations, the minaret in Kunya Urgench was built during the rule of Qutlugh Timur [136, 36].

* Ibn Battuta discusses Turabek Khatun earlier while describing his trip to Iran and retelling the story about the gift that she had sent to an

Indian Sultan [25, II, 73]. Refer to the latest data about the mausoleum of Turabek Khatun in [89, 121].

Page 96

* Muezzins were usually responsible only for announcements from the top of the minaret calling Muslims to prayer.

* The penalty to be paid for insufficient piety was more than the price of a horse (according to Ibn Battuta, the horse cost four dinars).

* This is the River Amudarya. Detailed references on the names of this river appear in 79, III, 325; 103, 12–13. According to Muslim mythology, which appeared in the latter part of the Middle Ages, four major rivers of the world start from paradise, flowing out from underneath the cristal cupola: Nile, Jayhun, Tiger and Ephratus.

* Itil [Idil] – one of the names of the River Volga. It was called so in the middle and lower parts of its flow [130, 66].

* Najm al-Din al-Kubra – Ahmad ibn 'Umar al-Khiwaqi (the famous poet and shaykh) is the founder of Kubrawiyya, the religious brotherhood. He was killed in 618/1221 by mongols in the battle for Khorezm. According to archaeologists, his grave is located near the outskirts of Urgench, just a few sagenes to the north of the northern manuscript of the city wall. This coincides with the evidence of Ibn Battuta [143, 59]. For information about Najm al-Din al-Kubra refer to 'Abd al-Rahman Jami. Nafahat al-uns. Manuscript of Oriental Studies. Institute of the Academy of Sciences of Uzbekistan, N.4409, 224a–224b; Qamus al-A'lam, IV, p. 4, 568; Khwandamir. Habib al-siyar, Bombay, 1857, vol. III, part I, p. 31–32; also refer to 79, I, 99, 440, 503, 504, 541; 82, 324–334.

* Please refer to sixth * note for page 93.

* Abu-l-Qasim Mahmud ibn 'Umar al-Zamakhshari – the prominent Central Asian scientist, philosopher, literary worker, philologist, geographer, poet and writer (1075–1144); for more detail about him, refer to 122; 131, 146-148.

* Zamakhshar (Izmikhshir, Zmukhshir, Zumukshir) – medieval settlement in Khorezm, the territory of the contemporary Takhta region of the Turkmenistan Republic [79, I, 203, 204; 81, 5; 130,66].

Page 97
* Reiteration of the notes about Ibn Battuta's servants is evidence for us to suppose that he was accompanied by a great number of escorts; it means that Ibn Battuta had enough means to pay for his trip.

* V. Tizengauzen translates the title "sadr" as "senior" ("senior qadi" [29, 310]). Probably, it would be appropriate to translate it as "elder" or not to translate it at all. R. Dozy, whom we prefer in general because he used mainly the Western (that is, Maghrib and Andalussian) sources, uses the connotation of "elder" [153, I, 822]. However, here we have the case where Ibn Battuta used the Eastern Arabic terminology, which does not always coincide with the Western one.

* *Mawlana* (Arabic) – means "our Master" if translated literally. It is used to denote the meaning of "honourable" addressing the most esteemed, authoritative people.

* V. Tizengauzen was right to translate: "I'tizal is prevailing in their teaching" but he explains it as "evasion from the existing dogmas, a split" [29, 310]. However, the teaching of mu'tazilits is not an evasion from the existing dogmas but rather a rational trend in Islam, proclaimed by the official clergy at the time of 'Abbasid Caliph al-Ma'mun (813–833), later persecuted. The basic theoretical provisions of mu'tazilits were the denial of the divine features and the statement that the Qur'an was created; they developed the teaching about the freedom of will. The founders of this teaching were Wasil ibn 'Ata' (died 749) and 'Amr ibn 'Ubayd (died 762) from Basra.

* "Adherents of the [orthodox] Sunna", or Sunnits – followers of one of the main trends in Islam. In this case, those who did not recognize the teaching of mu'tazilits.

Page 98
* The notificator – the official at court who met the noble visitors at the entrance and let the people at the court know about their arrival. In this case, Ibn Battuta denotes this title by the word "mudhakkir" instead of the popular "mu'arrif".

* The extract is very interesting from the point of view of medieval etiquette. The Muslim who visited "the sacred places", all the biggest Muslim cities, was appreciated so highly that the amir had to explain his

inability to receive him because of his illness. This fact seemed to be true, although we cannot deny the wish of the traveller to make clear to Abu 'Inan that the maghribian traveller was always received by the rulers of the East with great respect.

Page 99
* Bayalun – the third wife of Uzbek Khan, the daughter of Bysanthyne Emperor. Ibn Battuta recounted her in a detail [23, II, 393–394].

* In the Middle Ages, Iraq was famous for its manufacture of glass bowls.

* Ibn Battuta was not aware of this method earlier.

Page 100
* This information was of great interest to historians and numismatists. The Russian scientist G.F. Fedorov-Davydov made a conclusion based on this statement that the "ratio between the prices for silver and gold in Khorezm in 1330 was equal to 1:3,65" [129, 208].

Page 101
* Malaga fig – came from the name of the Andalussian city Malaga, famous for its dried fruits.

* Karbala'/(Mashhad Husayn) [54, IV, 249] – a city in Iraq, one of the sacred cities of the Shi'its. The grave of a Shi'i martyr, Imam Husayn, the grandson of the Prophet Muhammad – the worship place for many Shi'i pilgrims – is in this city. There are many notes about Karbala' by al-Tabari, Ibn al-Athir and other Arabic authors. Among the modern studies the most complete are by Th. Noldeke, G. Le Strange and Donaldson [165]. The word "sharif" has a terminological meaning. The sharifs were divided into many branches ('Abbasids and 'Alids) and very frequently the people who did not have anything to do with "the house of the Prophet" were included in sharifs and sayyids [63, 165].

Page 102
* Almaliq – the city situated on the bank of the River Ili, to the north-west of the contemporary city of Ghulja, China [130, 71], a very important trade centre on the caravan road leading from the Golden Horde and Central Asia to Mongolia and China. The residence of Chaghatayid Ulus khans [123, 215]).

* Mawarannahr (something that is over the river – that is Amudarya) – the most general name for Central Asia at the time of Ibn Battuta.

* Funduq (Arabic). R. Dozy gives the meaning of "a store-house for the merchants coming to the city to sell grain" [70, 292]. But the meaning of this word is wider – an inn with a warehouse for commodities. Ibn Battuta used it in this context. The glossary of Mu'in states its Arabic origin. This word is originated from the Greek word "inn" or "hotel". To denote the same meaning in the East the word "Khan" – "inn" was used.

* Hama – a city in Syria on the bank of the River al-'Asi.

* "With no settlement or city" [27, 314] – incorrectly translated by V. Tizengauzen. The right version is "sands with no permanent settlement in them save one small township". V.V. Bartol'd noted: "The difference between Khorezm of the mongol domination time and Khorezm of the Samanid epoch is clear from the words of Ibn Battuta, that there stretched the steppe between the capital of Khorezm (Urgench) and Bukhara with only one settlement in between – the small city of Kath" [79, I, 525].

* Every kind of dress, not just the robe, could serve as an honour dress to be presented. 'Abbasid Caliphs had special workshops to manufacture the clothes to be given as gifts.

* Kat (Kath) – the city on the right bank of the River Amudarya, the capital of Khorezm at the end of the tenth century; it was also called Khorezm. In the nineteenth century – Shabbaz (Shaykh 'Abbas Wali). In 973, the greatest scientist of the Middle Ages, Abu Rayhan al-Biruni, was born there; it was destroyed by Timur in 1372. Nowadays, the Biruni region of Qara Qalpaqstan (Republic of Uzbekistan) is located on the place of Kat [79, III, 475–476; 81, 6, 171, 173 and others; 70, 137, 65]. Yaqut wrote a few lines about that city and gave the co-ordinates, mentioning that in the Khorezmian language "kath" meant "a wall" [55, IV, 222].

Page 103
* Shaikh of the town (shaykh al-madina) – an official, a kind of "city leader".

* Sibaya (sepaya, or "sepoya" in contemporary Tajik language pronounciation) – meaning "tripod". It is also a technical term for a special bunch of logs used to prevent the banks of the river from being washed out by the water. Perhaps the city was so called because of the sepoyas reinforcing the banks of Amudarya [79, I, 59, note 48]; for references to sepoya in Khorezm refer to 95, 245.

* Wabkanat (Wabkant) – a settlement located 26 km south-east of Bukhara [79, I, 175]; see also O.P. Chekhovich: [78, 225, note 87].

* The Imām of the Scholars, the leader of muhaddiths – the scientists engaged in the collection of *hadiths*, making the contents of the Sunna.

Page 104
* Abu 'Abdallah Muhammad ibn Isma'il al-Bukhari (810–870) – the author of *al-Jami' al-Sahih*, comprised on the basis of 600 thousand *hadiths*.

* "The accursed Tankiz" – Chinggis Khan. The epithet "accursed" is used very frequently by Ibn Battuta in relation to Chinggis Khan, though he did not dare to use it with any other Mongol ruler, speaking with great respect even if they were not Muslims.

* Ibn Battuta means the Ilkhanids, the descendants of Chinggis Khan who ruled in Iraq. For more on Ilkhanids refer to [79, VII, 500; 83, 200–203].

* ". . . their evidence [in legal cases] is not accepted" – that is, they were not legally eligible, but here Ibn Battuta says that their evidence was not accepted mainly in Khorezm. Maybe it is the result of the political competition existing for a long time between Bukhara and Khorezm.

* Khata (Khatay) – the northern part of contemporary China (to the north of the River Yangtze) [123, 219; 130, 76].

* Khotan – a city in China [79, III, 553–554].

* Kashghar – a city in Eastern Turkestan of China Xinjiang; for more details refer to [79, III, 456–457].

* Please refer to second * note for page 102.

Page 105
* Jalal al-din Mankburni (on the reading of the last component as "Mankburni" and an interpretation of the meaning refer to 85, 143–146)

– the last of Khorezmshahs, who ruled 1220–1231. In 617/1221 Mawarannahr was conquered by the Mongols of Chinggis Khan and all the efforts of Mankburni to stop the Mongol flow to the Middle East were in vain [83; 84a].

* Utrar (Otrar) – a small city (Ibn Battuta sometimes calls it just "balda" – "a settlement"). In Otrar the Mongol merchants were detained ("Otrar catastrophe"). For more details refer to 79, 87, 234–236, 260, 420 and others; as well as 89, 315, 448, 459–461; 81, 193–195.

* Mahalla – a word of Moroccan dialect meaning a "military camp" of the sultan or amir.

Page 106
* Balkh – a city in Northern Afghanistan. In ancient times it was known as Baktra. The Mongol occupation put an end to its development. A new city was built in the vicinity of Balkh and was given the name of Wazir'abad [130, 60].

* Bamiyan – a city in the mountains, between Kabul, Hulm and Balkh. In the tenth century, Bamiyan was the central city of the region with Kabul and Ghazna as part of it and ruled by local rulers [79, I, 118]. It was destroyed by Chinggis Khan and was not rebuilt until the eighteenth century [38, 144a]. Bamiyan is famous for its ancient monuments and numerous huge sculptures.

* 'Irāq al-Ajam – the north-western part of Iran, sometimes the whole of Iran.

* "Fallen down upon its roofs" – an expression from the Qur'an [62, II, 261], which was generally used, mainly in colloquial speech. Ibn Battuta used it frequently.

* Khalifa al-Musta'sim bi-llah al-'Abbasi – the last of 'Abbasid Caliphs (1242–1258).

Page 107
* Ulem – 'Ulama', the Muslim clergy.

* Fath'abad – a settlement located 1 km to the east of the Qarshi Gates of Bukhara. Nowadays it is within the city; for more details refer to 78, 220, note 30.

* Sayf al-Din al-Bakharzi (Sayf al-Haqq wa-l-Din Abu-l-Ma'ani Sa'id ibn al-Mutahhar ibn Sa'id al-Bakharzi) – a Bukharan shaykh (1190–1261); for a detailed bibliography see 78, 215–216, note 6.

* "He was one of the great saints." The word "awliya'" (the plural form of "wali") was taken into the Turk language in its singular form as "saint"; Arabic dictionaries give the meaning as "God's friend", "God's neighbour". Thus, influenced by *sufi* terminology the word "wali" acquired the meaning of "saint", especially during the period of the late Middle Ages alongside the development of eventual or hagiographic literature. The feature of "saint" is karama; the meaning of this word seemed to appear from the Qur'an [62, X, 62]. The word karama can be explained as "wonderful ability, blessing granted by God to His distinguished saints" – in other words a miracle. For further information, refer to 62, III, 37. In the hagiographic literature of the eleventh to fourteenth centuries in Arabic and Persian languages we learn about the "karamat" of the local "walies" and very frequently the most common cases were interpreted as the phenomenon of karama. It also happened frequently with Ibn Battuta. Even Ibn Khaldun, Ibn Battuta's contemporary, recognized karamat [48, I, 169, 199; 160, 118–124].

* Yahya al-Bakharzi (Yahya ibn Burhan al-Din Ahmad) – the grandson of the famous Shaykh Sayf al-Din (see item 70). He came to Bukhara from Kirman in 712/1312–1313 and lived in a zawiya built at the grave of Sayf al-Din al-Bakharzi in Fath'abad; he died in 736/1335–1336; for more details refer to 133, 150-151; 78, 215, note 1.

Page 108

* 'Ala' al-din Tarmashirin – the Sultan of Mawarannahr, the nineteenth of the Chagatayids; ruled in 726–734/1326–1334. The name of Tarmashirin is a Persianized form of the Buddhist Dharmashila ("accepting dharma" – Buddhist legal code). He adopted Islam. But the too resolute denial of nomadic traditions became the reason for the uprising of the nomad Mongols of the eastern part of Khanate, the opponents of Islam. The rebels killed Tarmashirin. After his death the residence of the khans was moved to the bank of the River Ili [79, II, p.2, 33, 543; 83, 198].

* Nakhshab – an ancient city in Central Asia, 10–12 km to the north-west of contemporary Qarshi. In the Middle Ages it was called Nasaf [96, and 105, 147–148].

Page 109

* ‘Aqiqa – a Muslim ritual held a week after the birth of a child, when they first cut the child’s hair.

* Al-Jakhatay – this is what Ibn Battuta calls the Sultan of Mawarannahr, Elchigidey, who was in power for a few months in 1326.

* Kebeg (“a dog”) – the totemic name of the Sultan of Mawarannahr from the family of Chaghatayids, who ruled in 709/1309, with a second term in 718–726/1318–1326. He was the second to settle in Mawarannahr after Mubarak-Shah (1266) and Baraq (1266–1271), and built his palace two *farsakhs* (12–16 km) from Nakhshab. The name Qarshi came from the Mongol for “palace” [79, II, 2, 33].

* Fi ayyi suratin ma sha’a rakkabak – the words from the Qur’an (LXXXII, 8). There is a vocal correlation with the name of Kebeg. In order to get the name of Kebeg, the preacher had to pronounce the word “rakkabak” separately in a pausal form with “sukun” at the end (rak-kabak).

* This is a “hikayat” type of story, typical for hagiographic literature and peculiar to Ibn Battuta, who, while telling the story about the “good” ruler, underlines his goodwill and respectful attitude to the Muslims in spite of the fact that the ruler is a “nomad”. To our mind this story is a very good explanation of the legends relating to “nomad rulers and preachers” who, in many cases, were successful rulers and preachers.

Page 110

* This is a “didactic” story, which is close to hagiographic literature and distinguished by a certain sugariness despite the “rude” plot (a peculiar phenomenon for literature).

* Later, Ibn Battuta explains very precisely the meaning of all the given words and spells them with no less accuracy; here he reproduces the Turkish expression “khosh-mi-sen?” meaning “Do you feel well?”

* Qaba’ – street clothes, corresponds to the late “farjiyya” [152, 240, 244, 325 and so on].

Page 111

* Al-Khalil – the city in Palestine where the prophets Ibrahim, Ishaq and Ya‘qub were buried.

* Al-Nasir – Nasir al-Din Muhammad, the Mamluk sultan who was in power three times: 1294–1295; 1299–1309; and 1309–1340.

* ". . . he would never fail to attend the dawn and evening prayers with the congregation". Tarmashirin is represented by Ibn Battuta as an extremely devoted Muslim. That was why "the period of intense and perishing cold" was underlined.

Page 112

* Qaba' – "the robe warmed by cotton from inside" – in other words, "quilted robe"; see third * note for page 110.

* Qalansuwa – a conic shaped hat looking like "a head of sugar" [153, II, 409]. Such hats were popular in the West of the Arabic Empire (Spain and Morocco).

* Qirat – a small weight measure equalling 1/116 dirham [153, II, 335] used to weigh precious metals.

Page 113

* Buzun – (pronounced Buzan) – the Sultan of Mawarannahr (1334–1338).

* Yasaq (Yasa) – the collection of regulations imposed by Chinggis Khan, which reflected the Mongol tribal legislation. For more on "Yasa" refer to 87a, 375–381.

Page 115

* ". . . whom he used to address [in his letters] as 'brother'". According to a complicated system of etiquette, the way messages were communicated between rulers was very important. "Brother" meant one "who was equal", "Son" was used towards the junior vassal, "Father" was used towards the sovereign. Correspondence was very frequently the reason for political misunderstandings and even wars.

* Sind – the region located in the lower part of River Indus.

* Ghulam – a young slave, often from the Turks. The institution of ghulams began in the ninth century; the ghulams very often comprised the guard of Muslim rulers [39, 78], but at the same time the high military commanders, rulers and founders of different dynasties came

out of the class of ghulams (for example, Sabuktekin, the father of Mahmud Ghaznawi, the founder of Ghaznawid dynasty, was formerly the ghulam of Samanids).

Page 116

* Multan – the city in Panjab (Western Pakistan), on the bank of the River Chenab. In the thirteenth century it was the centre of a small principality, conquered by the Sultan of Delhi; for more details refer to 123, 233.

* Ibn Battuta tried to explain the word "sirraja", perhaps unknown in Maghrib, by using the similar word "afraj", known to him as meaning "the fence surrounding the camp of the sultan".

* ". . . went out to receive him" – according to etiquette it was considered to be the highest honour rendered to the superior or to the equal. Later in the text we have: "dismounted before him" – that is, he showed honour. One was supposed to mount down only before the superior by position or by birth. To ride inside the castle was the privilege of the rulers.

Page 117

* ". . . he was ordered to do homage" – the subordinates (vassals) of the lower range were supposed to stand before the rulers with arms crossed on their breasts unless the ruler ordered them to take their seats [59, 86]. That was the way to treat the lower range people and the example was the case of humiliation.

* In this case the province of Mekran is mentioned, which was sometimes called Kij wa Mukran [70, 332, note 1].

* ". . . allowed the Christians and Jews to rebuild their churches" – the Muslims usually did not allow the people of other faiths to build new churches and synagogues, they were allowed only to make repairs to the existing ones – by special permission [160, 133–135].

Page 118

* Husayn, the son of Ghiyath al-Din al-Ghuri – the Sultan of Herat Mu'izz al-Din al-Kart (1331–1370).

* Sharif, whose genealogy dates back to Husayn, the grandson of the Prophet; see also second * item for page 101.

* Taraz (Tiraz) – today Jambil, Republic of Kazakhstan [130, 74]. For more on the history of this city refer to 79, III, 495–496.

Page 119
* Qara-Qorum – the medieval city in the upper flow of the River Urkhun (Orkhon, Orqon) in modern Mongolia. This city was built after the death of Chinggis Khan by Ogodey, who was elected the Great Khan and moved to Mongolia [79, III, 443–444; V, 146; 130, 76].

* Besh-Baligh (Besh-Baliq) – the ruins of Jilisar near Guchen in Western China [130, 61]. Mahmud Kashghari explains the name in the following way: Bish-Baliq means five cities. The Uyghurs call the other city Yangi Baliq – that is, a new city (Mahmud Kashghari. Devon-u Lughot-it-Turk. Translated into Modern Uzbek by S.M. Mutallibov, Tashkent, 1961, vol. I, p. 145). For more on the name of Besh-Baliq refer to 79, III, 362, 371–377.

* ". . . he wrote to him demanding that the *khuṭba* should be recited in his territories in Khalīl's name, and that his name should be struck on the dīnārs and dirhams" – that is, demanded that the vassal be dependent upon him. Khutba (Friday prayers and preaching): at the beginning of Khutba the name of the supreme ruler of the country is proclaimed, then the name of the heir apparent and viceregent. The casting of the name on the coins was the privilege of the independent ruler only.

Page 120
* That is, in 1347.

* "The river of washers".

* Nawa'ir – water wheels with paddles used for irrigation; this word is not always translated because it has entered some European languages.

* Qutham ibn al-'Abbas ibn 'Abd al-Muttalib – the well-known Arabic commander who is said to have conquered Samarqand in the seventh century. His grave is still in Shah-i Zinda necropolis in Samarqand. For more details about him and his grave refer to 116, 122a, 15, 114, the legend of the "alive king".

Page 121
* Sadr al-Jahan (sadr-i jahan) – "the pillar (centre) of the world". At the

initial stage of the occupation, the Mongols did not interfere with the domestic affairs of the country. But, until the beginning of the fourteenth century, the local administration belonged to the leaders of pre-Mongol dynasties and partly to the Muslim clergy, with the title of the Sadr passing from father to son in the last case. Yet thirty years later, when Ibn Battuta was there, the Samarqand *qadi* like Bukharan Sadrs of the twelfth century, had the title of sadr-i jahan [79, II, part 1, 363].

Page 122
* Sahib al-khabar – official information man. In the earlier epoch the chief of information of the district (city) in Caliphat (he was also post institution chief) was called Sahib al-barid. For more details about his functions refer to 153, I, 347.

* Abu Hafs 'Umar al-Nasafi – the Muslim theological scientist from the city of Nasaf (Nakhshab), and the author of the work *al-Manzuma fil-l-khilafiyyat*. These are the four orthodox trends in Sunni Islam named after their founders – malikis, hanbalis, shafi'is and hanafis. Each can be distinguished by its own peculiarities.

Page 123
* Tafl (Moroccan dialect) – a kind of a "clay soap" in the form of balls, made from dried clay mixed with incense [153, II, 458].

Page 125
* Kadhdhan – a building stone like tuff [153, II, 458].

* 'Akkasha (or 'Ukkasha) ibn Mihsan al-Asadi – one of the followers (ashabs, sahaba) of the Prophet Muhammad. According to Muslim tradition, "the muhajirs" and "ansars" (the Companions of Muhammad in Hijra and the citizens of Medina who supported the Prophet) and the saints (awliya') will have their place in paradise without any questioning on Doomsday.

Page 126
* Mazarat – "the visiting places" – that is, "the worship places", the graves of the saints, mazars.

* Hizqil (Ezekiel) – the Bible prophet. Naturally he could not be buried in Balkh. It is not clear how this legend could appear, but the

twelfth to fourteenth centuries are very rich in such legends, which were created during the political riots and were one of the characteristic features of medieval thinking.

* Ibrahim ibn Adham – the famous ascetic from Balkh. He spent most of his life in Syria, working hard to earn his living, moving from one city to the other giving sermons. He died between 776 and 783 during one of the sea battles against Bysanthyne. Evidently, if the house which Ibn Battuta saw in Balkh really belonged to Ibrahim ibn Adham, then it proved he lived for a certain time in Balkh. However, here we may have the case which we mentioned earlier: the hagiographic literature that was intensively coming into being at the time of Ibn Battuta demanded the creation of detailed biographies of the saints. We may suppose that this is the same case of falsification that took place with the grave of the Prophet Hizqil (see item 119): it was known that Ibrahim ibn Adham came from Balkh.

* It is interesting that Ibn Battuta travelled in the same direction as Marco Polo, who also visited Herat, Balkh and the other cities [132, 104]. Nonetheless, Marco Polo does not mention either Herat or Nishapur. As for Ibn Battuta, he describes it in the following way: "Balkh is a big and famous city, previously it was bigger and better. The Tatars and other peoples robbed and destroyed it; in ancient times there were many more of the beautiful palaces, nice marble houses; and all of them are robbed and demolished. In this very city Alexander the Great married the daughter of Darius. They told me that the people in this city pray to Muhammad. The lands of the Eastern Tatars reach this city and here are the frontiers of Persia to the East and East-North [70, 73]". Balkh – the ancient Baktra; after 250 B.C. – the capital of the Greek-Baktrian Empire. In 1221 the city was destroyed by Mongols. Today, it is renamed Wazir'abad and is situated in the north of contemporary Afghanistan.

* Naysabur (Nishapur) – the main city of Khurasan, the motherland of 'Umar Khayyam and Farid al-Din 'Attar, the biggest cultural and religious centre of the Middle Ages.

* In the Middle Ages this city was called Marw-i Shahijan. In 1220 it was totally destroyed by Mongols. The ruins of Marw are close to the city of Bayram 'Ali (Republic of Turkmenistan) [81, 6, 8, 15, 43, 138–139].

Page 127

* It should be mentioned that Ibn Battuta omitted the reign of Shams al-Din Muhammad, the senior brother of Hafiz and Husayn. According to Khwandamir, the reign of Shams al-Din was as long as ten months [76, vol. III, p. 2, 74–75].

* Rafidits – here we have the case of the general name of the Shi'as. Al-Ash'ari, in his writing *Maqalat al-islamiyyin*, explains this name by the supposition that the rafidits denied the right of Caliphs Abu Bakr and 'Umar to possess the power (the verb "rafada" means "to deny, to reject"). By al-Ash'ari, the rafidit is just the version of the *imamits* [68a, 208–209; 77a].

* Shuttar (plural from shatir) – "the guys", "the dodgers". In the Middle Ages the stories about "the shuttar" – the swindlers, cheating the simpletons – were very popular. Alongside the negative meaning, the word "shatir" acquired a positive connotation, that of "a good boy".

Page 129

* Mar'ashi writes that the battle happened on 13 Safar of 743 (July 18, 1342), two *farsakhs* away from Zawa and continued three days and nights [64, 104–105]. According to the evidence of the witnesses, to whom Khwandamir is referring, about 7,000 people were killed in the battle [76, III, p. 2, 62].

* The story about Nizam al-Din, the pious man from Herat, which seemed not to be connected with the main plot at all. For Ibn Battuta, such stories are important because they comprise "the events parts" of his Travels with "saints", "pious men" and stories about the miracles accomplished by them.

Page 130

* Khatib al-madina – the chief preacher who performs "khutba" in a mosque.

Page 131

* ". . . with a mounted company of his disciples and mamlūks". Probably, the term mamluk came from the Qur'an usage of the word (XVI, 75): "The things that belong to You." Mamluk – a slave (a property

of the Master) – that is, the general definition of a slave without the specific detail (for example, ‘abd – black slave, khadim – the household servant, ghulam – white slave, bought especially for military service). Unlike the word "‘abd", the word "mamluk" had never been used in a religious meaning.

Page 132
* Suyustan – a city that stands on the bank of the tributary of the River Indus, the contemporary Suy (Soi).

Page 133
* This story is a typical example of the "eventual" genre. The plot of the story is typical not only for the "life stories" (*siyar*) of the Muslim saints and pious men but also for the hagiographic Christian literature, oriental and European folklore (the story of "a remorseful sinner"). This topic relates to the time of new Christians, very popular in the literature of Bysantine, in the legends and tales of various nations. (In Russian folklore and Russian literature it is presented in a very precise manner [see 89, 215, chapter VI, "The dispute about the great sinner", where the options about the sinners in the folklore of Eastern and Western Europe nations are mentioned]). Although with Ibn Battuta this topic lost the feature of a tale and legend, and acquired a very "real" and prosaic outlook, it is peculiar to the whole way of Ibn Battuta's narration (that is why it is strange that he is still called "a dreamer"). Ibn Battuta doesn't tell the tale; he describes the details of the biography of a saint as if they happened in reality.

* Islah halihi ma‘a rabbihi – to settle affairs (to reconcile) with one's Lord. We accept this translation because of its "businesslike" character, which is peculiar to Ibn Battuta, who regards "reconciliation with the Lord" as if it is a trade bargain.

Page 134
* Abu Hamid al-Ghazali (1059–1111) – the greatest Muslim theologist, mystic and philosopher; he was born in Tus, studied in Nishapur, and was a close retainer of the famous wazir of Saljuqs, Nizam al-Mulk. He taught philosophy in Nizamiyya *madrasa* in Baghdad. He travelled to Syria, Egypt, Palestine and to the Arabian Peninsula. *Ihya' ‘ulum al-Din* is the most famous of his works.

* Naqib – the leader of a squadron, the leader of the group; see also second * note for page 136.

Page 136
* Abu 'Inan acquired the title of Caliph, calling himself "the ruler of the faithfuls" and also "the caliph's name" – al-Mutawakkil 'ala-l-Lah" (a man leaving Allah to judge). This extract, containing the standard appraisals of Abu 'Inan, is distinguished from the general style of a narration, repeating word for word fragments of the preface to "The Travels" and undoubtedly fixed into the text by Ibn Juzayy, who found it impossible to mention Fez without praising Abu 'Inan.

* In the epoch of Ibn Battuta the complicated hierarchy of *sufism* was completely established. From this hierarchy, corresponding with the spiritual growth of "tariqa" with "ahwal" and "maqamat" as the stages of the latter, we can distinguish the main hierarchic grades: "naqib" – "a leader of a squadron" (the word has both a social and a religious meaning), there may be only 300 naqibs; "badal-abdal" – "substitution" (40 abdals); "amin-umana'" – "the confident" (seven amins); "'amud" – "a pillar" (four 'amuds) and one "qutb" – "a pole", "centre". This hierarchy was not strictly followed all the time and there were many *qutbs* (by territorial dimension, though it was known that the *sufis* used to have wide international ties). Evidently, in this very case, Qutb al-Din al-Naysaburi was the leader of Khurasan *sufis* (Khurasan was very important for the development of mystic studies in Islam).

Page 137
* Abu Yazid (Bayazid) Tayfur ibn 'Isa, was born in Bistam. One of the most well-known *sufis* of the ninth century. We know very little about his life but he was the hero of many legends. Thus his biography is mainly of a legendary character. It is known that Bayazid was persecuted by the sunnits traditionalists, he was exiled and the most part of his life was spent in Bistam, where he led an ascetic life. He was the founder of the Tayfuriyya *sufi* order. He died in 847. In 1313, on the order of the Mongol Sultan Oljeytu, a mausoleum was erected at his grave place. We have "The Revelation" by Bayazid which reached our time, where he told us about the ways of perfection of the *sufi* "tariqa". For further details, refer to 166.

Page 138

* "The traces of whom were wiped out . . ." Evidently, this expression belongs to Ibn Juzayy because it looks like an ordinary formula used in pre-Islamic poetry (the traces of the house of the beloved lady) which had been transferred to medieval Arabic poetry. Speaking about Bukhara, Ibn Battuta uses the colloquial word "kharab". The expression "the traces of whom were wiped out" belongs to another style that was common for Ibn Juzayy and seemed to be used in the same way as the elements of the rhymed prose.

Page 141

* In this case Mahmud Ghaznawi is mentioned (998–1030) – the Ghazni sultan-conqueror. His father, Sabuktekin, was the ghulam of Samanids, then he became leader of the Turk warriors, separated from Samanids and founded an independent state. Mahmud, the son of Sabuktekin, occupied Afghanistan, Panjab, a part of Central Asia and Iran. With the pretext of "the Holy War" he was undertaking devastating attacks on North India and surrounding states.

Page 143

* "Yuliyu" in the text means July. The name of the month by Julian calendar, known in Maghrib from the Roman period.

Bibliography

Primary Source

١ - **مهذب رحلة ابن بطوطة**، وقف على تهذيبه وضبط غريبه وأعلامه أحمد الاوامري بيك ومحمد أحمد جاد المولى بيك، المجلد ١ - ٢، ١٩٣٣ - ١٩٣٤.

٢ - **رحلة ابن بطوطة**، صححها الشيخ أبو السعود، القاهرة، ١٢٨٧هـ/ ١٨٧٠م.

٣ - **رحلة ابن بطوطة**، القاهرة، ١٣٢٢هـ/ ١٩٠٤م.

٤ - **رحلة ابن بطوطة المسماة تحفة النظار في غرائب الأمصار وعجائب الأسفار**، جرى تصحيحها ومراجعتها على عدة نسخ صحيحة، القاهرة، ١٩٦٤.

٥ - **رحلة ابن بطوطة**، بغداد، ١٩٦٢.

٦ - **رحلة ابن بطوطة**، بيروت، ١٩٦٢.

٧ - **رحلة ابن بطوطة**، بيروت، ١٩٦٨.

٨ - **ابن بطوطة نينك دشت قبجاق ده سياحتي**، مترجم رضا الدين بن فخر الدين، أورينبورغ، ١٩١٧ (باللغة التترية).

٩ - **سياحت نامه ابن بطوطة**، مترجم داماد حضرت شهرياري محمد شريف، استنبول، ١٣١٥-١٣١٩هـ/ ١٨٩٧-١٩٠١م، المجلد ١ - ٢، ايكنجى نشر، استنبول، ١٣٣٣-١٣٣٥هـ/ ١٩١٦-١٩١٩م، المجلد ١-٢ (باللغة التركية).

١٠ - **سفرنامه ابن بطوطة**، ترجمه دكتور محمد علي موحد. طهران. ١٩٧٠. المجلد ١-٢.

11 - *Descripte terre Malabar, ex arabico Ebn Batyta*, Itinerario edita, interpretatione et annotationibas instructa per Henricum Apetz, Jenae, 1819.

12 - IBN BATTUTA, *Voyages* (Extraits), Traduction annotée par R. Mauny, V. Monteil, A. Djenidi, S. Robert, Dakar, 1966.

13 - GABRIELI F, *Ibn Battuta*, Firenze, 1961.

14 - IBN BATTUTA, *Osoblivosci miast i dziwy podrózy 1325-1364*, Wybór, Tlumasczyli z jezyka arabskiego T. Majda i H. Natorf, Warszawa, 1962.

15 - *Ibn Battutahs Resa genom Maghrib*, Texst öfversättning och commentar at Herman Almquist, Upsala, 1866.

15a - IBN BATTUTA, *Reisen aus Ende der Welt*, Tübingen, 1974.

16 - IBN BATTUTA, *Travels in Asia and Africa 1325-1354*, Translated and selected by H.A.R. Gibb, with an Introduction and Notes. L., 1929.

17 - VÁNDORLÁSAI, *Ibn Battuta zarándokújja és*, Budapest, 1964.

18 - MOURA J.S-A., *Viagens extensas e dialatadas do celebre Arabe Abu-Abdallah, mais conhecido pelo nome de Ben-Battuta*, Lisbon, 1840.

19 - *De Mohammede ebn Batuta Arabe Tingitano ejusque itineribus*, commentation academica, auct. J.G.L. Kosegarten, Jenae, 1818.

20 - *Muhammad ibn Abdallah Ibn Battuta, Cesty po Africe, Asii, a Europe*, prelozil Ivan Hrbek, Praha, 1961.

21 - *Die Reise des Arabes Ibn Batuta durch Indien und China*, bearbeitet von Dr. Hans von Mzik, Hamburg, 1911.

22 - BURCKHARDT, *Travels in Nubia*, 2nd edition, L., 1822.

23 - *The travels of Ibn Battuta*, Edited by sir H.A.R. Gibb, volume I - II, Cambridge, 1958-1962, volume III, 1971.

24 - *The travels of Ibn Battuta*, translated from the abridged arabic manuscript by S. Lee. L., 1829.

25 - IBN BATOUTAH, *Voyages*, texte arabe, accompagné d'une traduction par C.Defrémery et B.R. Sanguinetti. Tome I - IV. P., 1853-1858, 1874-1879.

26 - KHRESTOMATIA, *Istoria Afriki*, Moskva, 1979.

27 - *Proshloe Kazakhstana v istochnikakh i materialakh*, Alma-Ata-Moskva, 1935.

28 - *Vestnik Russkiy*, Tome II, Saint-Peterburg, 1841.

29 - TIZENGAUZEN V.G., *Sbornik materialov, otnosiashikhsia k istorii Zolotoy Ordy*, Tome I, Izvlechenie iz sochineniy arabskikh, Saint-Peterburg, 1884.

30 - *Ibn Battutah*, Text, translation and commentaries by R.Agarian, Erevan, 1940 (in Armenian).

31 - DEFRÉMERY C., "Fragments de géographie et d'histoire arabes, relatifs à l'Asie Mineur" - *Annales des voyages*, 1850, décembre, 1851, janvier, mars, avril.

32 - DE SLANE M.G., "Voyage dans le Soudan par Ibn-Batouta" *Journal Asiatique*, P., 1843, mars.

33 - DE SASY S., "The travels of Ibn Batuta", translated by S.Lee, *Le Journal des Savants*, P., 1829, août-septembre.

34 - SEETZEN U.J., *Ephémérides géographiques du baron de Sach's*, Monatliche correspondenz, Bd. 17. B., 1808.

35 - DEFRÉMERY C., "Voyages d'Ibn-Batoutah dans la Perse et dans L'Asie" *Centrale-Nouvelles annales des voyages*, P., 1848, janvier-avril-juillet.

36 - BULGAKOV P.G., KHALIDOV A.B., *Vtoraya zapiska Abu Dulafa*, Moskva, 1960.

37 - BALAZURI, *Kniga zavoyevaniya stran*, text and translation from Arabic into Russian by P.K.Zhuse - Materialy po istorii Azerbayjana, Vypusk 3-4, Baku, 1927.

38 - بحر الأسرار، Manuscript of Tashkent Institute of Oriental Studies, No. 1385.

39 - *Puteshestvie Abu Hamida al-Garnati v Vostochnuyu i Tsentralnuyu Evropu (1131-1153),* Moskva, 1971.

40 - ZAKHODER B.N., *Kaspiyskiy svod svedeniy o Vostochnoy Evrope*, Tome I, Moskva, 1962; Tome II, Moskva, 1967.

٤١ - زيادة، محمد مصطفى، **رحلة ابن جبير وابن بطوطة**،القاهرة، ١٩٣٩.

٤٢ - ابن عرب شاه، **كتاب عجائب المقدور في نوائب تيمور**، القاهرة، ١٣٠٥/ ١٨٨٨ـ١٨٨٧.

٤٣ - **رحلة ابن جبير**، القاهرة، ١٩٥٤.

٤٤ - **كتاب الأعلاق النفيسة**، تصنيف أبي أحمد عمر ابن رسته.

Bibliotheca geographorum arabicorum. Edidit M.J. de Goeje (BGA). T.7. Leiden, 1967.

45 - *Puteshestvie Ibn Fadlana na Volgu*, translation and commentaries by A.P. Kovalevskiy, Moskva-Leningrad, 1939, 2nd edition, Kharkov, 1956.

٤٦ - **مختصر كتاب البلدان لأبي بكر أحمد بن محمد الهمذاني المعروف بابن الفقيه**. BGA, V, Leiden, 1967.

٤٧ - ابن حجر العسقلاني، **الدرر الكامنة في أعيان المائة الثامنة**، المجلد ٣. حيدر أباد. ١٣٧٣/ ١٩٥٤.

٤٨ - ابن خلدون، **مقدمة**. القاهرة،١٣٢٢هـ/ ١٩٠٤م.

٤٩ - ابن خلكان، **وفيات الأعيان**، المجلد ١ـ٣، القاهرة، ١٨٨٢.

٥٠ - أبو القاسم بن حوقل النصيبي، **كتاب صورة الأرض**، BGA, II, Leiden, 1967.

٥١ - ابن خرداذبه، **كتاب المسالك والممالك**، BGA, VI, Leiden, 1967.

٥٢ - أبو اسحاق الفارسي الاصطخري، **كتاب المسالك والممالك** BGA, VI, Leiden, 1967.

53 - *Ya'qubi. Istoriya*, Arabic text and translation from Arabic into Russian by P.K. Zhuze//Materialy po istorii Azerbayjana, Vypusk III - IV, Baku, 1927.

٥٤ - أحمد بن أبي يعقوب بن واضح الكاتب المعروف باليعقوبي، **كتاب البلدان**، BGA, VII, Leiden, 1967.

٥٥ - ياقوت، **معجم البلدان**، المجلد ١ ـ ٦، طهران، ١٩٦٥.

٥٦ - ياقوت، **معجم البلدان**، Ed. F. Wustenfeld. Lpz., 1866-1873.

٥٧ - **قاموس الأعلام**. استنبول، ١٣٠٦هـ/ ١٨٨٩م.

٥٨ - الكيلاني، **سوق الشاطر**، القاهرة، ١٩٥٦.

٥٩ - **كتاب التاج**، القاهرة، بدون سنة.

60 - KLAVIKHO, GONSALES Ruy, *Dnevnik puteshestviya ko dvoru Timura v Samarkand v 1403-1406 godakh*, Saint-Peterburg, 1881.

61 - *Kniga tysiachi i odnoi nochi*, Translation by M.A. Salie, Tome I - VII, Leningrad, 1929-1939.

62 - *Koran, Perevod i kommentarii I*, Krachkovskogo, Moskva, 1963.

٦٣ - الماوردي، **الأحكام السلطانية**، بون، ١٨٥٣.

64 - MAR'ASHI, *History of Tabaristan and Mazandaran*, edited by B. Dorn, Saint-Peterburg, 1850.

65 - VYPUSK, *Materialy po istorii kirgizov i Kirgizii*, 1. Moskva, 1973.

66 - *Materialy po istorii turkmen i Turkmenii*, Tome I - II, Moskva-Leningrad, 1938 - 1939.

٦٧ - المقدسي، **أحسن التقاسيم في معرفة الأقاليم**، BGA, III, Leiden, 1967.

68 - NARSHAKHI, *Istoria Bukhary*, Tashkent, 1897.

68a - AN-NAWBAKHTI Al-Hasan ibn Musa, *Shiitskie sekty*, translation, commentaries by S.M. Prozorov, Moskva, 1973.

69 - *Khozhdenie za tri moria Afanasia Nikitina, 1466-1472*, Moskva-Leningrad, 1948.

70 - *Kniga Marko Polo*, translated by I.P. Minaev, Moskva, 1955.

71 - *Proshloe Kazakhstana v istochnikakh*, Alma-Ata-Moskva, 1935.

72 - *Puteshestvie v vostochnye strany Plano Karpini i Rubruka*, translated by A.I. Malenin, Moskva, 1957.

٧٣ - الطبري، **تاريخ الرسل والملوك**، المجلد ٦ . بولاق، بدون سنة.

74 - TIZENGAUZEN V.G., *Sbornik materialov, otnosiashikhsia k istorii Zolotoy Ordy*, Tome II, Izvlechenie iz persidskikh sochineniy. Moskva-Leningrad, 1941.

٧٥ - ابن فضل الله العمري، **كتاب مسالك الأبصار وممالك الأمصار**، Edited by Klaus Lech. Weisbaden, 1968.

٧٦ - خواندمير، **حبيب السير**، المجلد ٣، الجزء ٢، بمبي، ١٨٤٧.

77 - *Hudud al-'Alam, The Regions of the World, An Persian Geography circa 372 A.H. - 982 A.D*, translated and explaned by V. Minorski, 1937.

77a - ASH-SHAKHRASTANI, *Kniga o religiakh i sektakh*, Perevod, vvedenie i kommentarii S.M. Prozorova, Moskva, 1984.

78 - CHEKHOVICH O.D. *Bukharskie documenty XIV veka* (Kriticheskiy tekst, perevod, vvedenie, primechanie i ukazateli), Tashkent, 1965.

Secondary Works

79 - SOCHINENIA Bartol'd V.V., Tome I - IX, Moskva, 1963 - 1976.

80 - BEYKER J, *Istoria geographicheskikh otkrytiy i issledovaniy*, Moskva, 1950.

81 - BELENITSKIY A.M., BENTOVICH I.B., BOLSHAKOV O.G. SREDNEY Azii, Leningrad, 1973.

82 - BERTEL'S E.E., *Sufizm i sufiyskaya literatura*. Moskva, 1965.

83 - BOSVORT K.E., *Musulmanskie dinastii*, Moskva, 1971.

84 - BULGAKOV P.G., *Svedenia arabskikh geografov IX - nachala X veka o marshrutakh i gorodakh Sredney Azii*, Avtoreferat kandidatskoy dissertatsii. Leningrad, 1954.

84a - BUNIYATOV Z.M., *Gosudarstvo khorezmshakhov-anushteginidov*, 1097-1231, Moskva, 1986.

85 - BUNIYATOV Z.M., *Sirat as-sultan Jalal ad-Din Mankburny an-Nasawi*, Izvlechenia Akademii Nauk Azerbaijanskoy SSR., Baku, 1963.

85a - AN-NASAWI, *Sirat as-sultan Jalal ad-Din Mankburny,* edited by Buniyatov Z.M., Moskva, 1996.

86 - VAMBERI A.G., *Istoria Bokhary ili Transoksanii s drevneyshikh vremion do nastoyashego*, Perevod A.I. Pavlovskogo, Tome I - II, Saint-Peterburg, 1873.

87 - VASILYEV A. K., *Khronologii Chingis-khana i ego preemnikov - Zapiski Vostochnogo otdelenia Russkogo Arkheologicheskogo obshestva*, Tome IV.

88 - VOROBYEV M.G., *Opyt kartografirovania goncharnykh pechey Sredney Azii,* Materialy k istoriko-etnograficheskomu atlasu Sredney Azii i Kazakhstana, Moskva-Leningrad, 1961.

89 - GAFUROV B.G., *Tadjiki. Drevneyshaya, drevnaya i srednevekovaya istoria*, Moskva, 1972.

89a - GIN M., *Ot fakta k obrazu i syujetu*, Moskva, 1971.

90 - GIBB Kh. A.R., *Arabskaya literatura*, Klassicheskiy period, Moskva, 1960.

91 - GORDLEVSKIY V.A., *Izbrannye sochinenia*, Tome IV, Moskva, 1968.

92 - GREKOV V.D., *Yakubovskiy A. Yu. Zolotaya Orda i ee padenie*, Moskva-Leningrad, 1950.

93 - GULIAMOV Y.G., *Istoria oroshenia Khorezma s drevneyshikh vremion do nashikh dney*, Tashkent, 1957.

94 - DAVIDOVICH E.A., *Denejnoe khoziaystvo Sredney Azii posle mongolskogo zavoevania i reforma Mas'udbeka (XIII vek)*, Moskva, 1972.

95 - ZAVADOVSKIY Y.N., *Marokkanskaya literatura na arabskom yazyke - Folklor i literatura narodov Afriki*, Moskva, 1970.

96 - ZIMIN A.A., NAKHSHEB, NESEF, KARSHI, *Ikh istoria i drevnost*, Tahkent, 1927.

97 - IBRAGIMOV N., *Ibn Battita i znachenie ego "Puteshestvia" dlya izuchenia* istorii Sredney Azii - Nauchnye trudy Tashkentskogo Gosudarstvennogo Universiteta, Vostokovedenie, Vypusk 456, Tashkent, 1973.

98 - IBRAGIMOV N., *Kult sviatykh v islame po arabskim istochnikam XII-XIV vekov* (Arabskaya sira i "Puteshestvie" Ibn Battuty) - Islam v istorii narodov Vostoka, Moskva, 1981.

99 - IBRAGIMOV N., *Nekotorye momenty ideologicheskoy i kulturnoy zhizni Sredney Azii pervoy poloviny XIV veka v"Puteshestvii" Ibn Battuty*- Nekotorye voprosy razvitia obshestvenno-politicheskoy mysli v stranakh Vostoka, Moskva, 1976.

100 - IBRAGIMOV N., *"Puteshestive" Ibn Battuty* (Perevody i publikatsii) - Voprosy vostochnogo literaturovedenia i tekstologii, Moskva, 1975.

101 - IBRAGIMOV N., *Sposoby opisania Ibn Battuty i drugikh avtorov proizvedeniy srednevekovoy geograficheskoy literatury* - Vostokovedenie, Nauchnye trudy Tashkentskogo Gosudarstvennogo Universiteta, Vypusk 497, Tashkent, 1976.

102 - IBRAGHIMOV N., *Stilisticheskie osobennosti i printsipy perevoda "Puteshestvia" Ibn Battuty* - Nauchnye trudy Tashkentsk Gosudarstvennogo Universiteta, Vostokovedenie, Vypusk 480, Tashkent, 1975.

103 - *Istoria Uzbekskoy SSR*., Tome I, Tashkent, 1967.

104 - KARRA DE VO, *Arabskie geografy*, Perevod s franstsuzskogo O, Kraui. Leningrad, 1941.

105 - KARAEV S., *Geografik nomlar ma'nosini bilasizmi?* Toshkent, 1970 (in Uzbek).

106 - KOTRELEV N.V. *Vostok v zapiskakh evropeyskogo puteshestvennika* - Tipologia i vzaimosviazi srednevekovykh literatur Vostoka i Zapada, Moskva, 1974.

107 - KRACHKOVSKIY I.Y. *Arabskaya geograficheskaya literatura* - Izbrannye sochinenia, T.IV, Moskva-Leningrad, 1957.

108 - KRACHKOVSKIY I.Y., *Arabskie geografy i puteshestvenniki* - Izvestia Gosudarstvennogo Geograficheskogo Obshestva, Vypusk 69, N 5, Leningrad, 1937.

109 - KRYMSKIY A.E., *Istoria arabov i arabskoy literatury, svetskoy i dukhovnoy*, Chasti I - III, Moskva, 1914.

110 - LUNIN B. K, *istorii goroda Termeza - Istoricheskiy zhurnal*, Kniga 4, 1944.

111 - MAGIDOVICH I.P., *Ocherk po istorii geograficheskikh otkrytiy issledovaniy*, Moskva, 1957.

112 - MASSON M.E., *Gorodisha starogo Termeza i ikh izuchenie* - Trudy Akademii nauk Uzbekskoy SSR. Seria 1. Vypusk 2. Tashkent, 1940.

113 - MASSON M.E., *O datirovke tak nazyvaemogo mavzoleya Tyurabek-Khanym v Kunya-Urgench* - Izvestia Akademii nauk Turkmenskoy SSR, 1952, N4.

114 - METS A. *Musulmanskiy Renessans*, Moskva, 1973.

115 - MILOSLAVSKIY G.V., *Ibn Battuta*, Moskva, 1974.

116 - NEMTSEVA N.B., *Ansambl Shakhi-Zinda v XI-XII vekakh* - Zodchestvo Uzbekistana. Vypusk 2, Tashkent, 1970.

117 - PETRUSHEVSKIY I.P., *Dvizhenie serbedarov v Khorasane* - Uchionye Zapiski Instituta Vostokovedeniya Akademii Nauk, Tome XIV, 1956.

118 - PETRUSHEVSKIY I.P., *Zemledelie i agrarnye otnoshenia v Irane XIII-XIV vekov*, Moskva-Leningrad, 1960.

119 - PETRUSHEVSKIY I.P., *Islam v Irane v VII-XV vekakh*, Kurs lektsiy, Leningrad, 1966.

120 - PETRUSHEVSKIY B. K., *voprosu o transkriptsii mestnykh geograficheskikh nazvaniy v Sredney Azii i Kazakhstane*, Izvestia Vsesoyuznogo geograficheskogo obshestva, Tome XC, Vypusk 2, 1958.

121 - PILIAVSKIY V.I., *Kunya-Urgench*, Leningrad, 1974.

122 - RUSTAMOV A., *Makhmud Zamarkhshariy*, Tashkent, 1971 (in Uzbek).

122a - *Samarkand*, Tashkent, 1970.

123 - SVET Ya.M, *Posle Marko Polo (Puteshestvie zapadnykh chuzhezemtsev v strany trekh Indiy)*, Moskva, 1968.

124 - SNESAREV G.P., *Relikty domusulmanskikh verovaniy i obriadov u uzbekov Khorezma*, Moskva, 1969.

125 - *Srednevekovye puteshestvenniki*, Chtenie v Imperatorskom obshestve istorii i drevnostey rossiyskikh pri Moskovskom Universitete, Moskva, 1964-1965.

126 - TIMOFEYEV I., *Ibn Battuta*, Moskva, 1983.

127 - *300 puteshestvennikov i issledovateley*, Biograficheskiy slovar, Moskva, 1966.

128 - FEDOROV-DAVYDOV G.A., *Monetnaya sistema Khorezma XIV veka* - Sovetskaya arkheologia, 1957, N2.

129 - FEDOROV-DAVYDOV G.A., *Numizmatika Khorezma zolotoordynskogo perioda* - Numizmatika i epigrafika, Vypusk 5, Moskva, 1965.

130 - HASANOV H., *Orta Osiyo joy nomlari tarikhidan*, Toshkent, 1965 (in Uzbek).

131 - HASANOV H., *Orta Osiyolik geograf va sayyokhlar*, Toshkent, 1964 (in Uzbek).

132 - HENNING R., *Nevedomye zemli. Moskva*, 1962.

133 - CHEKHOVICH O.D., *Noviy istochnik po istorii Bukhary nachala XIV veka* - Problemy vostokovedeniya, Moskva, 1959.

134 - SHISHKIN V.A., *K istoricheskoy topografii Starogo Termeza* - Trudy Uzbekskogo Filiala Akademii Nauk, Seria 1, Vypusk 2, Tashkent, 1940.

135 - YAKUBOVSKIY A., *Yu. K voprosu o proiskhozhdenii remeslennoy promyshlennosti Saraya Berke*, Moskva, 1931.

136 - YAKUBOVSKIY A., *Yu. Razvaliny Urgencha* - IGAIMK., TomeVI, Vypusk 2, Leningrad, 1930.

137 - YAKUBOVSKIY A., *Yu. Feodalizm na Vostoke*, Stolitsa Zolotoy Ordy Saray-Berke, Leningrad, 1931.

138 - YAKUBOVSKIY A., *Yu., Grekov B. Zolotaya Orda*, Leningrad, 1937.

١٣٩ ـ العربي، إبراهيم أحمد، **ابن بطوطة في العالم الاسلامي**، القاهرة، بدون سنة.

١٤٠ ـ بدوي، فؤاد، **ابن بطوطة**. القاهرة، ١٩٦٤.

١٤١ ـ جودت م، **ذيل على فصل الفتيان الأخي التركي في كتاب الرحلة لابن بطوطة**، استنبول، ١٩٣٢.

١٤٢ ـ ابن بطوطة، **تحفة النظار في غرائب الأمصار وعجائب الأسفار**، المجلد ١ ـ ٣، بيروت، ١٩٣٢-١٩٣٧.

١٤٣ ـ ميلوسلافسكي ج. **ابن بطوطة**. تهران. ١٩٧٧.

١٤٤ ـ **منتخبات من آثار الجغرافيين العرب في القرون الوسطى مع نظرات إجمالية في الجغرافية عند العرب وتعليقات وتوضيحات بالفرنسية**. بيروت ـ باريس، ١٩٣٢.

١٤٥ ـ حسبان، شاكر، **ابن بطوطة ورحلته**، النجف، ١٩٧١.

١٤٦ ـ الشرقاوي، محمود، **رحلة مع ابن بطوطة**. القاهرة، ١٩٦٨.

147 - HUSAIN Agha Mahdi, *Le gouvernement du sultanat de Delhi, Étude critique d'Ibn Battuta et des historiens indiens du 14ème siècle*, P., 1936.

148 - BEAZLEY R., *The dawn of modern geography*, L., 1897-1900.

149 - BLANQUE E., *Elmorabito de sidi Ahmed Et-Tanyi "Mawritala"*, Tanger, 1958.

150 - BROCKELMANN C., *Geschichte der Arabischen Litteratur*, Tome I - II Weimar-Berlin, 1898-1902, Supplementband, Tome I - III Leiden, 1937-1942.

151 - BROCKELMANN C., *Geschichte der islamischen Völker und Staaten*, München-Berlin, 1943.

152 - DOZY R., *Dictionnaire détaillé des noms de vêtements chez les Arabes* Amsterdam, 1845.

153 - DOZY R., *Supplément aux dictionnaires Arabes*, Tome I - II, Beyrouth, 1968.

154 - DVORAS R., *Zemepis u Arubu Ibn Battuta* - Zemépisny sbornik, Praha, 1887, 11.

155 - PONS BOIGUES F., *Ensayo bio-bibliographico sobre los historiadores y geografor arabigo-espanoles*, Madrid, 1898.

156 - *Encyclopaedia of Islam*, Leiden, 1934.

157 - FERRAND G., *Relations de voyages et textes géographiques arabes, persans et turks relatifs à l'Extrême-Orient du XIIIème au XVIIIème siècles*, traduits, revus et annotés par G. Ferrand, Tome I - II, P., 1913-1914.

158 - FISCHER A., *Battuta nicht Batuta*, Zeitschrift der Deuschen Morgenlandishen Geselschaft, Bd. 72. Lpz., 1918.

159 - GRUNEBAUM C.E., von. *Classical Islam*, Chicago, 1970.

160 - GRUNEBAUM C.E., von. *Der Islam im Mittelalter*, Bd. 1, Zürich-Stuttgart, 1963.

161 - HRBEK I., *The Chronology of Ibn Battuta Travels-Archiw orientalni, 30*, Praha, 1962.

162 - JANACSEK St., Ibn Battuta's journey to Bulgharia, JRAS, L., 1929.

163 - JANSSENS H.F., *Ibn Battuta, Le voyageur de l'islam (1304-1369)* Bruxelles, 1948.

164 - LE STRANGE G., *Baghdad during the Abbasid Caliphate*, Oxford, 1900.

165 - LE STRANGE G., *The Lands of the Eastern Caliphate*, Cambridge, 1930.

166 - MASSIGNON A., *Essai sur les Origines du Lexique technique de la mystique musulmane*, P., 1922.

167 - MEILLASSOUX C., *L'intinéraire d'Ibn Battuta de Walata a Mali, Journal Africain Histoire*, Tome XIII, N3, L., 1972.

168 - NEWTON A.P., *Travel and Travellers of the Middle Ages*, L., 1930.

169 - RUSKA J., *Zur geographischen Literatur in islamischen Kulturberricht, Geographische zeitschrift,* Tome XXX III, Lpz., 1927.

170 - SCHEFER Ch., *Notice sur les relations des peuples musulmans avec les Chinois, depuis l'extension de l'islamisme jusqu'au XVème siècle*, Centenaire d'École des langues orientales vivantes, P., 1895.

171 - TATSURO Yamamoto, *On Tawalisi described by Ibn Battuta*, The Oriental Library, N8, Tokyo, 1936.

172 - YULE H., *Cathay and way thither* Vol.ume II, L., 1915.

173 - YULE H., CORDIER H., *Ibn Battuta's Travels in Bengal and China* (circa). L., 1915.

174 - DUNN R., *The adventures of Ibn Battuta*, a Muslim Traveller of the *Fourteenth Century*, L., 1986.

175 - PAUL J., *Sheiche und Herrscher im Khanat Cagatay - Der Islam*, 1990, Bd. 67, Heft 2, 278 - 321.